PETER ROUTIS

FREE BESIEGED

NFB Publishing
Buffalo, New York

Copyright © 2021 Peter Routis

Printed in the United States of America

Free Besieged/ Routis 1st Edition

ISBN: 978-1-953610-98-0

    1. Title
    2. Greek History.
    3. Greece.
    4. European History.
    5. Nation/Greece.
    6. History, General.

No part of this book may be reproduced or transmitted in any form by any means, electronic or mechanical, including photocopying, recording, or by any information storage and retrieval system without permission in writing by the author.

NFB
NFB Publishing/Amelia Press
119 Dorchester Road
Buffalo, New York 14213

For more information visit Nfbpublishing.com

This book is dedicated to the students of the Polytechnique, the high school students, the Athenians, and those who fought for justice and lost their lives during the three horrifying days and nights of November 1973 at the Polytechnique and the streets of Athens. To those who dedicated their lives to the restoration of human rights, dignity, self-respect, academic freedom, social justice, and indeed democracy; this book is a tribute to them. That early morning of April 1967 will never be forgotten, when the colonels imposed dictatorship and martial law, suspending parts of the constitution, imprisoned, exiled, tortured, and killed civilians. The fabric of the Greek society fundamentally changed, and the picturesque Greek islands were populated with those who were called *Reds,* anarchists, nihilists, or radicals. Those who fought the evils of fascism. Those we will remember.

"Exiled poet, tell me, what do you see in your century?"
"Axion Esti" Odysseas Elytis

Waves and waves were hitting me, the demons; first the demons of the flesh, then the demons of the mind, and the last ones, the most powerful and dominant, the demons of the heart; they thrashed me, battered and ravaged me; I should climb up.

Nikos Kazantzakis

PART I

CHAPTER I

Those hours which I lived in such a depth, I was unable to name happiness and sorrows; as such, I would rest my body; but I would leave them inside my amateur and novice mind, deeper than the word, with a transparent carcass, with movement and rhythm. I was sunken into an ocean of sounds and light, but the light became rhythm and was beating on my temples. Now that I contemplated, the words seemed to me like exorcisms, and as soon as I pronounced them, the demons, good and bad, gathered inside those exorcisms and lost their strength.

*

The book I was reading since the train left the station, I now placed on the seat next to me. The words were jumping off the page and I was unable to halt them. Odd and peculiar Shakespeare seemed to me; he depicted death, lovers, betrayed loves, kings, queens and princes, revolutionaries and dictators, with the same fascination and ingenuity. I let my gaze wander on the fields outside the window. The train was struggling to drag its weight up the hill, heading toward the city, where new challenges awaited me to come to terms with, as the shadows of the trees were leisurely passing by the coach's window. My mind was drifting aimlessly, as thoughts of my challenges in the big city were consuming me. Taking into account the dire political situation, which devoured the entire country, since that ill-fated *Friday,* I was not prepared or even ready to face it in the capital. I was certainly not politicized at that point, which would make me politically unaware or utterly inactive. As such, I was oblivious to the processes of abstract concepts and specific entities and collection of facts, which were interpreted as political. I was not prepared to face the political dilemmas which people faced daily in the capital. My mind was pure and completely untainted, but yet, I expected to be open and ready, to consume and deal with any imminent hurdle, which might arise out of the current dreadful and appalling political and socio-economic state of affairs of the country.

Before the train left the station, I ventured into the town's bookstore, wandering along the aisles, contemplating and searching for a book to read on the train. I did not have the will since that morning to even talk. My mother with difficulty appropriated a *goodbye* from me, as I left home. My move to the city, being away from home, disturbed and distressed me; it traumatized me, interrupting my quiet life in the village. It was my first time away from home, away from the serenity and the peacefulness of my town, away from the mountains, the meadows, and the brilliant and magnificent starry nights. My studies at the university would commence in a week or so, and while I was feeling the excitement at the moment, butterflies were fluttering inside me from the anticipation. What would I find there, at the city which I read so much about? The city which had engraved the glamour of its past, deep inside my brain.

Roaming the aisles of the bookstore, now, scanning the shelves, considering my options, I came across a section of past and present philosophers but I did not dare draw near them, although the provocation was immense. What I was looking for to find, I confess, was not clear in my mind. I was certain, if I explored every book in the store, I would not have found the book I was yearning for to cascade over and devour every page, every syllable. Perhaps it was not a book I was considering; perhaps it was my anxiety that was overwhelming me, contemplating my trip to the city and my studies at the university. My attempts to find the perfect book to take me to the city were futile; perhaps it was something else I was looking for, giving it reluctantly the shape of a book. I was pondering my options, but I didn't raise my hand to grab the one which mesmerized and captivated me. Nothing fascinated me and nothing attracted my attention or even remotely engrossed me until I got to the poetry section. Poetry had always fascinated me, giving a special intensity to the expression of feelings and ideas; it's the splendor, the beauty, and the intensity of emotions that had attracted me from a very early age.

I got a glimpse of Shakespeare's love poems and picked it up. There were four photographs on the front cover, which depicted the black Shakespearean hero Othello with his beloved Desdemona. The first photograph revealed Othello with an astonishing gentle and obliging expression, admiring his beloved Desdemona with adoration and affection, standing at a wharf in Venice. The caption below read: *"startling creature, calamity to fall upon my soul if I don't love you."* Astonished by his pledge, Desdemona looked at him astounded. The cruel tragedy of the couple went on and those who were envious of such love had made their mark already. *"If she's a liar oh, then the sky would be laughing at itself. No, I don't believe it,"* he said to the sycophant who was determined emphatically to expose to him the misadventures of his wife. The third photograph depicted the black figure of Othello, in contrast with the white form of Desdemona, emphasizing that tragic scene. *"The cause … the cause this is it, my God … but I will not spill her blood, and neither would I destroy her body which is whiter than snow."* The antithesis remained; he began his tragedy inevitably with thunderous and disturbing words, where he gave his beloved his oath of love, while she was still alive and the hand, which he held, was still warm. But she was warm no more; the body which he was holding, was now cold. His love for her, his affection, and his jealousy were merely the causes to murder her and put her to sleep forever. But then again, he didn't want to accept it as true and believe it. She was alive, as far as he was concerned, and his love for her, which was nothing more than its real persona, remained pure. The black officer had locked inside her body the whitest and fairest soul, which was arrogantly given to her forever. To her, who he had killed and who he had loved so dearly, he uttered: *"stay dead as such and if I kill you, I will love you in advance."*

Astounded by what the book would divulge to me reading it, I walked hurriedly to the cashier, I paid and drifted out of the bookstore. The fresh warm air gave me a different perspective of life and death, contradicting Othello's verses. The obscure and sinister world of Othello was replaced by the brilliant and luminous warm day which was promised ahead. The book was scorching my hand, oxidizing my senses. I didn't open it. Not yet. Not at the station. I needed to get to the train as fast as I could, to find a quiet corner in a coach. Reaching the station, I was informed that the train was delayed and had not yet arrived. I sat on a bench and opened the book.

I was so absorbed and captivated by the book, that I was awakened from a lethargic sleep, it seemed when I heard the whistle of the train. I was enthralled and immersed in the paths, which Shakespeare took me through. Sometimes to Denmark, where he acquainted me with the tragic essence and existence of Ophelia and her melodious full of pain song; other times he would drug me to some other meadow or mountain of Wales, to introduce me to the resplendent love of young people; and other times to some kingdoms somewhere in Scotland or at the wharves of Venice.

I found a seat by a window and I opportunely claimed it. A fellow traveler got up and disappeared behind the door of the coach, which was shut behind him. I was left alone. I felt tired. With a big jolt, which my entire body felt, the train left the station and started down the hill, leaving the village behind me. The grief and anguish, abandoning my village behind, conquered my senses. Looking at her, which was spreading in front of me and to the right, my village, which I adored since I got hold of my feelings and impressions at a very early age, diffused my senses. I was left alone with my thoughts. Further away in the distance, I could see the hill where I spent most of my youth. I adored the precious mountains, the river, the meadows, and the deep blue sky. I was very much attached to this place, which I held so dear to my heart. I turned to my book.

The words started to jump out of the page and I could not hold on to them. I was saturated. I turned to the window. I couldn't read any longer. It was early afternoon and it was still rather hot, enduring the presence of summer. Obscurities and silhouette traces, like shadows, were passing by the window, the trees, tailing each other. The enchanted city, I was so anxious to visit, was still far away, and my yearning to see her was immense. I read so much about her; historical events and tales were overwhelmingly engulfing me, as her imposing and splendid sites could not be narrated. I wanted to speak to her; I had so much to divulge to her, to comfort her and ease her pain, as my words were obstructing my throat, eager to reach my lips. She was so discrete, aggrieved, and offended. Her white marbles were shamed, dishonored and tarnished, since that ill-fated *Friday*. The city, which hosted the birth of democracy was now no more. But her beauty was untarnished and brilliant. Hemmed by the three mountains: Hymettus, Aegaleo, and Parnitha and the Saronic gulf unfolding to the south, were submerging her to such beauty, which was so brilliant, stretched under the blue sky. The white marbles, the temples, and statues complimented her magnificence.

*

I was surrendered to deep sleep, embracing in my memory the images I had seen of the city, which offered me the essence and soul of her. The train blew its horn three times and reduced its speed. Metal upon metal was the distinct sound that woke me up. As I opened my eyes, a beautiful city was emerging. I could see the mountain which partly concealed the aged metropolis.

The foundations of the world shifted; the hearts of the people were rearranged and shuffled. The city was sheltered and concealed by the marbles which are called Athens; it was concealed from the curses and the anathemas; concealed from the Persians and the Romans, from the Venetians the Turks and the Germans; from the rich who had plenty and the poor who were hungry, and it was concealed from gods and devils. Suddenly, a soft wind blew, not from the sky but from down the earth, and the leaves of the hearts of people moved; they bowed and bent over, turned and curved and twisted and fell first inside their heart, then inside their mind and then on top of the earth. The stones, which are called Athens, the prophesies and the anathemas, the Turks the Persians and the Venetians, took again the measuring tape and the hummer and started demolishing the former, rebuilding the new.

For thousands of years, she lived there, falling on the hands and mercy of numerous and diverse brutes and ruffians throughout the centuries, ravaging the city. Friends and foes alike stole from her; first, the Romans stole most of the works of playwrights, poets, and philosophers, and on the way to Rome, they were placed in a ship which regrettably and sadly went down in the middle of the Adriatic Sea, during a cataclysmic storm. Several important manuscripts of philosophers, dramatists, and mathematicians were stolen from her and were placed in the great library of Alexandria; in 48 B.C. Julius Caesar accidentally burnt the library down, when he set fire to his ships, and the fire spread from the docks. Then the British lords came, during her occupation by the Ottoman Empire, and removed statues from her most sacred and consecrated temples, and to this day, they refuse to return them. Then the Turks blew up the Parthenon. But she still stood there in shreds, wrecked but not defeated, among the white marbles, the ruins, and the unprofaned temples. They told us that gods had built that city. I supposed that was why she was so pure and absolute. Aristotle had written extensively about its citizens and its untainted society: "... *nor was civil society founded merely to preserve the lives of its members; but that they might live well for otherwise a state might be composed of slaves, or the animal creation ... nor is it an alliance mutually to defend each other from injuries, or for commercial intercourse. But whoever endeavors to establish wholesome laws in a state, attends to the virtues and vices of each individual who composes it; from whence it is evident, that the first care of him who would find a city, truly deserving that name, and not nominally so, must be to have his citizens virtuous.*"

*

THE train blew its horn three times and reduced speed; we were entering the station. Many travelers waited to board the various trains. I disembarked and picked up my suitcase. I took a deep breath, and I walked out of the station. That was my first assignation to the old city. The warm summer breeze was blowing leisurely across the city, which unstiffened and mollified my chest. I had never seen so many people and vehicles, and never heard so much noise in my young life. The streets were lined up with taxis, streetcars, trolleys, and busses as the other vehicles were competing for space on the road. The sidewalks were busy with pedestrians, tables, chairs, umbrellas, vendors, retailers, and shopkeepers. All were muddled together in clutter, as people tried to navigate among these obstacles. I walked amid a myriad of people, who were either in a hurry to get to their destination, or were trying to sell me something; politely I refused by smiling at them, or by just simply saying *no thank you*. Despite this, there was something I had also noticed about the people; something I could not put my finger on. They seemed to be in a hurry, in some kind of urgency, but there was no eye contact, and the faces were gloomy, melancholic, and expressionless.

I was famished, and I looked for a place to eat. There was an enchanting café down the street, which seemed inviting and alluring. I inquired about a hotel in the area to put my suitcase down and go and explore the city.

"Are you a new arrival to our city?" requested the waiter.

"I'm coming from up north," I said with my timid and subdued voice.

"There is an inexpensive hotel in the corner. What will you do here?" he asked.

"I'm attending university," I said with a gratifying and prominent tone.

"My son is also at the university. Come by again, and I'll introduce you to him," the man said with pride.

"What is he studying?"

"Engineering. It's in high demand right now, and especially when the economy gets any better, if ever with this government..." he said, drifting his low voice to an inaudible sentence which did not reach my ears, "there will be a lot more jobs in the future," he resumed.

"Let's hope. Which university is he attending?"

"The Polytechnic."

"I haven't seen it yet but I will visit it tomorrow. It's a beautiful building," I said.

"Yes, it is, and it's close to home," he said as he traced my face with his eyes.

That was my first taste of the city and its people. I noticed a trace of contentment toward the government, and that surprised me, because under the current circumstances, people, I would think, would be fearful talking openly to a stranger against the government. But I liked his honesty; this man had fortitude and backbone; he was not afraid to express his dissatisfaction with the regime. Nevertheless, I pondered: how did the people here feel about the political situation? How bad was it in the big city? Everything was nearby: the police stations, the army, the *Yellow Building*, neighbors, even ruffians; one wouldn't know who to place their faith on. Although, seemingly, the people in a big city --as opposed to those who lived in small towns-- would be a lot more contented with their lives, having access to a lot more fascinations, and a lot more services obtainable, jobs and different experiences, still, none of these captivations were enough. Something essential was missing; something so indispensable, so fundamental: freedom. One could not materialize freedom. Freedom is the essence of living a complete life, essential to the development of one's self. A basic need, necessitating a struggle to be able to obtain it and preserve it.

I finished my meal, and I picked up my suitcase to leave.

"If you're looking for a more inexpensive place, there is another hotel further down the street," the waiter said as he exited from the kitchen and came toward me.

"Yes, I will look into that. Thank you," I said and I withdrew, walking out the door.

"Be careful with this city. She's ..." I didn't hear his last words, although I guessed his allusions about the city.

It was a century-old building with the sophistication and intricacy that many old buildings of the city possessed. A few steps, which were adorned by two lion statues at either side, led to the entrance of the hotel. The heavy oak door opened with exertion, to reveal a small but pleasant lobby, with a desk at the opposite wall. His back was against a set of small shelves with keys rested in them, reading the paper. When he saw me, the front desk clerk, lifted his head from the newspaper, and he got up to welcome me. I checked in, and I went to my room. It was a sizable and generous room, with a substantially large window overlooking the busy street. The wardrobe in the corner was timeworn, as was the large bed. The ceiling was hanging excessively high and the floor, built with large heavy oak boards, gave one the sense of an exceptional and extraordinary building this might have been in its prime. Remarkable decorative oak trimming embellished the perimeter of the door, window, and ceiling, garnishing them with flair and elegance. The view from the window was astonishing: small shops, gift shops, restaurants, and bistros were streaking along the sidewalk, while the traffic and the pedestrians were competing for commotion share. I left the room, and I went downstairs. I walked out on the street. The sounds of the city were prodigious and overpowering for my virgin village ears. There was an idiosyncratic smell coming from the streets, the houses, the small hill on the east side which was alluring and provoking. It was the smell of the city. The calm and tender wind caressed and embraced my open chest.

*

THE sun had escaped the embrace of the eastern mountain and was rising above the city, illuminating it with that lucid brilliant intensity which the city was renowned for. I walked among vendors, newspaper stands, flower stands, and myriads of people. The overcrowding at this part of the city and the cramming and congestion on the streets, were exceptional and extraordinary, to say the least. I walked in the direction of the university, to get a glimpse of the campus, and get a sense of where I would spend my next four years.

The Corinthian architectural design of the main building and the statues of ancient personalities, scattered around its perimeter, enhanced the spirit of high education and engulfed the heart. Plato's view of education signified the virtue of the spirit, the nobleness of the person, and the security and the protection of the state. The intention of education, according to Plato, was the wellbeing and prosperity of both the person and society. His directorial principle was: *"Nothing must be admitted in education which does not conduce to the promotion of virtue."* Socrates somewhat agreed with Plato, insisting that he rejected the idea that human virtue depended on a person's sex or age. He hinted toward the idea, that virtues were common to all people, who exercised self-control and justice, refraining from harming others. These were virtues even in children and old people, Socrates insisted. Behaviour, which showed high morals, was a quality that was considered morally good or desirable in a person. The congenital eminence of Socrates, regarding the assets of virtue, was a great part of his life and his thinking. Holding the weighing scale, however, he measured his life against his ideology, which seemed to be heavier, and tipped the balance. He considered the equilibrium, and he could only give it stability by taking the cup. The cup ended his life, but his ideals remained untarnished. They offered him the cup as a tender, to drink that noxious substance of hemlock. He did not protest; his demise was his four words he carved upon a rock at the Acropolis: *"to the unknown God."* This inherited eminence of virtue, which had endured for centuries, had shaped societies and molded people to the form which was instigated by him.

*

THE exhaustion, fatigue, and sleeplessness, caused me to lean over the windowsill, but my eyes never left the street below. It was my second morning in the city, and I intended to take it all in. There was that old antiquated part of the city, which I was familiar with from my past readings. But also, there was another part that was a more prevalent, innovative, and progressive part of the city. I was trying to make sense of it, juxtaposing the new city with the old. There were old Byzantine churches and multi-leveled modern buildings, scattered among ancient ruins. The neo-classic architecture was widespread and dominant among the eighteenth and nineteenth-century buildings, a reminiscence of its antiquity, which once was the center of civilization.

I left the window, and I approached the bed. The white sheets on the bed were luminous, as the first glimmer of the sun was showering them. It was almost noon when I woke up. My head was burdensome, and I felt greedy, for I wanted to take it all in at once. The noise coming from the street through the open window was oddly welcomed, and my disposition was clear. It was hot, and I was sweating to the bone. I was still tired but I didn't want to sleep. I wanted to put my thoughts in order, as time was approaching. The people, the city, and its beauty were all exquisite, but where was my journey taking me? I came from a village full of passion and eagerness. Where was I progressing? Was I anticipating seeing Socrates speaking to the youth of the city at the agora? What was I to see? Whatever was there, I had already familiarized myself. There was nothing else. I went downstairs, and I ventured out again. My thoughts and reflections were extinguished in the obscurity of time.

I was left alone.

I existed within the boundaries of anticipation and optimism. I didn't sob, I didn't beg, I didn't shout; it was endured intimately within me. Every step on the cobblestone street, every deliberation, every concept and line I wrote, deliberated and negotiated with me. It was concealed obscurely within me. It was not inclined to reveal itself, as I was not prepared to accept it. I needed first to liberate myself from my chains, so I could open the door to unleash it, like a hurricane into the streets and exclaim the truth with candor and integrity. But the gates were bolted, fastened with the shackles of eternity; my uncultivated political notions immobilized me. As if in a prison cell, my conceptions were sheltered within me.

*

THE broad thoroughfare was lit up, gorged with people and vehicles. With a heavy and demanding head, I left the main boulevard to avoid the boisterous street, and leave behind the constrain I felt. I got onto a cobblestone street -- who knows how old it was – with whitewash yards, red and blue windows, and a lantern hanging in front of each door. The music, which was coming out of the taverns I passed by, was trickling into the street. The disciples of Dionysius were coming in and out of these establishments, with their eyes brilliant from the wine, and their feet unsteady on the ground. The small, well-built, and decorative balconies were supporting the inhabitants, enjoying the warm evening, eavesdropping on the music coming from the tavern below. The street lanterns, which were lit earlier in the evening, were giving a soft brilliant light to the cobblestones of the narrow street. The water truck of the city had passed by earlier and saturated the streets, relieving it from the heat and washed away whatever remnants were left behind from people of that eventful and demanding day. I found a small staircase and I climbed it. Sitting at the top step, I was taking in the pleasant evening, assimilating to the marvels of this picturesque neighborhood. The small lantern above the door welcomed me, as I was looking at the deserted street, attending to the exchanges taking place on the balconies above.

I don't remember how long I sat there; I was not asleep, but neither was I awake. I was not dreaming; my brain was immersed within this immense city, trying to unearth memories and past events. I looked up in the sky, and it gave me the impression of an otherwise brilliant sky. Only a few stars were visible, competing with the illumination of this metropolis. For a moment, I envisioned I was on the hill at my village, looking at the sky inattentively; reflecting further, I brought to mind the time I encountered the old shepherd playing his fife with gusto and passion at the side of the mountain, minding his herd. Further in my thoughts, I brought forward the last time I spoke with the old shepherd, the mountain musician. That was a period in my life when I would jump out of the window and run up the hill to gaze at the stars, sitting on a rock; I was consumed by the need to put them all in my small palm to warm me up. I would ask them about the divinity, the mysticism of nature, about my worries, anxieties, and uneasiness, and they would answer me with a discrete indulgent: discard all your worries and keep one; that is your god. Abandon that star and harvest a stone, a flower, a tear; that is your god. Smell a flower, taste the sea, become fond of the sun, befriend a bird, get wet in the rain; that is your god. Abandon everything and touch your heart. Every heartbeat is a step towards your god. You're coming closer to him. He's carrying with him, spirit and passion to invigorate you in his embrace. Accept it. Your heart is beating; your blood is trickling drop by drop; it's yours. Every droplet is a stride toward him; every dewdrop of the early morning is a cobblestone. Count the rhythms of your heart; count the cobblestones. Your heart is beating. You're alive. Accept it. Fly over the seas and mountains; the birds will guide you to warm lands with laced seashores. He's coming, accept it. Now you're crossing the desert: solicit water. The water droplets are following one after the other in a rank as manna, falling from the sky to help you attain your next step. Hover over peaceful countries: smile. Hover over oppressed countries: cast a tear. Hover over jungles, and speak the language of the animals. He's coming. Expose the door of your soul, and welcome him. Your heart rhythm holds on. His approach is imminent. Lift your hand without fear and salute him. Hold him and feel his warmth. Smile and confess. Your heart rhythm, which was progressing with the droplets of your blood, has hastened. Plant him inside your heart. You've traveled in the depths of exultation and despair. You sensed every flower, and you sampled every ocean. You looked everywhere. You summoned him and he came. Get hold of him. He will accompany you to higher grounds. Continue the climb. You must reach extraordinary heights; you must remain with him unaided; you must communicate with his soul; you must acknowledge your soul.

*

SINCE I was very young, one word always brought me to a desolate state: freedom. I was young then, and I didn't recognize its meaning, but I could see its shadow in my mother's wet eyes. As I was growing up, I began to extricate the meaning of the word elsewhere. I could see it in people's faces, in their eyes. Everyone had adopted and embraced their meaning. At some point, I saw the word subsequently next to another one; I understood then, that the road to freedom was by way of the road to death.

Whatever the consequences, people's demise became a struggle for only a piece of land to cultivate and a piece of bread on the table. To be able to survive with their hands, and be free-spirited, as their conscience mandated.

CHAPTER II

Above all books and schools, even deeper than the first happiness and sorrows which the wonders and marvels of the world gave me; deeper than the torments, eagerness, and enthusiasm, truly solitary, only one notion influenced my life so immensely: the struggle to defeat the Junta. The political situation was becoming horrific, and the oppression was depraved and merciless. Severe penalties had been imposed on citizens, who defied the authoritarian rule of the regime. Consequently, their existence became insufferable, while their fear escalated, since that ill-fated early *Friday* morning, when the soldiers and tanks paraded in the streets of the city. There had been two years since the military took over the government, and life had become horrendous and atrocious. Political prisoners populated the islands. Coming from the Headquarters, of that dreadful *Yellow Building*, one could hear screams of pain and agony, as the basement holding cells were full. The oppression was unbearable, and the restrictions uncountable.

The ideology of neo-fascism, ultra-nationalism, and despotism, were the emblems of this government, which led to subjugation, tyranny, and repression. Violence against groups of people was carried out, based on their political believes and convictions. The government's misgivings and mistrust for those people, their perceived threats to the native ethnic group, the nation, or to the ultraconservative traditional social institutions, was the pinnacle of their paranoia, and which the government explicitly exhibited. That astonishing disrespect to the constitution of the land, which the colonels exhibited, instigated a temporary change to the fabric of the Greek society – I might remark here only for a short period since it lasted only for seven years. This authoritarian government was characterized by a single leader, who didn't belong to any political party. There was no mass mobilization and no political pluralism. The top dog, who was identified as a dictator, preferred to refer to himself as *the leader*.

The common aspect that characterized dictators, was their strong personalities. By suppressing freedom of thought and speech of the masses, they succeeded to achieve and maintain complete political and social supremacy and constancy. They employed political propaganda to decrease the influence of advocates of alternative governing systems. Several underground radio stations were cascading all over the country, but they were quickly shut down, and the perpetrators were jailed. Rumors were circulating in cafes and around kitchen tables -- which were particularly true—that the regime was murdering people, jailing them, or exiling them to remote islands, as a result of their beliefs their subversive activities.

*

I decided to go back to that cafe I visited when I first came to the city. I craved fine homemade food, which I had missed since I left home. I also needed to meet the waiter's son who was also at the university. He would be a good advocate for me, as I was beginning my endeavors as a freshman at the university. When I arrived at the cafe, a little before the dinner rush, the place was almost empty. The same waiter greeted me, shaking my hand, recalling my name. He mentioned that his son was in the kitchen and he would send him right out. I thanked him, and I placed my order. While waiting for the arrival of my first to-be-friend in the city, I glanced at the few patrons scattered around the bistro in small groups. It was fairly quiet, which added to the prodigious ambiance of the place. The light blue walls supplemented the blue doors and windows, while several pieces of art hanging on the walls, portraying scenes from around the country in vivid water colors. The floor was an old oak floor, disclosing the many years of memories and reminiscences, which an old building such as this was allowed to recall. The two big fans on the ceiling were dispersing a sound, which was effortless and tranquil to the ear, while an unruffled breeze was descending upon the benefactors of this placid milieu. The sounds from the street were invading this tranquil environment, with vehicles and people rushing by in this warm early evening. The buildings across the street were casting their long shadows on the sidewalks, suggesting that the time for the sun to depart and repose was near.

A man, a few years older than me, approached me from the kitchen, extending his hand to me.

"I'm Ari," he said, extending his hand with a lenient and casual smile enveloping his face.

"I'm Daniel," I said, receiving his hand to a warm handshake.

He took off his apron, and placed it on the back of the chair in front of him, and sat down. He wore jeans and a shirt with the sleeves rolled up to his elbows. His smile showed two healthy rows of white straight teeth, while his brown hair was slightly blowing from the soft breeze, which the fan was dispatching from the ceiling above.

"My father told me you will be attending university here," he alleged with his soft voice.

"Yes, this is my first year, and I'm a little anxious. It's a new city for me, you see, and I feel somewhat alien and unacquainted."

"Where do you come from?" he asked.

"I come from a small village up north, and this is my first visit to this astonishing city," I said, as I tried to relax and feel at ease with this young man.

"What will you be studying?"

"Philology and Philosophy are my passions since I was a little boy," I countered with relish, savoring my words.

"The Philology and Philosophy departments are very respectable and world-renowned. The professors are masters of their virtuosity and have studied here and abroad. Most of them are leaders in their art, dominating the intellectual world with their concepts and principles. They have written several books, exposing their principles and values masterfully, but ..." he hesitated.

"Yes?" I said awaiting his explanation.

He looked around the café, and with a voice almost hardly audible he said:

"You have to be careful. There are some elements on campus, due to the current political situation, that you must not get involved with."

"Why is that?" I asked surprised.

"You'll find out. Have you read the papers? The university campus is not as safe as it used to be. There are cops and sometimes soldiers strolling the campus, spreading fear and uncertainty."

"But aren't the university grounds sacred, protected from these kinds of goings-on?" I asked, but he didn't have a chance to answer; the waiter brought my food steaming and smelling deliciously.

"You have another week before you start. Come by the café again and we'll talk more extensively. It was a pleasure meeting you, Daniel. Enjoy your dinner," he said, offering me his hand for a handshake.

"It was my pleasure indeed, Ari meeting you. We'll talk soon."

He picked up his apron, and with a smile, he turned and went back into the kitchen.

These enigmatic and obscure revelations from Ari struck my heart so deeply, I was left with no answers, no remedies, while my head was trying to make sense out of all this. The contamination of the sacred grounds of the university taking place was unthinkable and immoral. Since ancient times, these grounds had been sacred and no weapons, soldiers or police were allowed in, to pollute and infect its soil, its essences, and its ethics. But this was not the case now, as we had witnessed the barbarism and savagery in the last few years by the government. Reverence and principles did not exist, but only contempt.

Freedom had been folded! It was buried deep under the soil, as with so many other precious fundamental principles. The junta had shown no regard to the constitution, and they had shown no respect for human dignity, integrity, and self-worth.

Freedom had been buried!

*

THE newspapers' headings at that momentous and ill-fated *Friday* read: *Dark days in the city*. It was a time of discontent and disgruntlement, when the tanks rolled through the streets of the capital, as the colonels imposed dictatorship and martial law. And indeed, dark days had fallen upon the dishonored and tarnished city, across the entire country and indeed its citizens. The junta, by oppressing all democratic values, morals, ethics, and principles, sent thousands of citizens to exile, torture them, and ultimately sent them to their death. This group of right-wing army officers, who planned and executed the coup d'état, seized power quickly by using elements of surprise and confusion. Tanks were placed strategically throughout the city, effectively gaining complete control. At the same time, a large number of small mobile units were dispatched, to arrest leading politicians, authority figures, literary personalities, and ordinary citizens, who were suspected as being left-wing sympathizers, according to lists prepared in advance. Within hours, the entire country was under the ruthless rule of the colonels, and by 6 a.m. the announcement came that eleven articles of the constitution were suspended. Consequently, as a result of this suspension, anyone could be arrested without a warrant at any time and brought before a military court to be tried.

There were some US critics of the junta, including then-Senator Lee Metcalf, who criticized the Johnson Administration for offering aid to a *"military regime of collaborators and Nazi sympathizers,"* while Phillips Talbot, the American ambassador in Athens, disapproved of and protested the coup, complaining that it epitomized *"a rape of democracy,"* to which John M. Maury, the CIA station chief answered: *"how can you rape a whore?"* Such a statement was anathema and abhorrence to the country and to the city, which stood for centuries, symbolizing democracy and freedom, and which both could be traced back 2500 years to its laced shores. This onerous state of affairs, which concealed the entire country, could not be exempted or discharged, and return, by some means, to the quality of life it once enjoyed, or a state of elation, unless something dramatic and remarkable took place. This remarkable event, the return to democracy, took seven years to materialize, but not until thousands of people died at the steps of the university, at the streets of the capital, and in remote and improbable islands.

As I left the restaurant, my mind was drifting; I felt alone and abandoned. The square was almost empty, except for a few passersby hurrying home. A soft breeze was coming from the south, as the clouds, orange and yellow, were piled up one on top of the other over the mountain. I walked to a newsstand and I purchased a newspaper. My surprise was, that, although this city used to print at least a dozen daily newspapers, there was only a handful on the newsstands. I picked up one closest to me; after paying for it, I walked away. What kind of news would I read, when eleven articles of the constitution were suspended, including freedom of the press? Where was the integrity of the press? What happened to the truthfulness and veracity of the news reporters, when their hands and mouths were bound, and they were counseled and directed on how to move their pen? There were a few soldiers hither and thither, and military trucks were parked on the road. I was of course aware of this tragic political situation, but it never occurred to me that it was as bad and cruel, as when I walked the streets of the city. Were my future and the future of the country in jeopardy? Were my studies going to be impacted? I needed to speak to Ari. I needed to know what I can do to elevate the burden I felt in my heart. I craved answers.

*

THE atmosphere on the street, as I perceived it that early morning, was inimitable and idiosyncratic. There was something I had not understood yet, since I first arrived in the city. There was something that didn't seem to be genuine, sincere, or authentic. The people on the street were always in an imperativeness and urgent disposition and didn't dare have eye contact with anyone. Although at a first glance, the city looked engaged and eventful, one would also notice the electrifying atmosphere, concealing any sense of exhilaration and contentment. An atmosphere that was launched and authenticated the early hours of that awful and horrifying *Friday.* The sidewalks were freshly washed, and the tables and umbrellas were consigned to their location on the wet pavement. A few patrons were sitting quietly under an umbrella, shipping their morning coffee reading a newspaper. My head was filled with apprehensions and doubts about my future. Was it the right time for me to come to the city and commence my studies at the university?

The freshly washed sidewalks, the flowers decorating every window, every balcony, the brilliant blue sky, and the warm breeze, which was caressing my face, were lingering around from the past; from more fortunate and blissful days. But my eyes were not looking at this animated, deceitful and fallacious personification of life, but far beyond; yonder than the clouds, the mountains, and the oceans; yonder than the limits of the mind; yonder than my heart. My freedom was lost and disoriented. Life meant freedom; but my life was adrift along with my freedom, I thought. I consigned out of the way the flesh, the bones, and the entrails to find it but I couldn't. I secured a ladder against the sky, and I climbed it; perhaps I would find it that way. I felt anguish inside my heart tormenting me. I felt it was an ovary, a capsule, a product of my soul, which was struggling, held by the chains of the oppressive and tyrannical regime, since that ill-fated *Friday*, when a bunch of colonels took over the country in a coup d'état. I was submerged in the webs and lattices of my world, and anguish was hanging over my head, as if I were resting my head on a guillotine and my executioners, having covered their faces with black cloth, prolong my beheading, persisting and elongating my death. The dictatorial regime in Athens had confiscated freedom and ashamed and humbled the white marbles. The desperate voices of the tormented and agonized prisoners of the *Yellow Building*, the police headquarters, were heard throughout the city and indeed throughout the country and the world. Freedom had folded. The political situation was putting a damper on my heart and my aspirations. The disposition of the city had changed. It was far gone.

*

WALKING swiftly among tables, chairs, and unresponsive and mechanized people, I was headed in the direction of the café. When I arrived, I ordered a coffee, and sat inside the café at a corner, waiting for Ari to join me. Our conversation was interminable and prolific. I was pledged and ensured contacts, which would assist me in getting through my apprehensions and fears. I learned that there was a student anti-government rebellious organization, to which many students belonged to. They were organized and were planning something inevitable and decisive. Many other organizations were in support of the students, including trade unions, banned radio stations, which were operating now from secret locations outside the country – of which I was given their frequencies -- and several outlawed anti-government organizations operating abroad. I felt a sense of alleviation and reprieve. The activities of the students were promised to bring about some deviations to our lives, and possibly a changed political situation. This idea, although very optimistic and buoyant, brought some sense of normalcy and reprieve to my distressed and unsettled heart. I left the café and Ari, after promising to meet again the next day.

CHAPTER III

The morning came about the city with its usual noise, hassle, and bustle on the streets as if suddenly everyone woke up at the same time and spilled into the avenues of this metropolis. I distilled my mind to retrieve any fragments of the discussions I had with Ari the day before. The situation was dreadful and appalling, and I was terrified of what might come next week when I started my classes at the university. The capital was veiled by fear and trepidation, obscuring in its entirety everything magnificent, which characterized the city. Gentle and delicate was the breeze, which blew from the south, and it drew me to its earthly smells. Upon it, the stones and sidewalks were in a haze. Without warning, the air became thick and agitated; the warm exhale of people and animals was lifting in the air, and a pleasant smell of fresh bread was mixing with the sour smell of human perspiration. But swiftly, the noises and the human voices blended with engines roaring, disappeared; and suddenly and amid the silence which overtook the entire city, a scream, a shout was heard from deep inside its entrails, the people and the white marbles: *"until when? Until when?"* It was not one man; it was the entire city which was shouting; it was the bones of the dead; it was the roots of the trees, the white marbles: this land. It was this land that was in pain, and could not give birth.

I met Ari at the café on Wednesday morning, and he treated me to a cappuccino and a piece of spinach pie. He introduced me to a friend of his,

Avgy, who was helping in the kitchen. I discovered, during our conversation, that she also belonged to the students' organization and she was in her second year in Philology. I asked her several questions about the program, and I was disappointed and saddened to find out that a great number of writings of prominent authors, philosophers, and philologists, domestic and international were proscribed from the curriculum of the university. But she assured me, that the organization had a vast library of most of the banned books. The time I chose to enroll at the university was not the right time, considering the prohibitions and restrictions imposed upon the students, professors, and the institution itself.

The conversation was carried over to the activities of the students' organization, tactics, and engagements in subversive activities and plans. "We still have to organize," Avgy added, "and bring into the organization more people from the university and the community. There is a great deal of interest, and we are exploiting this opportunity," she said carefully choosing her words, speaking in a low voice, which induced confidence within me, nodding with the conviction of indeed being aware of the risks and consequences.

"Tomorrow we'll visit the campus, and I'll show you around," Ari said, bringing me back to reality and nearer to my purpose, which at that point had become obvious that there could be turbulent days ahead. "I'll be waiting for you here at nine to walk to the campus. Then you'll get a sense of the environment which exists there."

"I'm discouraged about what kind of education I'll receive because most of the books I wanted to study have been banned," I said, as Ari nodded with a shade of concern in his look.

"Things will change," Avgy said with confidence.

Things will change, my heart echoed.

I left the café in deep thought. I walked the streets looking for answers in faceless people, which had no expression, utterance, or feelings; they had just departed long ago. I disappeared among the countless people on the sidewalk, as the sun was battering my face, feeling the late morning warmth, sensing that I was trapped in the tentacles of the regime, afflicted by its wrath. I thought of my father who was struggling in the village with the properties and the animals, enduring the political situation, trying to stay away from any controversy, which might escort him to unsolicited and undesirable places. I had an inexplicable and arcane desire to be there with him, hearten him and relieve him from uncertainties and ambiguities. I was certain, his apprehension of me being here alone, was a great discomfort and agonizing for him and my mother, not knowing what I might find here, amidst the current circumstances. I thought of the animals which were brutally slaughtered, and the animals my father lost and squandered around the river; his anguish to cultivate the land, which he might lose to a new highway the government was proposing; the loss of his son who was so supportive helpful to him and who loved so dearly.

This inexplicable loss of confidence and buoyancy in one's existence was a dramatic switch of fate; the uncertainty and apprehensiveness of the future of this land and mine were genuine and authentic. I sat at a park bench, observing my surroundings. Suddenly I heard sirens erupting from the end of the street, as flashing lights were coming from a speeding police vehicle. It stopped in front of an apartment building. Several policemen got out of the armored vehicle, and run through the doors of the building up the stairs. A short while later, they carried out a man in handcuffs and led him inside the vehicle. They sped away again with the flashing lights of the cruiser flaring and with a deafening sound of the sirens. As the sound of the siren perished, silence engulfed the park again. Some passersby had stopped to observe the spectacle of this fateful man, dragged away in a cruiser, and taken to the interrogation room of the chief of police while others, bending their heads to the ground, hurried away as if they were next in line.

This inhumane way of treatment stopped the heart and smothered the brain, desperately trying to find a reason, an explanation for all this mistreatment of one's ideology. The life uncertainties, which the regime had brought and the fearful tactics, which they executed daily, demonstrated the imminent failure of the regime, and they acted as such as if we were immersed in a war. I was aware of the *Yellow Building* downtown, where most of the interrogations took place. The fate of each one who entered that building was uncertain, resulting in many cases being tortured, held with no warrant, or sent to isolated and far away islands. The tentative existence of citizens was sadistic and atrocious. Life had become worthless and futile in the hands of the colonels.

CHAPTER IV

Dusk fell about almost stealthily, with a warm breeze coming from the south, as the lights of the streets veneered the city. I quickened my pace reaching the hotel, climbing the short staircase into the cool lobby. I took the narrow staircase to my room, while the tales of the street, I witnessed that day, were going from place to place in my head unsettled. I laid down on the bed, while the echoes of the street followed me to a deep and immersed sleep. It was quite late when I woke up, and I was annoyed by the fact that I wasted the entire and unqualified evening. I felt that I lived adrift and in shadows. I got up and I set out to write a letter to my parents. The ongoing dreadful and appalling political situation, the wildfires burning outside the city, and the slaughter of animals in my small village, were enough to be concerned about the imminent future of the peasants and of this country.

My parents were always quiet about such issues; never engaged in any brawls or arguments with the villagers, making sure that the animals and the land were taken care of, although recently they had lost a couple of sheep in the hands of intruders and murderers. I was certain, my parents were very concerned about my safety in the big city, where everything was taking place. I needed to reassure them, but how could I have done that? I heard that mail was being opened by the authorities before it was delivered to its destination. I ought to be careful, exploiting such uncertainties. As a renowned celebrated German playwright wrote once, *"when you go through Germany, hide the truth under your coat,"* which Galileo uttered to his aid. I must hide the truth under my tongue.

I met Ari at the café at 9 in the morning, to accompany me to the university grounds. The morning was pleasant, with the sun rising high above the eastern mountains, casting its long shadows about the city. There was a sense of excitement and anticipation which I felt in my gut.

The short walk to the university was quiet. We walked without speaking to each other, observing the passersby curiously with a flare in my eyes. The walkway to the university buildings from the street was lined with orange trees, whose branches stoop full of fruit. I was amazed at the splendor and magnificence of the building climbing the stairs. There were two columns, as the illustrious and imposing statues of Athena and Apollo were resting on them. Upon entering the building, there were enormous columns that filled the foyer. Across from the entrance, there were two massive double doors, which led to a lecture hall. This impressive and enormous room was lit with the natural light glow from a skylight, while remarkable and inspiring paintings lined the walls. This Neo-classical style architecture which was imposing and inspiring, decorated with sculptures of ancient Greece, is one of the oldest institutions of higher education in the country. The building of the University of Athens is part of a trilogy which includes also the National Library and the Academy of Athens, which are situated next to each other. The National Library, also Neo-Classic, is a masterpiece and a historical building with exquisite architecture. The books, neatly stacked tall on various floors – I was certain the stacks of books were much higher before that inauspicious *Friday* -- were visible from the lobby of the library, which was used for research in historical, scientific, and philological matters. A few other buildings were neighboring the National Library, with equally impressive and astounding architecture, ornamented by ancient statues.

We entered this impressive and inspiring lecture hall. Looking around, I could feel the presence of Socrates lecturing the youth of Athens. I could sense the arguments the students were making, challenging the great philosopher. I could sense the profound answers and counteroffers given by this great and nobleman. My timid and timorous outlook, esteeming these exquisite buildings, the statues, and the thousands of books piled up in the library, gave me a sense of purpose, gratification, and fulfillment. My studies would commence only in a few days.

It was past noon when we left the university. The heat was bearable with a few feathery nomadic clouds drifting across the sky, pilling up on top of the mountain. The streets and sidewalks were busy with hurrying pedestrians and vehicles, engaging in their world, however occupying a great deal of whatever space was available. I allowed my thoughts to wander around inside my head, reminiscing of what I experienced that morning, recalling memories of the past, evoking emotions that were still raw inside me. Ari turned and faced me; he had a contemplative and reflective expression on his face; he looked at me, and his lips parted to a solicitous smile.

"Daniel, the other day we talked about the situation here, around the country and at the university; I mentioned implicitly the organization; I suggested that we should talk some more about it, and the role you may potentially play," Ari said.

"Ari," I said after a moment of silence, "Ari, lift your hand and hit me; hit me until I come to my senses. I'm tired of being afraid."

Ari slowed down his pace, and he turned to me. His eyes now had a supportive gaze, looking deep into my eyes. "Does your heart agree with you, Daniel? Are you really afraid, or you're speaking off your cuff?"

"I'm drained and exhausted, Ari; today I'm repulsed and dismayed; it churns my stomach. I disgusted my soul. Show me the way, Ari, I'm ready. My only thoughts turning around inside my head all day long, were how I will be able to complete my studies within this environment. I wasn't thinking of the struggles our brothers and sisters are going through; I was thinking about myself and my studies. I'm ready. Show me the way."

Ari looked around, then turned to me. "Daniel, can you put your life on the line for the cause?" he said in a low voice.

"Yes Ari, I can," I said, and my heart quivered.

I had read a great deal in the media about the *outlawed* organizations, fighting the evils of fascism; the *Reds* as they were called. The media characterized them as terrifying people, with their bombings and sabotages; a fearsome bunch of anarchists, they said; they walk around armed with weapons and bombs, spreading death and destruction; disorder, chaos, and rebellion.

"Have you killed anybody, Ari?"

"I haven't; but when the time comes, we may have to result to that. Only time will tell," he said, and he looked at me again with a broken smile on his face. "Are you afraid? We're not murderers, you know, don't be alarmed. We're fighting for freedom, to unchain our country from the chuckles, which suffocate and smother our soul, Daniel. Get up, the time has come for you to show concern, take an interest and be a fighter; come with us."

I had my head down, meditating on Ari's words. Ari came closer, bent over me, and gently touched my arm.

"What's our life, Daniel?" he said, "what is it worth to you, to me to anyone? Nothing, if it's not free. We're fighting for freedom; come with us."

I was listening, and my heart was filled with butterflies. "Daniel, do you have it in your heart? Make a decision and settle on it," he said as he grabbed me by the arm and shook me. He was right; we were fighting for freedom; we were fighting for a much bigger cause, bigger purpose than studies and universities. I made up my mind.

We walked in silence and deep in thought. We came to the café exhausted. Avgy had left a few books at the café for me, which was as brave and daring of her as defiant. They were in a dark plastic bag.

"Take them to the hotel," Ari said, "safeguard them and don't bring them to the university. You can read them whenever you're alone. These books are banned, and the consequences are enormous if they find them," Ari said cautiously, offering me the plastic bag with the books.

I thank Ari, and I left the café. That afternoon I spent hours going through the books, reading paragraphs, pages, going from one book to another. I felt frantic, that someone might barge into my room and snatch them away from me. I wanted to read them, lock them deep inside my brain, engraved forever. I wanted to be able to expose and bear my brain to throw them in, thus no one would ever find them. This thesaurus of knowledge, now hidden under my mattress, was the kind of knowledge I could never acquire at school under the current circumstances. I heard of raids which the police would contact habitually, especially on students, regretfully, looking for relevant banned material. And B. Brecht's phrase, *"hide the truth under your coat,"* was indeed alive and well here. The truth was hidden under my mattress; it was well guarded.

CHAPTER V

The life of the villagers was becoming increasingly challenging and elusive; the slaughter of the animals, been discovered all around the countryside, tormented them, creating disputes and allegations among villagers. Furthermore, the plans of the government to misappropriate a great deal of land to build a highway would disrupt the livelihood of the farmers, leaving smaller patches of land to cultivate, and for their animals to feed. In a letter from my father, protesting intensely the government's plans, he indicated that the government would defraud –that's the way he put it— defraud a significant piece of his land, resulting in splitting it into two. The village dwellers didn't concede to that idea; they couldn't see the need for a thoroughfare going through their properties. There was plenty of municipal lands which could be used for this purpose. This expansion would obliterate the fabric and the structure of small towns and villages, displace animals and people alike, and create an atmosphere, which would be disruptive for the peaceful and productive existence of the residence.

The suspicion was that the killings of the animals were associated directly with the proposed development of the highway -- although there was no evidence to that -- trying to force the inhabitants out of their land, and compel them to sell it to the government at ridiculously low prices. My father's land had been in the family for generations, and the prospect of losing part of it was unthinkable and excessive. With the surging trend of commercial exchanges among nations in Europe, and the development of many cities and towns to prepare them for the possibility of joining the union – which was, of course, inconceivable and improbable, considering the current political situation – the government had falsely advocated that possibility. Joining the union was mostly just talk in the media, because the colonels will never agree to that, and the community will never accept them, considering their revolting record of human rights abuses, they've displayed.

Progress, evolution, and prosperity were the words the government used, to describe the heisting of their land, while the killings of their animals were taking place in broad daylight. What kind of logic and rationale permitted such actions? Was it done by a deranged person, who enjoyed the sight of blood, and who had a thing about seeing the blood rushing down the throats of these innocent creatures, or was it set off by the government, instigating such actions as to drive the villagers out of their land? Was the government as malicious and callous as to take these kinds of measures to such an extent, as to destroy the livelihood of the farmers to obtain its goal? That brought to memory the wildfires, set across the outskirts of the capital a little while ago – presumably by developers -- to attain permission to develop the land, which would have been unthinkable under different circumstances. Hundreds of acres were burnt, vineyards, orchards, and large sections of the hills and mountains. Pure destruction.

*

THE state of being free was non-existent; it had vanished. People were restrained, muted, keeping them in check; a free choice had been eluded along with their freedom. What freedom was, or the concept of it could have gone in a very inexplicable direction. Freedom had perished, democracy had departed. I heard the cries and whispers coming from the ancient monuments and the fallen pillars, from the streets of the city, from the hearts and souls of those who had been denied that basic human compulsion. I heard voices, which had been lost in the essence and embodiment of society, distilled by the restrictions imposed upon them.

But this eschatological human condition was capable of extracting out of the combated people's hearts other significant and expressive qualities, which were seen only under pressure, and under the loss of self-respect and dignity. The intensity and ardor, which one felt upon the loss of their liberties and autonomies, were enough to bring about transformations, alterations, and undeniably unrest and ultimately revolutions. The core beliefs and principles of people were undeniably very strong, and when it came down to the possibility, that their core values might be destroyed, annihilated, or even be replaced by other undesirable, uninvited, or even unsolicited beliefs, their consent was never in submission. True beliefs never surrendered, and capitulation was disputable. A feeling of cognitive discord instinctively was fashioned within them. That realization was very important and imperative, permitting the sheltering and guarding of their core values, rationalizing it as being outside the realm and jurisdiction of their existence.

*

THE morning was unfolding slowly, as the sun left the embrace of the eastern mountain, plummeting into the firmament of the blue sky. The soft breeze, blowing from the west, was giving some relief to the morning heat. The merchants had spread out their products on tables, blocking partially the sidewalks, as the day, still young, was seizing every corner of the city. The pigeons, in large flocks, concealed a great deal of the sky, diving onto the sidewalks and parks. I approached the window and opened it, to marvel at the new day, arriving with glitter and great expectations. A policeman, holding a baton on his right hand, hitting the palm of his left hand with it, and with a sense of intimidation and coercion, slowly approached a group of youngsters standing at the corner of the street talking, and asked them to disperse. The sidewalks were already lined up with chairs, tables, and umbrellas, as the patrons of the cafes were enjoying their morning coffee, reading the latest news. I dressed quickly and climbing down the narrow staircase. I ventured outside.

   I read through the entire night the books which were hidden under my mattress. The fresh cool breeze hit my face, and the airiness and crispness of the early morning were refreshing and invigorating. I walked to the café among blossomed trees and colorful flower pots, set at various corners and staircases. The fruit and vegetable stands were loaded with the daily production, and their fragrance elevated from every cart. A magnificent Chopin's piano concerto, which was heard coming out of the open window of a house, was received pleasantly, filling my senses with gratitude. An armour military vehicle sped up the street, and turned the corner ahead of me, roaring at incredible speed, as people were rushing to get out of its way. Sirens were heard from a distance, while another armored vehicle took the same direction. It was offensive and insolent to hear the sirens blasting from a speeding military vehicle, over the soft and thought-provoking Chopin; equally as offensive was to the aromas coming from the flowers and the fragrance from the fresh produce. Those adverse and contrasting notions mystified and bewildered my mind, plunging the spirit into the abyss of feelings and sentiments. Is the end near?

I reached the café sweaty, sticky, and out of breath. I found an empty table outside under an umbrella and I claimed it. Several people were walking the sidewalks while others were sipping their coffee quietly, in this pleasant but hot Athenian morning. Two policemen, stationed at the corner, were watching the toing and froing around, while a military truck was parked in front of the park further down the street; the soldiers inside the truck were contemptuous and sardonic with each other. The waiter brought my steaming coffee, acknowledging me with a charming smile. Ari came out to greet me, announcing that we were to meet certain people that evening. He would introduce me to them, indicating that they were good connections for several reasons. Would that soothe the conflict I was fighting inside me? Would my devils be extricated and free me and allow me to breathe the sterile and unadulterated air of my eagerness and anticipation? A conflict which was arisen from the fight between my survival as a student, and my survival as a citizen of an oppressive city? This enormous conflict, which occupied my mind with immense questions, could not be wrestled down without hesitation. My imminent involvement in the student organization was imperative and necessary, to fight the hostile environment, which was defective and deficient in freedom and human rights. My studies were also critical and eminent, in which the success of it depended heavily upon the moral and comprehensive educational system which was non-existent at that point. But my conflict was still raging furiously inside me: fear, panic, and distress, products of the current political situation, were fighting with my other devil: the devil which was commanding my growth and my advancement, to move forward and complete my studies as I had promised to my parents.

I left the café heavy-headed, walking the noisy and crowded streets. The meeting that night was encouraging and prolific. I was introduced to Stephan, Mary, Lisa, Jason, and Michael. Ari and Avgy also attended, which made it easier and more comfortable for me. Upon the launching of the meeting, Stephan began by welcoming the members, and particularly me, the newest member.

My first meeting at the organization was with apprehension and skepticism. The danger, involving myself in any subversive activities, was enormous, which could lead to very serious consequences, putting my studies in jeopardy, or perhaps end up in jail or even worse. That was the beginning of a long and difficult journey, which I was asked to embark on. But why such hesitation? Why such reluctance to accept this responsibility and carry it out? Was I afraid? Afraid of what? Why was I so terrified of the prospect, that I might not achieve what I set out to accomplish here in the big city? How much was my freedom worth? What was the price that I had to pay? My studies? My life? Years in prison? What frightened me mostly? Suddenly, I felt a weight pressing upon my heart, and my temples were beating like a drum.

CHAPTER VI

It was Saturday evening when my spirits were boosted upon a telephone call from Avgy, inviting me out to dinner. It was a very pleasant and quiet evening, with a soft wind blowing from the south; the shadows were long on the street when I stepped out of the hotel. The heat had subsided, and the air was refreshing and crisp. The children's laughter was echoing from the side streets, and a few birds were flying low over the umbrellas on the sidewalks. I walked up Academy Street. I could have taken the yellow trolley, but I felt like walking in this amiable and congenial evening among people, looking at the windows of the shops. We met at a friendly and meticulous small bistro by the Parliament building. She looked very elegant and gracious, with her brown hair combed to the side, her green eyes bright and luminous; her white shirt was falling over her shoulders with flair and elegance, while her blue stylish jeans were somewhat tight. She wore sandals, which revealed her polished toenails. Her smile, confident and bright, exposed a row of white teeth which gave her bright and photogenic defiance. Her posture was elegant and assertive. She shook my hand, and I felt the softness of her palm as if I were caressing velvet. The waiter showed us to a table by the large window overlooking the square, and I asked for a bottle of wine. We talked for hours. We touched on several topics: my new semester at the university, the current political situation, the concerns and fretfulness of the people, the brutality of the government, and her father's situation.

"Where is your father now?" I asked her with a sense of concern in my voice.

"Ah, my father," she said and shook her head. "I'm not ashamed to tell you, Daniel, that he's in prison. He's a political prisoner, not a criminal," she said sadly and with pride.

"A political prisoner! What happened?" I asked, and my voice validated my concern.

"He was caught distributing leaflets to unionized workers," she said, "one of those things which you somehow expect."

"When did that happen?" I asked.

"About a year and a half ago. He's been in jail for over a year now."

"How is he treated?" I asked rhetorically, of course, knowing very well what kind of treatment he would be subjected to.

"We hardly see him. We're allowed to see him only once every two months. His hair has turned completely white, limping at one side. Twice they woke him up early morning to take him for execution and twice was returned to his cell. Tactics of intimidation. He's treated very badly, and I'm not sure how long he will survive, to talk about his saga," Avgy said, and her eyes went teary. She wiped them with the back of her hand, and she blew out a sad sound declaring her grief.

"Did he have a trial?"

"Ha, yes; if you call that a trial," she said with a mocking and sardonic laugh.

"How about a lawyer? Did he have one?" I asked, thinking perhaps it was again a rhetorical question.

"He was assigned a lawyer by the department," she said, and she chuckled again.

"Assigned a lawyer?" I echoed, "what kind of a trial was that?"

"It was a classic *mock* trial. He didn't have time to defend himself; but again, how could he? The trial lasted less than half an hour."

"Less than half an hour!" I echoed her words. "What was the charge?" I asked.

"Distributing subversive material which was prohibited under such and such a law."

"A law which was made up on the fly, I'm sure," I said, extending my hand placing it on top of hers. "I'm so sorry about your father, Avgy. This isn't democracy. In a democracy, one is allowed to demonstrate, distribute literature, or express grievances that one may have with the government or its policies," I said, and I was sure no grievances or objections to any of their laws could have been heard.

"Oh, Daniel; no, we don't have democracy; we have a totalitarian regime. They make up their laws as they go, to move forward their agenda."

"What was the verdict?"

"Five years. Five harsh years."

"That's a very severe penalty for distributing leaflets," I said, and my stomach turned with disgust.

"Yes, it is, and I don't know if he will endure such a sentence. He has health issues which need attention, but I'm not sure if he gets the treatment that he needs in prison," Avgy said, as her face turned red, and she erupted into a silent sob.

"How do you cope Avgy? I mean, it must be very difficult and distressing for you. I'm sure you're yearning for his presence; you worry about his health and the condition he will be in when he gets out."

"If he ever gets out. I'm missing him enormously. His health is very poor, and I worry that he may give up and die in prison," she said, as tears were traversing her sad and attractive face.

"You must hope, Avgy; you must hope something will happen, and he will be released from prison before his sentence is over," I said, kissing her hand.

"I hope so; I don't want him to die there," she said, as she kept her hand under my kiss."

"People are very resilient in these kinds of circumstances, and they hold on. Injustice and prejudice feed the heart and soul with the desire to break the chains of slavery, yearning for freedom, aspiring them to fight back with all the strength they have. If he dies in prison, it will be a triumph for the regime. He will fight, I'm sure," I said, looking at her brilliant eyes.

"Yes, he will fight; he's a fighter but he's also old," she said, and her gaze turned toward the square, where it got lost among people, streetcars, and policemen.

*

SUCH were the tactics of the junta; they were aiming to destroy and crush the people's confidence, poised to force them to offer false confessions; then the government would have a motive to keep them in prison, send them to exile or execute them, and at the same time justify it. I mentioned to Avgy the tribulations which the small-town folks were enduring with the government, including my parents, attempting to take their land away, to construct a new highway. There was no help for the farmers coming from the ministry of agriculture, while their crops and produce were sold at ridiculously low prices. The government defended its actions by insisting that the low prices were a result of international low prices for wheat, fruit, and vegetables, which was partially true. The inflation rate of the country was 6.6%, compared to the United Kingdom's rate which was 6.4%, and unemployment was high. The economy all around the world was not very healthy; the Watergate scandal was unfolding, and the war in Vietnam was still ravaging. One hundred thousand demonstrators were voicing their displeasure against the war in Vietnam in many U.S. cities. Twenty-two bombs exploded in Belfast, killing 9 people seriously injuring 130 on Bloody Friday; and on Bloody Sunday the IRA exploded a bomb at the 16th Parachute Brigade Headquarters in Aldershot. Martial Law was declared in the Philippines, which was very familiar to our people here, as we had it very often since that ill-fated *Friday*. The entire world was in a state of hysteria and chaos. Dismay and confusion were governing the people, while discontent and frenzy were expressed on streets and in front of parliaments around the world. The world was unkind and hostile; it was ailing by the day, and something was about to happen. The people here had tasted in their palate similar emotions and sentiments but were terrified to react, oxidized by the brutal measures and exploits of the regime.

Thrusting away the apprehensions and agonies of the world for a while, I felt quite comfortable with Avgy, having a bottle of wine with dinner, overlooking the parliament square. There were a lot of people on the plaza, exploiting this attractive and warm evening. Although soldiers and police were visible here and there, in armor trucks or on foot about the square and the neighboring streets, the scene was quite serene and placid. Conversely, in introspect, such a scene of armed soldiers and police, seemed, to many reflective and brooding people, very disturbing; realizing, of course, that one lived in a police state environment, putting a dumper on the emotions and feelings of each one of us. Happiness had become a far-reaching sentiment, and self-esteem had been annihilated. Reading the newspapers, or listening to the radio or television, the newscast was covered with a blanket of restrictions and false news, while the journalistic freedom, rights, and integrity had been abandoned somewhere back a few years ago.

Liberal and left-leaning newspapers had either been forced to close or follow the protocol which the government dictated. Several journalists had been jailed, while others had been sent away. The fabric of the society was constantly changing with the rise of extreme right-wing ideologies and neo-Nazi sympathizers, while the fear and trepidation which people felt, made the environment electrified, dangerous, and fearful with apprehensions. I had set my goals: I would concentrate on my studies, and congeal my duty to minister the organization, abiding with its decrees, offering my services for whatever the state of affairs would be, searching and fighting for justice, and freedom. What is justice after all, when it's stripped of appearances? *"Justice is the first condition of humanity,"* the Nigerian poet and playwright Wole Soyinka -- who won the 1986 Nobel Prize for Literature -- put it bluntly. It was a necessary human condition as apparent and intimate as the air we breathe. Freedom, in its pure and virtuous form, was unavailable, as we were trying to recollect and reclaim its true meaning. There was no justification for merely existing and being exploited, persecuted, and tormented by the authorities, but it was rather revolting, trying to salvage the freedom we all held dear in our hearts.

Leaving the restaurant, we walked along University Avenue, looking at the lavishly decorated shop windows, loaded with exclusive imports and expensive merchandise for the few.

*

AT a confined and sheltered corner, where the wind was contained, there was a ragged man in rather scruffy clothes, who looked quite intoxicated. He was wearing a rather long gabardine, shoes which seem to be missing most of their outsoles and heels; his long and unshaven face was twisted to expose his cheekbones; his eyes were dilated, and their deep grey color was reflecting something hallucinogenic about them, while bodily fluids, extricated from his nose, were meeting those from his mouth. He was rickety and unsettled with his posture, and he seemed to be agitated with the ground, which was not steady under his feet, or so he thought. He was moving his hands around as if he were attempting to catch invisible insects in the air. He was moving back and forth and bending at the same time as if he were ready to fall. Avgy and I approached him, looked at him with a sense of curiosity and desolation, as we greeted him *hello*.

"Ha… ha… hi there fellow," he replied trying to focus, squaring his eyes on mine as they were squirming around. "He… he… hello you pretty lady," he said trying to focus on Avgy, taking a couple of steps forward and backward.

I reached in my pocket, and I took out some change, placing it in the cup he was holding. He raised the index finger of his left hand, bent his body a little, and took a few steps backward and forward uncontrollably.

"Tha… tha… thank ou ma frend," he said and bowed to the ground ready to fall forward. Attempting to catch his fall he waved me away. "I … I'm… I'm okay," he said, steadying himself as best as he could, despite the influence of the alcohol and the amount of it he had in his veins.

"I noticed this young lady over there was making calf eyes at you," I said laughing, pointing at a young woman walking away on the sidewalk. "You know," I said, turning to the intoxicated panhandler, "you need to watch out for ones like her. The maids are easy to buy off, but one like her…"

"Essackly," he said with a hiccup, "she's one a' those respec … restec … reseptable types. Mi … might … might even have some ideas about climbin' a few rungsh a' the social ladder," the intoxicated man said trying to stabilize his feet on the sidewalk.

"Would you like to come for a coffee?" I asked him.

"Ju… ju… ju… jus' a moment … okay," he put his hand in the inside pocket of his coat, recovered a flask with alcohol, and took a mouthful. He placed it back in his pocket, took a couple of steps forward and backward tottering, as he tried to focus on me again. "I … I … I rathe stay here. You… you… you see, people move back and forth and… and the light show there, is a… a… amazing," he said, pointing in front of him into emptiness. We left him in his perceived happiness and walked away.

*

Listen, you affluent and prosperous people; and you prevailing and mighty of the world; we cannot endure and accept dishonesty, corruption, disloyalty, and hunger. For how long would you be laying on your soft mattresses? For how long would you be eating the meat of the poor? For how long would you be drinking the sweet wine, the blood, and the tears of the deprived and unfortunate ones? Society cannot sustain you any longer. Fire is coming; the dead are exhumed and arisen; the end of your reign and control is coming.

*

We talked on the way to her apartment, exploring the harshness of daily life, life at the university, and the horrific and terrifying conditions which our environment and the earth were facing. We stopped outside her building; she turned and kissed me on the cheek. My skin welcomed with ecstasy her warm soft lips, embracing her warm touch. She turned and disappeared behind the door which led to the lobby. I walked to my hotel, still feeling the convivial and tender touch of her lips on my face. I must declare, this was the first time I was kissed by a girl. This confession, however gratifying and mellifluous as it were, made my face twinkled and ostentatious.

My adverse economic situation led me to believe that I needed to work my way through school, without waiting for my parents to take all the burden for sending me to the big city to attend university. There were many jobs I could do, I thought; it was just a matter of finding something, making a start. Many students worked during their academic ventures. I would speak to Ari, I thought. I went to bed reflecting on Avgy, pondering in my mind how beautiful she looked, and how tender and affectionate her kiss was.

CHAPTER VII

Wherever I looked, the faces I glimpsed on the streets, the newspapers I read, everything was a reminiscence of that *Friday,* recollecting memories, recalling the misfortunate and unprincipled events of that day. The disastrous results of that calamitous and ill-starred day had stigmatized and branded the fabric of society; denouncing and censuring human dignity; deploring compassion, fundamental and elemental human rights, and civil liberties.

The shadows were cuddling at the side of the buildings, under the scorching sun of high noon, which looked like a nibble of fire in the sky. I returned to the hotel after a long walk. There, amidst my society's afflictions and its desolate silence, I relived my sort journey in the inconsolable streets; allowing some order to the sorrows and miserable existence, encountering my people on this ancient metropolis, suffering the anguishes of their everyday life under the shackles of conformity and submission. Where was my responsibility resting? I could no longer flee my duty; it had attained a heart and soul within me now. The temples and the white columns had spoken; the dead had risen, divulging to the country and to me, as an enormous Golgotha --such was its destiny since the beginning of time -- their plight and tribulations. What then? What was my obligation? But then again, was it to exert me and toil with her, to toss my life and heart and soul into the battle, at her side? Our freedom? Then, the beyond emanated. It emanated beyond freedom and justice, validating our existence, legitimizing our spirits; soothing and consoling our heart.

Have courage.

But why did I seek freedom? I was not going to the mountains or the border, rifle in hand, to combat our common enemy! Our battleground was here, in this city, its boulevards, its cobblestone streets, and the university grounds. We knew our enemy, it had an identity; it had been acknowledged and recognized; whatever decisions I assembled, I would accomplish them with reverence, integrity, and rectitude; I was certain of this. My perseverance and honor were engraved inside my heart, and my blood was caring them all acros my body. Freedom was a primary and ultimate human desire. But there was something else that was tormenting me: dignity. Freedom was in sync with dignity. Was that mankind's utmost and absolute model? Could we have gone beyond the limits of freedom and dignity? Could we have taken our country beyond that? It seemed as if destiny had driven its sword through the living substance of the land to slit away a piece of its troubled heart.

*

"*I'm afraid to go further,*" the fears inside me would admit, "*my potency and intensity stretch merely so far. I cannot endure.*" But the soothing voice inside me would nobly say, "*your contractual obligation has been done; you precipitated and brought about an order higher than I can endure; you remain here as a symbol; I will venture further and I will fight.*" Tightening my belt and holding my rifle in one hand, I glanced at my brother, raising my other hand to a farewell. Embracing him, I felt his anxieties and his apprehensions; he beamed, as his essence was issued with inflammation and affection, roguishly.

I left, as our hearts and souls departed for the unknown; I made my decision. My battle was unfolding in front of me; I should grab it by its horns. My consciousness had declared its highest obligation and its sense of duty; I should follow.

Only two primordial obsessions, or rather trepidations, reigned within me until that moment: the struggle to unshackle freedom and the longing for it, and now, these two obsessions were ignited inside me. The world was greater than this land. The world's anguish was greater than our anguish, and the longing for freedom was not the absolute privilege of ours; it was indeed the persistent struggle of all mankind; and although my brothers and sisters did not cease to exist in my mind, all mankind, along with my brothers and sisters, unfolded within me to become one.

*

My heart was heavy; my senses were mirroring the turbulent sea. My impatience and intolerance had reached high ground, and I was burning. The severity of my people was such, coming from above, that I looked for kindness and gentleness. Was God heartless, merciless, and unkind? Was he testing his people to see who would endure, and survive the calamities which had fallen upon their heads? That my grief were thoroughly weighed, and my calamity laid in the balance together! For now, it would be heavier, and my words were swallowed up. What was then my strength that I should hope for? What was my end that I should prolong my life? Was my strength the strength of stone? Was my flesh of brass? Now, be content and look upon me. Return, I implored you, let it not be iniquity and return my righteousness. Was there iniquity in my tongue? Couldn't my taste discern perverse things? Now, my God, I would not refrain my mouth. I would speak in the anguish of my spirit; I would complain in the bitterness of my soul. When I said, my bed comforted me, and my couch eased my complaints, you frightened me with dreams so that my soul chose to struggle and death rather than life.

I turned my eyes full of tears toward the window, and gazing out at the burned hearts of my people, I said, *"brothers and sisters, even those will get justice one day."* I bit into the day; not a single drop of green blood dripped. I shouted at the gates of God, and my voice took the grief of murderers. In the earth's centre appeared the dark tanks, growing darker and darker, and the sun's rays, look, became the guiding threads of death. I opened my mouth, and the whole world trembled; it carried my words to its darkest caves … and you whispered them gently to the innocent foolish men, who wept in the night over their troubles. I carved my veins, and my dreams turned red, to become hope and courage, and nightingale for the foolish men lying awake, secretly listening to the marvels of life. Dizzy, with human whispers, I went down to the valley, to bury the bodies of my secret dead, and cut the golden cord of their betrayed stars, so they may fall free into the black abyss. The iron turned rusty, as were my dreams, and I expelled the night. I, who suffered the myriad piercing points of my darkness out of fire and sulfur, fashioned a new knife fit for heroes. I bared my breast, and the winds were unleashed. They swept away ruins and broken souls, and cleared the earth of its murky clouds so as to reveal and expose the meadows of bliss.

With the lanterns of the stars, I went out into heaven. How in the deep forest, at the top of the mountain, the world's only shore, could I find my soul? Weeping Myrtle, silver with sleep, sprinkled my eyes; I propelled and went alone. How could I find my soul? Leader of rays and the creator of the universe, a vagrant who knew the future, speak to me. How could I find my soul? Nights, with a hundred hands, stirred my entrails throughout the firmament. This pain burned. How could I find my soul? With the stars as lanterns, I roamed the heavens, the deep forest at the top of the mountain, the world's only shore. How can I find my soul?

The night blew, and the houses went out, and it was late inside my soul. No one heard me when I knocked on His door, and memory killed me. *"My brothers and sisters, black hours are near, time will tell. The joys of men have soiled the guts of monsters,"* I shouted, as I turned my eyes, full of tears, toward heaven. I shouted at the gates of God, and my voice took on the grief of murderers; and in the earth's center, a black phantom, that looked like the prince of darkness, appeared growing darker and darker, as the sun's rays, became the guiding thread of death.

The world, this world was the same world of suns and dust of turmoil and quiet evenings, weaver of constellations, the silver gilder of moss, at the warning of memory and the exit of dreams. This world, this world was the same world. Soaring above floods, plunging under typhoons by night with the syrinx; by day with the lyre; on the cobblestones of cities, the jibsails of meadows. Flat-headed, long-headed, willing, unwilling, both god and son of man. This world, this world was the same world of ebbing and orgasm of remorse and clouding. Inventor of zodiacs, daredevil of domes at the rim of the ecliptic, at the farthest reach of creation. This world, this world was the same world. It was both brass-sounding brass and a vain distant cloud!

There I was before you, with my troubled soul dedicated to you, as my heart groaned under your wings. The years, one after the other, had passed, as our people were slain day by day. I saw their blood running down the white marbles, and I prayed for it to reach you. Pity me and give me my freedom. The winter came and I darkened; the spring came and I hoped. Give me my freedom, and I'd walk the desert under the hot scorching sun; then I would be yours once again. I would bring you twelve doves and place them on top of your temple, and their blood would run down my hands as I raise them high above my head with ecstasy.

I'm Greko, and Greko is my God; he opens roads, builds temples, brings water to the cities armed in bronze. He goes out to war. Marching at the front is Him, guiding us on foot, under our own steam behind him. Our flesh and our soul are one. When we die, the flesh dies; what's left is the soul and our sons who will continue the battle. This is immortality.

My chest was heaving and blowing up at the same time. I felt my heart beating in my chest and I shuddered. My blood touched my heart and I groaned. It touched my soul and I was filled with a deadly agony. *"Give me a sign,"* I shouted, *"give me, oh, give me a command; give me a word, a curse, or a blessing. The last one for my people. Give me a command. That which should throw me either in the abyss or in my climb."* You fought me in the white unprofaned temples of Sounion; you fought me at nights; those endless nights in my sleep, and during the day, you sent me to my slow death. The flame would launch from here. I'm afraid. The dark uphill road didn't have an end. My head was aflame, but the spirit of the night eternally blew and extinguished it. My fight was in danger at any moment; the fight of everyone was in danger. I stepped among the carcasses like in a war, and I yelled for help. *"Roundup and gather together all your terrifying and fearful experiences,"* the voice called, *"the exultation of liberty is a circle; close it."*

I couldn't sleep any longer; I'd get up in the middle of the night, I'd look at the sky; it was still sealed and wrapped in darkness; not a glimpse of the flame yet. The day would come, and I'd run to the streets. I'd speak to them, my people, and I'd startle and frighten them. I'd point to the sky, I'd command, I'd curse the flame to come down; my voice vanished, went astray, and became disoriented; the sky was closed and bolted, still and muted above me.

Your curse upon my country burned me. I'm going around inside the rooms of your labyrinth to find an exit. You placed in my palms burning coals. I couldn't sleep any longer. My agony burned me; my duty suffocated my heart; the duty to my people and my country chased me. *"Give me your last word. I'm at your mercy. The weight of this sad time we ought to obey. Speak what we feel, not what we ought to say. The old has seen a lot. We, the younger, will neither see as much nor live as long. But the years we live, we must live them with fidelity, for the new land, free, will soon rise."*

I had made my decision. The two forces inside me, my studies and my struggles against the junta fought endlessly.

CHAPTER IIX

"A_{VGY!}"

Her lips, moist and luscious, glowed with pink lipstick. There are faces one remembers and faces one dreams of; for me, Avgy was like an illusion: you don't question its authenticity and candor; you simply follow it until it vanishes or until it destroys itself. She knocked on the door of my hotel room that early morning, and I was disconcerted and surprised because no one knocks on my door. She was standing at the threshold with a grim smile in her face. Her hands were folded in front of her, and her hair was falling over her left eye which gave her a sensual and lascivious look.

"What's the matter? Are you all right?" I asked, letting her in, closing the door behind her, wiping my eyes from the deep sleep, full of dreams, I was engrossed in.

"I'm sorry I came unannounced," she proclaimed, and sat on the chair by my desk, crossing her legs and leaning back. I tore my eyes away from her face, concentrating on the picture hanging on the wall behind her. Her beautiful face was corrupting my senses. "Michael's been arrested," she said suddenly, and my blood rushed to my head. I sat on the bed setting my eyes on her. This revelation came like an explosive device going off inside my head. She had a poignant and desolate look on her face, and her eyes were wet.

"What happened?" I managed to ask.

"A few days ago he was questioned by the police about the people he associates with, the places he goes to, and the newspapers he reads. He was let go with a warning but last night they came to his house and took him away."

"Where is he now?" I uttered, and my concern was cresting.

"At the Police Headquarters," she said. The ultimate visit to that building; the *Yellow Building*, which thunders every night.

"That grief-stricken and distressing yellow building," I said, asserting my concern.

"We haven't heard from him since then," she said, and the tears were transversing her face, marking it with sadness.

"Have you told anyone about his arrest?"

"No. I'm sure Ari and Stephan know. Apparently they have been following us for some time now. Of course, not you yet," she declared with poise, self-assured, "but they will, sooner or later; they follow and investigate many people," she said, exposing her fright in her voice, while her eyes gazed outside the window with sadness.

"One would think that the police would not have all the resources they need to follow and investigate as many people as they do. But apparently, they do, somehow. Everyone is fearful for their safety," I said, sitting down next to her. I didn't know much about Michael; I wanted to know more. "What can you tell me about Michael? I met him only once, but I didn't have the opportunity to talk with him," I said, as I placed my hand on her shoulder.

"They took him from us, Daniel, and I'm afraid we may not see him again. I cannot envision what they're doing to him now. I can hear in my heart the screams of those tortured by the police at that notorious *Yellow Building* and my heart breaks. He was very dedicated and devoted to the cause; he was one of the first to join the organization; he has been involved with some of the most unsafe and hazardous undertakings, and he has been engaged in recruiting members," Avgy said, wiping her eyes.

"Do you think that maybe someone has infiltrated the organization, acting now as a mole and a squealer?"

"I don't think so, although we have to be a lot more careful who we talk with, and who we invite to our meetings," she said with concern and apprehension.

"Do you think he will talk?" I asked and my mind wandered back to our last meeting. There were a lot of things happening now with the organization, and Michael had a lot to divulge if he was pressured.

"The police uses many diverse and unethical methods of torture and interrogation techniques to compel people to talk, or to get a false statement out of them, so they can detain them, send them to the islands or even murder them. I hope he doesn't talk," she said.

"Is he strong enough not to talk?"

"He's strong enough to endure the physical pain, but there is no telling about his spirit."

"It makes me sick to my stomach thinking about the torture methods they use. Waterboarding, hitting the bottom of the feet with a baton, deny them sleep, and awakening them in the middle of the night for another horrific session of interrogation. These cruel and harsh methods of torture they employ will eventually break the person at some point," I said, bringing into mind the thousands of people tortured in the hands of the police.

"The human body may endure a lot of abuse, but not the mind. It's very fragile and brittle," Avgy said with a frown.

We spent the next few minutes in silence, looking at the floor perplexed and disconcerted. The cruelty, the police has demonstrated the last five years, was absurd and inconceivable; and now they had Michael.

"Daniel, are you all right?" Avgy asked, raising her head to look at me.

"How can I be? I'm an idealist. This kind of news takes me far away to a place where I struggle to hold on to my principles and the essence of them. Whether one is fundamentalist, perfectionist, optimist or realist, one may feel the threat and menace, which engulf people's minds when they face such prejudicial, indoctrination and propaganda."

"Pragmatism and rationality are also virtues. Let's go for dinner at the café. We may see Ari there," she said with an enticing smile. As she got up, she took hold of my hand to boost me up and kissed me.

It was past eight on the clock when we arrived at the café. The dinner crowd was already occupying most of the tables. Selecting one against the wall—although not too many were available at this time of night—we claimed it for the evening. The gluttonous crowd, which conquered the tables earlier, was noisy as if they were taken away for some time to some desolate and austere deserted island, and now they were dubiously let out. Soft classical music was saturating the space, giving it an amiable and jovial ambiance. Incredible smells were coming from the kitchen, invading my nostrils, prostituting my senses. I was looking at Avgy eating with such elegance and modishness, that my mind started digressing, losing concentration, drifting far away into the future, deviating from the ephemeral and transitory moment. She turned and smiled at me, and my entire body was immersed in goosebumps.

"You're beautiful," I managed to say with a trembling voice. She smiled again, and pushed a cluster of hair away from her eyes. I was not sure if the food was succulent and delicious, or the esprit de corps of Avgy was compelling and captivating, that my senses were flattering. A violin concerto was feeling the room, while the sounds of forks colliding with plates were competing for superiority over Mozart.

The evening was warm and I could see, amidst the street lights and the brilliance of the city, a few bright stars. We walked on Academy Street in the direction of the Academy and the National Library. Both were closed but the amazing architecture of the buildings was an inspiration to any architect. We didn't talk much. The fate of Michael was going around my head and the brutality and torment he was enduring under the hands of the police.

" How can we help Michael?" I inquired with that rhetorical question which was indeed in vain.

"We can't. He's in their hands now. We just hope they will let him go soon. He doesn't have a criminal record, and any accusations or allegations would be fabricated, " she said with an appreciation for buoyancy.

"Hopefully there will be no fabrications; then he would have a chance to come out alive. What's the likelihood of them infiltrating our organization?" I asked.

"If they have infiltrated our organization, then we are all in some kind of trouble."

"We have a scheduled meeting again for Saturday evening. We should perhaps put it off until later in the week. It's hard to know if they have discovered our meeting place. We should change the location and the time and day of our meetings."

"The university may be a good place," I suggested.

"Perhaps, but some members won't be able to make it as they have no access to our meeting rooms, " I said, daring an attempt to hold her hand. She did not draw away. The warmth and softness of her hand penetrated my entire essence. We continued walking without a purpose. The comradeship of Avgy walking next to me, holding hands, was ethereal.

*

THE words of Avgy and my thoughts of Michael, which I was spinning around in my head, brushed aside all the gratification and indulgence my visit to this city had left in me. At dawn, after I spent the night wide awake, engrossed in Avgy's words, the voice I sensed behind her words, and the perseverance of Michael, I left my room. I dressed quietly, I left a note with the front desk that I had some errands to run returning in the afternoon, I went down the narrow staircase and stepped out on the street. The blueish shadows of early morning darkened the paddles left in the street by the night's drizzle. I button my jacket, and I accelerated my pace towards that *Yellow Building,* which was holding Michael. Looming closer to the building, I was discovering a new part of the city. Dawn was breaking slowly, and a purple blade of light cut through the clouds, spraying its shade over the fronts of apartment buildings, houses, and shops. The citadel of the *Yellow Building* was on the opposite side of the street, from where I was standing, guarded by a large wrought-iron railing, woven with ivy and dead leaves, which confined this fortress. Set in the iron bars, barely visible, was a small gate, firmly locked. I tried to peer into the property, but I could only make out the angles and the arches of the front door of the building, a tangle of weeds, and the outline of what seemed to be a dilapidated fountain. That was not the door that Michael had crossed, handcuffed, and hustled inside. I walked the perimeter of the building's fenced yard, to get to the other side where it seemed to me to be the entrance. A policeman was guarding the entrance. He examined me carefully with some kind of reluctance and aloofness. His eyes looked blurred, and a few wisps of hair was creeping under his cap. I noticed that he gave me a puzzled and mystified look as if he'd seen me before but couldn't remember where; or perhaps he was pondering, deliberating what I was doing there, as people try to avoid that place at all cost. He looked perplexed. I approached him hesitantly and cautiously. "How can I find out if a friend of mine is held here?" I asked. My voice echoed against the building coming back to me with a sense of fear and apprehension.

"Go inside and inquire at the front desk," he said, as he looked at me again. "Was he involved in any subversive activities, that friend of yours?" he came back with that piercing question before I had a chance to thank him.

"I'm not aware of any such activities my friend has been involved in," I said.

"What's your name? Can I see your ID?" he asked approaching me closer. I took my identification card from my pocket and handed it to him. He examined it carefully. He pulled a book out of the side pocket of his trousers and opened it. He was going through the pages of the book shaking his head up and down with a smirk on his face. He lifted his head, he gave me a look for a long time, then he closed his book, put it back in his pocket, and gave me my ID card back.

"I suggest you go home and don't come back here again. If you do, you'll be arrested."

Without giving him a second to think and change his mind, I turned around and walked hurriedly off crossing the street. A cold sweat covered my forehead. I can still hear his voice harsh, demanding, and threatening: *"you'll be arrested."* His face appeared in front of me as quickly as it vanished, and all that remained of my conversation with that officer vanished as well. I was left holding my identification card, my words still hanging on my lips, gazing at passersby until they melted in the heavy shadows that preceded the rising of the sun. I put my ID card in my pocket, and I slowed my pace. The intimidation of the policeman was melting away, and I began to enjoy my morning walk.

CHAPTER IX

My studies at the university were progressing rather miserably, under the current deplorable conditions, which were unbearable, consuming most of my concentration and intensity. The repression and restriction of free speech was suffocating and throttling the students. The restrains and controls imposed upon the curriculum of the university, further stifled the students, hurting their studies, impairing their progress. The professors were very careful with their methods of teaching and the kind of concepts and viewpoints were putting forward to their students. The curriculum was limited, and the field of study of a particular discipline was constrained and confined within the bounds, which the ministry of education had outlined. My philosophy course was hacked severely with the absence of Plato's *Republic* and Aristotle's *Politics*. Jean-Paul Sartre and Frederick Nietzsche were not to be seen on campus, and Sophocles and Aeschylus were just phantasms in the theatres. The pedagogy of the students was taking a downward spiral, seizing with it knowledge, excellence of education, and the aspirations and ambitions of future scientists and scholars. But one cannot restrict the young minds; their resilience and pliability strengthened their spirits, avoiding defeatism at the heels of the Colonels' boots.

*

"What are you planning for the summer?" was the question that came from Avgy that night, walking down Academy Street.

I began my story with the distant dawn when I awoke and could not remember my brother's face, and I didn't stop until I paused to recall the world of shadows, I had sensed that very day in my hotel room, recalling what Avgy had told me regarding Michael. Avgy listened quietly, making no judgment, drawing no conclusions. I told her about my parents' difficulties with the ministry of agriculture; I told her about the killings of animals taking place in my small town; I told her that I would visit my parents to talk with them to understand what kind of troubles they were having. I had not realized, absorbed by my thoughts, that this was a story about me, my needs, and my yearnings. I told her that I had the feeling, I was neglecting my duties as a son. I had not yet written to my parents a letter for a long time. I spoke about my brother and of his death, my anxieties, having conquered the hills and mountains around my town myriad of times, counting the stars. I spoke about meeting an old shepherd, who played his fife as good as my brother did. I told her that I had never been kissed by a girl, until the kiss I received from her the very first time, at the doorstep of her apartment building. What was I planning for the summer?

I wanted to go back to my town.

*

THERE was a time, in my childhood, I recall, where everything became real, and the place, where I was born and raised, was a sanctuary for my young mind. I often recalled the place where I had been raised among the green fields and yellow trees of the silent slopes, loaded with the leaves of the beach tree; among haughty cypresses and pine trees, while the silent wind caressed my white downy face. It was all peaceful and orange and blue, as I saw my shadow chasing the moon, which grew smaller that very night. Under the golden stars, I implored him: *"let me be the shepherd once more, and my wishes will race through the notes of my fife, and my tears through the sea."* It was blue and green, as the morning song raised from the petals of my eyes, wet with the morning dew, and red from the chains of my youth; I recalled time and time again, as I ran my pathos up my naked eyes. Running among the blades of the green grass, which were caressing my naked feet. My open hairless chess was resisting the wind, under the sun which was born that very moment; I was famous among the trees, and

I was happy and carefree, as I was left in the mercy of the winds, allowing me to be free once again and sing, as the fields were home, and the sounds from the mountains were mine.

*

My ambitions, apart from the marvelous simplicity with which one sees the world at the age of ten, lay in a prodigious book which was exhibited in the town's bookstore, behind the Ministry of Agriculture government building. The object of my devotion, a book of Africa, adorned with forests, animals, and heaven knows how many different colors it was ornamented with, presided over the shop window as if it were the crown jewels. Every time my mother and I went into town, I couldn't stop nagging her to take me to see the book. I was secretly convinced that with such an astonishing book, one would be able to discover new untouchable and brilliant worlds in faraway lands. Thus, my love for books began to flourish.

CHAPTER X

I MET HIM AT the Small Harbour. That was the name of that small port, of no consequence, at the edge of the village: small, poor, and neglected, but it was charming. The wharf was the extension of the bow of a German warship, which was sunk during the second war by the Greek fleet. It was pulled out of the water and secured to form the front of the wharf. There was a lighthouse installed at the front of the bow. It welcomed the ferries which brought provisions to the village and visitors alike. The ferries came only twice a week. I was at that harbor that early morning, waiting to embark the ferry to take me to the island across the way, as the sun was deserting the embrace of the deep waters of the sea, and the day was unfolding with the heat which was promised ahead. My classes at the university had ended for the summer; I needed a rest, and I found myself in that village. It was one of those excursions I embarked upon, to escape from the torment and distress of the big city, thus afflicting on myself the luxury of the open space, the pure air, and the vastness of the sea. I was inspired by those elements, the few weeks I spent at that island; the peacefulness one might find in such an astonishing and magnificent place.

Quite colorful and quaint was the village, a short walk from the seashore among pine trees, olive trees, and vineyards. The narrow cobblestone roads were wide enough to squeeze between a donkey and the whitewash stairs to the houses. The whitewashed yards and front steps, the flowers with vibrant and vivid colors, the red and blue windows and doors, decorated the small village as if a painter had splashed the canvas with the colors of the rainbow. Small balconies were extended over the narrow streets, ornamented and adorned with bright and multi-colored flowers. The mountain on the background, behind the village, was bare and rocky. Rough to the naked foot, overwhelmed by rocks and thistles; the kind of thistles which are flowering plants, characterized by leaves with sharp on the margins; its prickles could also occur all over the plant which was an adaptation to protect the plant from being eaten by herbivores. A large river crossed the village, with its water trickling among rocks and bushes in the summer, where the animals would visit often to gratify and mollify their thirst. In the spring, the river was fiercer, and some of the villagers had drowned over the years. The township tried to widen the river, but many obstructions and hurdles popped up which made the work difficult.

The fishermen attended to their nets, spread over the sand every morning after they return from their nightly fishing expeditions. The village square characterized the nature and the spirit of the villagers. The small but impressive Saint Nicolas church with whitewashed walls, stood on one side of the square, as its steps were decorated with numerous flower pots, which the women of the village attended to. The village folk graced the church with their attendance every Sunday morning, and on December sixth, Saint Nicolas Day, the entire village celebrated the event with festivities and carnivals which took place all over the village. At the other side of the square, and across from St. Nicolas, there were a few cafes and tavernas lined up, displaying the colorful chairs and tables, resting under the shade of maple trees. The view from the small picturesque town was extraordinary. The deep blue sea could be seen as far as the eye could stretch, and behind the village, the vast and bare mountain with the thistles and rocks walled the village between the mountain and the sea.

I marveled at the sun through the silver leaves of the olive trees. The fields of corn and wheat, which looked like a waving sea gesturing to the wind in amazement with their lean torsos, were stretching from the sea to the mountain. The fishermen were toiling with the nets, the villagers worked the land, water ran down the river downstream, and the orchards were consuming the water that was offered to them. Such was the simple life of the inhabitants of this small village during the day.

*

I wandered around the cobblestone streets, until I couldn't anymore, as the day had culminated, and the people had abandoned the square. Dark blue became the air, the sky had lost the sun, he hadn't found the stars yet, and it was getting dark. The day birds had returned to their nests; the night birds had not yet awakened and opened their eyes. In this uncertain dusk, the lanterns of the sky started to light up one after the other, until the entire sky was lit up. I remember that night. I had plowed the village all day; the night was falling, and I felt I wasn't alone; I was resting under a tree, gazing at the sky where I could see millions of stars, small and large, illuminating it. I closed my eyes, and I had a vision; an aforethought vision which took me to a different place. It was as if I were looking at the moon for the first time, unprepared, ill-equipped, and unwary. What was that, which emerged over the mountains, and the wolves put their tail down, raised their heads, and howl at it? Was that why it arose, in this startling and fearsome desert, thunderstruck, astonished and wordless, dripping venom? Was that the man's heart which became an enormous pit, and it was filled with that venom, gashing down from the moon? That terrifying and fearful thought made me shiver. I left that place blissfully, as good luck would have it, and returned to that magnificent starry sky

As I was following the moon's voyage, I fell asleep. Early morning came, and I felt the cool air coming from the unruffled sea. I opened my eyes and the mountain was irradiated by the sun, as it was rising from the depths of the sea that same moment. As the sun was warming up the soil, the mist was rising from its entrails, giving an eerie feeling to the surroundings. I got up, placed my satchel over my shoulder, and walking in the early morning breeze, I gazed at the sky where a small group of poignant white and orange clouds was traversing the sky. I lowered my gaze concentrating on the small harbor, far down the hill. I started walking towards it as if it were pulling me with an enormous force. I decided to visit the island which was noticeable across the way. With a clear horizon and no humidity feasibly, I caught a glimpse of the small town, the mountain, and the charming laced seashore, as that small island was stretched across the calm sea. Lost in thought, I didn't notice the carriage with a large horse that pulled next to me and stopped.

"Where is you going young man?" the voice came from my left, and I turned. His face had a friendly disposition, with gray hair crowning his head, as his face was growing a well-trimmed beard. He smiled. "Good morning. I'm Andreas. Can I offer you a ride?"

"Thank you, Andreas. I'm Daniel," I said, and I looked at him who seemed like a friendly sort.

"Where is you goin' young man?" the old man inquired.

"I'm going to the small island across the way," I said, feeling the excitement inside me.

"Ah, the captain's wife went there yesterday. You know, she said she went there to mend the pains and aches she has on her back. It has special springs she said, with hot water coming up from underneath the ground and you're cured," the old man said sardonically.

"Yes, it is true, old man. That water is therapeutic for certain infections and ailments," I said with conviction.

"You going to the island for the same reason?" asked the villager.

"No, no," I said avoiding the debate.

"Then, why?" he insisted again.

Why am I going there? I thought. It was not yet clear in my mind, but I'd find out when I got there.

"When is the ferry coming?" I asked, changing the subject.

"It's not coming today. It came yesterday. The next one is in two days," he said, and I felt the disappointment and discontent covering my face and my heart, squeezing out any untreated feelings I had. I wanted to go today. I could not wait.

"Is there another way to get there? Another ferry?" I asked with a great deal of fretfulness in my voice.

"No, but you can stay with us until then. Where is you from?" the inquiry came.

"I'm from the city," I said reluctantly.

"What'd you do there? There is no meadows there, orchards, nothing. Only wide roads, tall buildings, and shops. What'd people do there?" he asked apprehensively.

"They work in the factories, the offices, and the shops," I said abstractly, sensing that old man's untainted and innocent soul.

"You're on vacation?" he asked.

"Yes, on vacation, if we can call it that," I said, thinking of the writing I had to do.

"Why's that?"

"I do a lot of writing. With the school's out for the summer, I seized this opportunity to come to a quiet place to write."

"What do you write?" he asked with interest.

What and why do I write? My thoughts were soaring inside my head. Do I find serenity when I sit down, pick up the pen, and empty my brain on the paper? Do I feel content when I line up my characters one next to each other, inserting in their mind my thoughts, my anxieties, and fears, just to liberate my soul?

"I write about people, their anxieties and anguishes; their fears and worries."

"That shouldn't be very difficult to do. God knows, we have a lot of that," he said, shaking his head.

"Yes, we do; we have a lot of that in the city, too. There are a lot of poor and homeless people who are destitute; but nobody cares about them," I said, looking ahead.

"We have them here too; the government don't care about them, but society does. People help each other."

"What do they do?"

"They work the fields or they fish the seas. They may have a little hut to put their heads down at night after an entire day in the fields, or fighting the waves and the wrath of the sea, but they're happy," he said and looked over the fields. "They," he continued, "they may not have their land or their hut, but they're happy and fortunate with what they've got: a roof over their heads, and bread on the table, mostly every night."

I found refuge in the silence that followed, and I allowed myself to descend to my thoughts. The big frame of the horse was moving at a slow pace as we were casually leaving behind olive groves, vegetable gardens, and vineyards. The dirt road was dry, and dust arose from the horse's hoofs. It was blistering hot.

"Do you have your land, Andreas?"

"Yes. I have ten acres of vineyards and an olive grove of two acres. A lot of work for an old soul like me to spend the entire day working the land," he said, and a sigh came out of his chest.

"Do you have any help?"

"Only in the fall; I hire people to do the harvest of the grapes and the olives," he said, as he stroked the horse's behind.

"It must be very hard for an old person like you to take care of your fields with no help, isn't it Andreas?"

"It is, and it's getting to me now."

"Have you thought of selling your land and retire?"

"Yes, I have. One of these days I'll sell everything and get out of this harsh business."

The old man's house appeared hidden behind tall trees and bushes. Andreas, pulling at the reins, slowed down the horse, and neatly guided the animal and carriage through the narrow gate. Chickens scattered at our approach, disappearing behind the house. The house was a modest and humble one, with a window at either side of the blue door in perfect symmetry. The upper floor had a door that led to a small balcony with a window at either side. Chickens were roaming the yard, and at the back and to the side, there was a good size stable; two bales of hay were positioned next to the stable door, and an old carriage was leaning against the wall. As we reached the old man's house, we were welcomed by his wife: an old woman with grey hair falling on her shoulders, and with a mantilla covering her head. She had a black dress on and a floral apron. She was sitting in front of the door working on something. As soon as she saw us coming, she got up, to greet me.

"Welcome young man," she said and rushed into the kitchen to prepare the table. It was almost noon; I was famished. I turned, and I noticed a smirk covering the old man's face.

"You know," he said in a low voice as we were entering the house, "my wife don't interrogate no visitors before they sit at the table," he said and smiled. It was a peculiar confession coming from the old man, which was a declaration of guilt, as I was not expecting anyone to interrogate me.

The two days went by with a great deal of anticipation and eagerness, waiting for the ferry to arrive; my readiness and expectations were growing by the minute. I prepared my suitcase; I thanked my host and hostess for their hospitality the night before and I left.

The last two days staying with Andreas and his wife, the small island across the way never left my thoughts. There was something that was attracting me there; something that I had to discover; something that amazed me and astounded me. I was stunned by its beauty and desolation. But was it, indeed, the short ferry trip to the island or the discovery of something new? My mind blundered.

*

Now, sitting at a bench at the harbor, waiting for the arrival of the ferry, I was enjoying the cool early morning breeze coming from the serene and calm waters of the sea. As the smells of salt and iodine were piercing my nostrils, I was reflecting on the reasons to embark on that small island in such a hurry. The ferry was coming at ten in the morning, but I woke up at three. The anticipation was a carnage. I don't remember if I slept at all the night before; I only remember the large wooden clock on the wall on the hallway striking three times. My thoughts were meandering in distant lands, and I had a dreadful headache. I left my bed and went to splash my face. Those inconceivable thoughts were torturing me, and my mind was exhausted and worn out as if I had dispersed and scattered around all my body parts into the four horizons. I opened the window and looked toward the meadows and the sea. I was trying to remember what my thoughts were during the night. I didn't think of anything; I saw nothing. Only eternal darkness. I closed my eyes. The meadows and the sea were covered with a dark veil. Maybe it was better that way, earning the ability to reflect.

I must have placed all my passions and obsessions under that black veil of the night, I thought. All of a sudden, I felt chilled; the open window was allowing the cool breeze in and the smells of the sea, and the scent of the meadows were bouncing against my nostrils. I shut the window, and I laid down on the bed; I closed my eyes, and I could feel the headache pounding my head. Morning came before long; I got up and started to get ready for my trip.

Now, sitting on the bench at the wharf, the salted smell along with water drops from the sea were invading my face and nose; I utterly surrendered to the elements. The baker, who was wakened very early in the morning, now had the first loaves of bread coming out of the oven. Their aroma was spilling into the street, engulfing the entire small harbor. The first customers were arriving at his doorstep to purchase the freshly baked bread, which seemed only the magic of nature could produce such an ultimate and decisive miracle. The fishermen returned from their all-night fishing expedition, with a legion of seagulls following them. They settled on the beach, unloading some large some smaller fish that fell victims to their nets, still jumping and shuffling in the baskets.

As I was looking at the vastness of the sea contemplating my trip, witnessing the events of an early morning at a village, declaring my reflections, I didn't notice a man who came and sat next to me; I was deeply immersed in my thoughts.

"You waiting for the ferry? I said, you waiting for the ferry? Mr. you going to the island?" the man said, and he looked at me. The sound of the word *island* suddenly flinched me, and I turn to look at him. He was smiling.

"The island. Yes, that's where I'm going, to the island," I said inattentively and abstractedly.

"You waiting for the ferry? I'm waiting for it myself. They said it's coming at ten," the man said smirking at me.

"Ten … yes… of course, at ten," said I, while my mind was jumping around as if it were looking for a place to settle.

"What time is it?" asked the man trying to get a glimpse at my watch. I raised my arm and looked at the time.

"Eight-thirty. An hour and a half on this bench," I said, as I looked at the man's face which was trying to exhume a moment of tolerance.

"I'm Daniel," I said, extending my hand.

"I'm Mark," he said, shaking my hand.

I kept on looking at him with curiosity. He had a small round face, which was covered with a thin layer of skin, as the veins were visibly marking the skin wrapped around his nasal and zygomatic bones. His two small grey eyes, deep inside their sockets, were sitting below his bushy eyebrows; he had a piercing glare which penetrated one's inner thoughts. His torso was thin, and the bones were noticeable through his shirt. He wore shorts that came down to his knees and a pair of sandals. His arms were covered with hair, and his fingers were thin and subtle. He pinned his gaze at my face, and rolling down his eyes throughout my entire body he stopped at my suitcase.

"You an engineer Mr. Daniel?" he asked with no evidence of accuracy in his question.

"Why… yes, oh yes, of course," I said with conviction.

"What will you do at the island?"

I didn't like my lie. Then the question, what was I going to do at the island? Very peculiar. That was the question I was asking myself for the last two days. What was so essential that I had to go there? What was drawing me to that magnificent island? What was so enticing at that island, which kept me awake all night, thinking about it? And why such a hurry? I was trying to place all my thoughts into some order, to find symmetry, something! And now, a strange man sitting next to me asking me that same question, demanding an answer.

"I'm sure the old jailhouse is at the other side of the island," he said apathetic, breaking the silence, pointing to the direction of the island. "Only a few inmates are left. The others were moved to another island. It was very crowded there, and the old building was falling apart. Shame, what a shame," he said, as silence covered the perimeter of the bench again, with the two strangers confined and wedged on it. Deceiving the silence, I claimed it for myself as well.

*

In the 19th century, the prison system was an overcrowded disaster and in disarray. Prisoners were kept in large holding inclusions, like horse corrals, and were left to their own devices. Abuse by fellow inmates and guards was rampant; an extensive proliferating disaster. In 1887, the government at the time decided to build a proper house of repentance. A large structure was erected on that island. It was divided into cells, which provided for the solitary confinement of such inmates as were of a refractory temper. The building was furnished with material and instruments for carrying on such manufactures as could be conducted with the least instructions, or previous knowledge. Gardens adjoined the structure in which the inmates might occasionally work or wander around its paths. That new revolutionary prison at the time was designed to have a beneficial effect, not only upon health but also upon morals, because it would lead the prisoners to familiarity with that pure and natural environment, which was thought to renew the connection of fallen men with nature.

"It's a beautiful day today. It'll get very hot and humid, Mr. Daniel," he said, breaking the silence.

I let my gaze roam at the surface of the sea. A notion came to me at that moment. I didn't have a soul waiting for me at the island; I would be alone. I had plenty of time to think. I needed someone to be there with me, to talk to, eat with me, and gaze at the stars at night, when the weight of the pen became unbearable. I turned and looked at him for a while.

"Mark, is there anybody waiting for you at the island?" I said, trying to explore his face.

"No, Mr. Daniel, I don't have nobody waiting for me. Not even in hell. I live alone," he said, and I detected a hint of surprise in his voice.

"How long are you staying at the island?"

"As long as it takes. I'm floating and gliding," he said, laughing to himself. "I have my tools with me," he continued, "in case I want to stay the entire summer."

He called them tools; I call them necessities if that was what he meant.

"I don't have definite plans of coming back soon either," I said, "I'll stay as long as I need to."

"Is there a project that you're working on?"

"No. I'm a student at the university. I'm traveling for a while before I go back to the city. I have a lot of writing to do, but I would like to have someone with me as a companion. Would you like to come along?" I said reluctantly, looking at his reaction. He looked perplexed.

"Come with you?"

"Yes, you will do your own thing while I write. You have no obligation to me or anyone. You're your own man," I said. He looked at me for a while, then he got up and started to walk around the bench. His look was apprehensive but with a smile. He turned and faced me.

"Thank you very much for your offer, Mr. Daniel. But …" he said hesitantly, and he stopped.

"But what?" I requested dreading his answer.

"You're an engineer. I'm no engineer. I haven't went to no school Mr. Daniel; what will I do there with you?" he said hesitantly and aversely. I felt his nervousness in his voice. He was a bit cautious as if he were afraid of something.

"I'm not an engineer, Mark; I'm sorry I deceived you. I'm a student at the university in liberal arts," I said embarrassed and humbled.

"But you told me you was," he said again, irritated about my lie. I didn't say anything, although the insistence to know the veracity of my lie was evident. I didn't explain why. Maybe he wouldn't understand; maybe I wouldn't know how to explain it. He sat down on the bench again silently, gazing at the sea, hoping for the ferry to appear on the horizon. The sun was up a few yards by now, mining the sky, as there were no clouds to destruct its path, displaying its brilliant blue color. It was getting hot. Mark, sitting next to me on the bench, took out of his pocket a hunter's knife, and he started cleaning it. The concentration given to this knife was astounding. He would blow on it and use his shirt to polish it. After a long time's undertaking, he put it back in his pocket and looked at me.

"I use this knife to carve. I have a few more which are smaller," he said.

"What do you carve, Mark?"

"If I ask my eyes, fixations; if I ask my heart, everything and in between;

my brain keeps on hammering, so I execute. Different ideas that come to my mind."

"Is that your profession?"

"No. That's my hobby. I'm a painter," he said with pride.

"What do you paint?"

"Landscapes, portraits, that sort of thing."

"Do you sell them, or do you paint for yourself?"

"I sell some, others I donate or keep for myself. It relaxes my mind, and gives me something to do."

"That's very interesting. I would like to see some of your paintings. What media do you use?"

"Oil and water. I like water better because you can do so many different things with it. It's more flexible," he said proudly, describing his art. He let his gaze fall upon the water, and he plunged into silence. "Sometimes," he resumed, "sometimes when I listen to a classical piece, a painting unfolds in front of me. The tempo and the themes of that classical piece speak to me in colors, lines, and landscapes. If I had a canvas twenty meters long, I would paint the entire fifth symphony," he said, and he laughed. "Those images I envision, listening to music, turn out to be incredible colors, lines, and landscapes. The heavy baritone sounds speak to me in terms of dark colors of straight, curvy, and wavy heavy lines; the high notes inspire me with the lighter colors with thinner lines. Any variations, make me imagine faces, places, and landscapes, and most importantly, nature," he said with an inspirational flair.

"That's very thought-provoking," I said genuinely, finding it truly fascinating. "I never thought of classical music in those terms. Surely, the great composers were inspired by nature and by their environment," I said, and I took an instant to think about it, as silence had authority. My brother's fife playing, inspired in me many different notions and reflections, as I dreamt of fairies, climbing down from the glows of the moon and the flickering stars.

"When I was a little boy," I said, "my brother before he died oh so young, played his fife as we were minding the sheep. Many times, I closed my eyes and imagined distant and extraneous places, creations of my mind with colorful trees, birds flying high and low. My mind would jump up, and get lost in colors and places which I'd never seen before," I said, as I remembered how far my young intellect would travel, the worlds which would occupy, and the thoughts and feelings it would spawn. I reckon the beautiful landscapes I would have created if I were a painter. The outlandish and remote places which I traveled, as my mind seized me and removed me from the rock where I was sitting with my eyes closed.

From deep in the horizon, the ferry appeared like a dot. I took a deep breath. My anticipation was mounting. The sleepless night had not hindered and obstructed my eagerness to visit that small island. I felt fatigued and weary, but my spirits were winged very high. I considered staying there for a few weeks, to challenge my brain to empty its essence and release me into oblivion. I heard the voice from inside me calling on me to discharge and allow me to rest. That voice, which many times commanded me to brave the obstacles and climb and liberate myself. The sun was striking, battering my face, as its luminous rays were also reflecting on the water.

Mark got up, put both palms together with force, and yelled like a child. "It's finally coming. The ferry is coming. See, over there," he said, pointing toward the black dot which was getting bigger that instant. He placed his suitcase by the edge of the water, and he came back to pick up mine.

"I can manage that," I said, moving closer to my suitcase. But he had already taken hold of it, carrying it and placing it next to his.

"I'm putting them here 'cause when it comes Mr. Daniel, we won't have no time to think," he said delightedly. Why such a hurry?

As the vehicles were driving up the ramp to the ferry, we embarked. I walked directly to the back of the ferry, looking for a shady spot to sit, while Mark was following in my wake. There were several lawn chairs lined up overlooking below, where the men were tying up the cars securely to the floor of the ferry. That process did not take very long; the captain blew the whistle, signaling our departure. The ferry pulled slowly away from the wharf, turned around, and I heard the engines raving full strength forward. The wind picked up as the ferry was gaining speed; the sea galls were flying above, following us at very close proximity. A line of white fluffy water was left behind the ferry, creating waves, which would reach the shore before long. The wind carried drops of salty water splashing my face, as the sound of the seagulls gave me a sense of impartial and objective independence. I was finally on my way. The anticipation was over. I waited two days for this. I spent the entire morning, since three o'clock, waiting to board this ferry, forestalling and expecting something, but I didn't know what it was. The isolation? The loneliness? The place where I would regenerate? Where I would resurrect my spirit and reincarnate it into my carcass again?

I was terrified and at the same time yearning to find out.

*

We disembarked, picked up our suitcases, and started walking on the hot sand with the spray of the sea dowsing my face as the scent of the salty sea penetrating my nostrils. It was late morning; the sun was hot, submitting my body to its perpetual and enduring heat. It was awkward and demanding walking on the hot sand, carrying my case, sweating under my shirt. A crab was laboring to reach the water, as I stopped to watch it, beholding its stature. Such an amazing creature, fortified with extraordinary means and methods to defend itself. The sea looked inviting and alluring, but I wanted to settle down first at a place somewhere before I ventured into the cool clear water. My companion took his shoes off, walking in the water, splashing, and jumping, and getting wet like an adolescent. I was walking behind him, trying to keep my balance on this perpetual and never-ending shoreline. We walked for a long time, which seemed like we walked all around the island, as the sun was lingering above our heads. The perspiration was running down my face and my spine, and I picked up the pace.

"Slow down, Mr. Daniel, no stunts with the sand. Nobody's pursuing us. We're free. Aren't we Mr. Daniel?" he said with a smile and conviction. We're free. Yes, but I didn't dare utter it. Away from the big city, the people, the noise and pollution; away from civilization and any social order; away from any kind of evolutionary progress. In this deserted seashore alone. Alone with nature, away from any deception and deceit. Only the sound of the waves, which was carried across the way from Africa.

We're free! It sounded as if it were true. We were free within nature, but that was all. Freedom is not a state of mind. It's authentic, and it can be sensed and experienced. It can be intuited, and one can feel it in one's bones. The current political situation did not allow freedom to blossom and thrive. It had been oppressed, and any kind of freedom, which the books and the constitution had described, were non-existent. It had been arbitrarily and despotically limited or obliterated.

I was amazed to look at Mark the way he accepted life, consenting to circumstances, tolerating the actions of the government, seemingly, and resigning himself to be artificially happy. But was it artificial his sense of freedom? But then again, it was astonishing to see how he responded and countered the concept of it. Freedom for him would be a concept that was limited within the confines of nature. But isn't it a natural need to desire, crave, and yearn for freedom? Isn't it what we unearth from within our soul: the need to be able to express feelings, emotions, grievances from oppression and suffocating muzzle and suppression imposed by a government? Stifling the mind, gagging the soul, hightailing the spirit? Hijacking the only dignity and humility left in us; commandeering and seizing the only precious and cherished values we have as humans: identity, pride, and self-respect.

*

THERE was a sign visible among the trees; I approached it. There was a room for rent right on the beach, among the trees, at the foot of a small hill. The sea was unfolding in front of it, and one can hear the waves crashing on the shore. The hot sand was stretching from the sea all the way to that little house.

"There," I said, pointing toward the house, "over there; we'll stay at that place. It's close to the beach, and it looks charming," I said, pointing to the small house among the trees.

Mark did not object; he followed me. I negotiated with the landlord the price, and I got the key. The room was spacious with two beds on either side, a table, two chairs, and a dresser. There was a small counter in the corner with a small stove, a refrigerator, and a sink; a light bulb was hanging from a wire from the middle of the ceiling, and a large window was facing the sea. I opened it. A warm breeze filled the room with the scent of the sea. I put my things away, laid down on the soft bed, put my arms under my head, and closed my eyes. I could hear the waves softly breaking on the shore.

Sleep swept me away for a while because when I was awakened, I noticed the shadows were longer, the sea was calmer, and the sun was entering the spacious room from the open door. I couldn't hear the waves crashing on the shore anymore as an eternal silence was discreet, surrounding the room. The bed on the other side of the room was empty. I got up and went outside to sit by the water on the sand. The magnificent view of the island across the way, where I spent two days waiting for the ferry at Andreas' place, the mountain behind me, and the small village at its foot, gave me the sense of an enchanted place. *"Here,"* I thought, *"here I will kill my beast. I will gather all my tools, all my strength, and I will fight the demons within me; those demons which tormented me for such a long time."* A struggle, a conflict which I felt, had spilled all over me and had overpowered my senses with its strength and with such intensity. The trees, the blue calm water, the clear blue sky, and the stillness, would be my devices and contrivances to overcome my anxieties. I had so much to disclose. My brain was spilling over, and I could not stop it. I had so much to divulge and declare to my forefathers; so much to divulge, that my mind hurdled and leaped all over impulsively.

I felt a hand on my shoulder, and I turned. Mark had an amusing and genial smile on his face.

"I got some food from the village. I'm incredibly hungry, and you must be too Mr. Daniel," he said, indicating the paper bag of groceries he was carrying.

I looked at him, but I didn't move. He sat next to me, placing the groceries on the sand.

We scrutinized the sea together, which yearned for and craved to pull the moon back in its embrace; it aimed to intoxicate the moon with its sweet wine to make it even redder. The night was coming slowly, drawing its lazy veils over its children: the birds, the trees, the mountains, the sea, and the houses, as if it were singing a soft and enchanting lullaby to put them to sleep. A great gift, the night; it's the mother of man. She comes slowly, amiably, and covers her children with its dark veils. She places her warm hand on their forehead and extinguishes from their minds and their flesh the anguishes and pains of the day. It's a miracle; everything is a miracle. Lower your head, look; the most irrelevant and insignificant blade of grass is guarded by a cosmic spirit; raise your eyes high up; how brilliant and magnificent the starry sky is! And if you close your eyes, how superb and astonishing the world is inside you; how unblemished and brilliant is the starry sky of your heart!

"What brings you to this island Mark?" I inquired looking deeply into his eyes.

Mark looked at me with a revealing look, as if he were to disclose something very private, something very surreptitious.

"Do you remember Mr. Daniel the old jail on the island I told you about? I was an inmate there for a couple of years. I came back to visit some old friends," he said, with a sense of shame.

"How, interesting," I managed to say. I was shocked. There are sentiments, feelings, and emotions which are concealed within a person, sinking them into obscurity, disguising them to the naked eye. Their heart and soul conceal so many fascinations and events that are not apparent.

"Are there any inmates left in that prison? I thought it was closed for good," I said, not knowing how to approach the subject.

"A lot of them have been moved elsewhere, but some remained," he said, looking deep into the blue waters of the sea to the direction of the jail. I was stunned and saturated by his revelation.

"Of course … but …" the doubt in my voice was perceptible even to me.

"It's not a very pleasant story, Mr. Daniel," he interrupted, "we all make mistakes. Mine was stealing a loaf of bread to feed my family," he said.

"Don't worry about me, Mark. I will not judge you and your actions," I said, reassuring him of my intentions.

"It was one of the most difficult times in my life. I didn't have no employment. I lost my job right after the changes of the guards…"

"You mean when the colonels took over," I interrupted.

"Yes, the colonels, on that dreadful day. I was marked because of my past activities. My employer told me that I was not needed no more. My past had stained my existence, and I couldn't find no employment."

"Many people had the same fate as you, Mark; many lost their job because of similar circumstances." Mark gazed at me with a remorseful and embarrassed look; he withdrew his gaze and let it fall to the ground.

"My survival," he said, "and that of my family's, depended on my ingenuity and my innovation. I tried to do some odd jobs, but they didn't bring enough money."

"At least you tried to make ends meet," I said, trying to make him feel unapologetic.

"One day I was at a grocery store when I decided, in my desperation..." he stopped, he got up, and he started to walk up and down, digging his heels in the sand; his face was red, and his eyes had the cries. "It's very difficult for me to recall that day," he resumed, and he sat next to me again.

"I understand your anguish, Mark," I said, and touched his shoulder tenderly.

His gaze left me and fell on top of the open water as if the waves were bringing back memories from far away.

"In my desperation," he said with a low reprehensible voice, struggling to fashion his words, "in my desperation, I stole a loaf of bread, a can of sardines, and a piece of cheese. I was apprehended immediately, and was arrested," he said, and he stopped, hugging his head with his hands, placing his elbows on his knees. His look was wretched and sorrowful, and his irresolute gaze was wandering over the water, uncertain and unsettled.

"Please go on," I said with encouragement.

He lowered his gaze; his fingers were digging the sand deeply, and he looked perplexed. "When I came to live on this island, I was ignorant and oblivious to any communal responsibilities or societal concerns," he said. "It's shameful even to admit that, but it's true. That's where my ignorance originated."

"Society may be harsh, sometimes. It condemns people for these kinds of actions, without realizing, of course, the state of mind you were in when you committed the crime. I'm sure there was something inside you, something telling you not to do it; but then, seeing your family hungry and no prospects insight, you had to do something and take action," I said, offering my empathy.

"The judge said, after he discovered the depths of my ignorance, it was most imperative that I took personal charge of my affairs and provide to my family after I served my sentence at a penitentiary."

"That was a punitive and severe punishment."

"It was; two years without bail."

"Did you serve the entire sentence?"

"Yes, I did," he said, lifting his head to look at me. "Is it possible to imagine, Mr. Daniel, to what degree my entire being was put out of place? I was given a jail sentence for trying to feed my family. I was put away for two years, leaving my family alone to care for themselves. But I didn't wish to be no hypocrite and pretended to believe that I didn't do nothing wrong."

"Recognizing you've done something wrong, is very admirable, Mark."

"Are you aware, Mr. Daniel, that there is societies in this world where a person may lose his hands for such actions?"

"Is that so, Mark?"

"Yes, it is. So, you can imagine, Mr. Daniel, how disgusted I was with myself, before deciding that there couldn't be no cause for reproach in proceeding with my way of thinking. That was the best possible time for contemplation and repentance," Mark said. He turned away to look over his shoulder, in the direction of the jail. Mark's confession was disheartening.

*

From the opened door I noticed the sun emerging from the depths of the sea, red and orange, abandoning its cool embrace, as it was soaring toward the high sky. It was promising a hot day ahead. I got up and ventured outside. The cool salty breeze coming from the sea penetrated my nostrils. The sand was moist from the morning dew, and a few crabs were edging to the direction of the water. The seagulls were out already, screeching with their high pitch tone, shattering the stillness of the morning. Many thoughts penetrated my brain. Mark's imprisonment, his punishment for stealing a loaf of bread. I misjudged him. I thought he was oblivious to the political situation; I thought he went along. But he lost his job because of his past political activities and beliefs. I tried to push the thoughts aside and enjoy the morning. I got up; I started walking in the direction of the small hill next to the water. It was a small hill, resting in front of the mountain, as a child resting in his mother's embrace. The few pine trees on it were leaning toward the mountain, deformed from the strong winds coming from the sea in the winter. I walked slowly fighting with the sand, trying to steady and balance myself. I climbed the small hill, smelling the resin from the pine trees. Each step was slippery walking on the pine needles, covering the ground. I saw him sitting on a rock, carving with his knife a pine bark. I approached him quietly.

"Good morning, Mark," I said, looking at what he was carving with such a concentration. He raised his head and smiled.

"Good morning, Mr. Daniel," he said.

"What are you laboring over this morning?"

"I'm carving to pass the time; also, it helps me forget," he said with pride and gratification.

"Forget? What do you want to forget?" I asked with interest.

"Forget my troubles and misfortunes."

"We'll always have them, Mark. They turn up and show their faces unexpectedly. We just have to manage them and get along with them," I said, as I picked up a miniature boat he had placed on the rock. "Sometimes life is ungrateful and thankless, and saturates our heart," I said. Mark was a wounded soul. I came closer and gazed at his hands working the pine bark. "Life is giving us the good and the bad; we just have to bring about peace between them, get along with them, and live our lives," I alleged, hoping to bring some peace and harmony within his senses.

"All my life I'm trying to navigate those two, trying to reach a deal or go around them," he said exasperated.

"Yes, we become weary and exhausted; but sometimes we bypass them or we just ignore them; but at the end, they always come back. They were always there; they never left," I said, placing the small carving back on the rock.

Mark looked at me astonished as if what I said was so insightful and profound. I tried to approach his mind, his spirit, carefully without disturbing him; without scaring the stillness and tranquility he felt inside. Silence covered the slope of the hill. Mark was using his knife splendidly, raising his carving over his head in the sun, looking at it from every direction, every time he took a small piece of bark out of it. The piece of bark he was holding was taking form, as if he were a great creator, giving life to it. I was looking at him with a great deal of regard for his art. I sat down next to him.

"Mark," I said, and my voice seemed to startle him; he turned and looked at me. "Mark, what happened to your family? Where is it now?" I asked as that thought was going around my head for some time now. He raised his carving closer to his eyes and marveled at it, as his gaze surrounded the piece of pine bark.

"My wife died seven years ago, and my son left for Germany shortly after," he said, without any sign of despair or concern.

"Do you see him at all?"

"Curiously enough, I haven't heard from him. He's been a stranger for a long time. He alienated me from his life," he said, without any sense of dismaying.

"I'm sorry for your discords, Mark."

"My family expected so much from me, and I gave them so little," he said, looking at me, "but we accept what life gives us and what God allocates to us, Mr. Daniel. When we die and we knock on the big gate, where St. Peter stands guard, he will say, 'you had your share of life and troubles; you've eaten your share of loaves of bread. Come in,' or he will say, 'you have been deficient and flawed, and the gate will not open for you. Take the road down to your left; you'll find another gate. Knock on that one. He's waiting for you.' With God's help, Mr. Daniel, I'll follow my heart."

"Oh, I forgot about him," I said with a sardonic sense of humor. Mark turned and looked at me with apprehension.

"Did you know what someone said about God's last visit?" Mark asked. "God decided to visit us," he continued, "dressed in a white robe, bare feet, holding a walking stick; his white beard and hair were covering his chest, blowing in the wind. He said, 'the earth and heavens are not adequate for me, but the heart of a person surely is. Be careful, he said, don't hurt the heart even of the most marginal of people because I may be in there.'"

"Wise words, Mark."

Despite his plight and tribulations, despite his troublesome life, Mark didn't hold any grouch at his life or anyone; he took life as it came, and he manipulated it and deployed it to his advantage. The fact that his son didn't write to him, seemingly did not bother him; he was a wounded parent, but he endured the negligence and selfishness of his son.

"Have you tried to contact your son?" I asked with apprehension.

"I found out from a villager that he was in Germany. I don't have his address, and he doesn't write. It's impossible to contact him."

"If you get in touch with the embassy in Berlin, perhaps they may know where he is."

"I gave up on George, Mr. Daniel; that's his name. He knows where to find me. If he wants to write then I'll respond; until then, I wish him good luck and good fortune," he said, going back to his carving with an enigmatic and peculiar smile covering his sunburnt face.

"Have you eaten yet?"

"No, not yet. But I will make something for us. You know Mr. Daniel," he said, getting up collecting his carvings and his tools, "you must eat 'cause you have a lot of work to do."

I didn't say anything. I just felt a very peculiar cheerfulness and sadness at the same time. I was watching him walking ahead of me, jumping over the stones, whistling a tune. He was a very misfortunate and wounded man. But he had taken life on his shoulders and carried it, bearing its wrath.

*

AFTER breakfast, I got to work. He was sitting across from me on his bed, carving imaginary figures of his fancy. He seemed very happy and content sculpting, shaping and fondling the pine bark, creating new entities, fascinations, inventions of his illusionary caprice. I let my gaze fall upon him, observing him. Nothing agonized him more than what shape he should give to the pine bark he was holding. But my anguishes and torments were diverse and unlike his. I turned my gaze toward the sea through the open window. "Mark, what does life mean to you?" I asked. He raised his head, looked at me, and stopped carving.

"Happiness, fears, burdens ... doubts ... agonies ... sorrow, and loneliness."

"Have you ever been happy in your life?"

He smiled, and his eyes bounced off the floor. "Yes, when my son was born; later on, when I bought my fishing boat."

"I didn't know you were a fisherman," I said, captivated with fascination.

"Yes, for some time, until one day the sea decided to swallow up my boat to its depths."

"You survived a shipwreck, Mark?"

"Yes, with my heart clinching to my teeth, and me to a piece of lumber from the boat," he said, and he went back to his carving. "Then," he continued, "Then, I had to get a job."

"Tell me about your life as a fisherman."

"What is there to tell? I fished all night; in the morning I would take my fish to the market, and mend my nets."

"Was there ever a moment where you were content with your life? Enjoying being out there in the middle of the sea, relishing the stillness of the night?"

"There have been many moments like that. Sitting alone in my boat, I'd gaze at the starry sky; I'd hear the fish jumping, and stare at the moon over my head. It was peaceful, and I had time to think and reflect. Life was easy then. The fish was plentiful; they would clutch to my nets; I'd take them to the market, and I had the resources to look after my family."

"Why didn't you go back to fishing again?"

"I did; I was employed by a very wealthy man who had a fleet of fishing boats," he said, as he lowered his gaze again, and fondled a piece of bark.

"What happened?"

"One day, after the changing of the guards in Athens, the poli…"

"You mean when the junta took over," I said interrupting.

"Yes. One day the police sergeant came to see my boss. He asked questions about me. I don't know what they talked about, but in the end, I was let go. No explanations, and no options. Since then, my life has changed fundamentally. I gave up fishing all together, and became an artist."

Mark had a fascinating life. He came amidst my solitude and seclusion, holding up a new god. He grabbed him, prepared and complete from the Bazar of Olympus, and he brought him to me. Everything seemed so suitable, as it should have been; an ephemeral diversion of the eyes: a vision, a spectacle, which became more and more tragic, filled with ecstasy and exultation, as we sprinkled it with empathy and compassion, with the blood of our hearts.

*

THERE were times when my pen would not move. My mind was idle, and I was in a state of exhaustion; but not that day. That day my mind was gushing, rushing ahead, and I could not stop it. It was asking me questions; such questions which I could not answer, and for which I had no remedy. *What is a spirit? Where is the consciousness of man veiled and concealed?* There are limits and constraints which must not be traversed. Once, long ago, I fathomed that *one step from the chaos is the abyss*. I also recognized and became conscious of the fact, that if the spirit descended into chaos, then there was no remedy but to plummet into the abyss. I picked up my pen, I gazed into the calm sea outside the open door, I took a deep breath, my lungs were filled with the salty air coming in through the door. His voice inside my mind came again as if it were coming from the very depths of the sea. I moved the pen over the paper. The words were jumping up at me, feeling the page, and I couldn't stop them; and so, I was immersed into my thoughts, as the voice inside me, again and again, was prescribing, commanding my hand, ordering the words, determining the consequence.

> For an internal tiny moment ... yet,
> And I would have left the dream
> Meandering, promenading there,
> Where imagination denies hope ...
> But, I died last night,
>   The time of silence

In the kingdom of yellow and red flowers,
And I woke up with the first kiss of the sea,
    In dawn,
To live a day of charity,
With a formidable reverence,
To reach the sun
As if I were already human.

And then, in the endless night,
Where the waters meet the pebbles,
Under the silver sphere of the moon,
I got hold of my life
Setting among yellow trees
Of the silent slope,
Loaded with the leaves of the beech tree.

Innumerable hands carry me away,
Under the simmering of the empty moments,
    Of the leaves of dew!
It's dawning.
Ashes of the event,
Deadly shapes,
Which try to process the fibers of the day,
Let me be young again and free,
Among haughty cypresses and pine trees,
To race my wishes through the white temples,
And nothing I would care more,
Than the sky and the earth,
Which will allow me to run with my naked feet,
Among the waves
And the friendly winds of my thoughts;
And then, it was blue and yellow and green
    As in a dream,

And the heart was long of the trees,
As the sun was born over and over,
Among the legs and the bosom of the nymphs,
The clouds… the fibers of the day.

I put my pen down. It was time, I thought, as I saw myself battling with words; such was the very depths of my being, plunged in anguish and agony, tormenting my soul to the same degree my mind was tormented. I scooped up my tools, shoveled them inside my head, and I went for a walk. The fresh and unblemished air cleared my mind, and the morning dew refreshed my soul. The sun was rising triumphantly above the opposite mountain, dragging with it its warm rays, which fell upon the earth and its creatures to warm them up. The trees and the earth were smoldering, as the hot sun was evaporating the morning dew. Like a caterpillar of the earth, I was also enjoying the warmth of the sun. The smells from the pine trees were coming alive; I felt my strength plunging onto the earth, but it would bounce back again stronger. I was tired. I wanted to lay down and close my eyes. *It's summer*, I thought. *It's summer and it's a great temptation. Even the most unable bodies come out to warm up; even the hardest bark of the body flourishes in the summer.* I closed my eyes.

*

THE sea lifted heavy and fat waves. The south wind was blowing, warm and tender. Autumn was coming, and the air was saturated with the prejudicial smells of vine leaves and pine. The moment had come to end my journey. It appeared as, time had gone swiftly and hastily; I hardly had time to enjoy the sea, the mountain, and the sun. But autumn was coming, and I had to take my leave; the ferry was arriving in three days. The last days at the island were days of repose. I hunted my brain all summer; now it was time for that to rest. I placed my papers in a case, yearning for my return to the city to continue my studies. The sun was positioned now halfway up the sky, and the heat was agonizing. I walked to the beach where Mark was sitting. Under the scorching sun, the intense light was falling upon his head, as he was bending over his creations. The sand was hot, and the splashing of droplets of water from the waves was hitting my face with indulgence. He had positioned all his creations of his fantasy on the sand one next to each other, marveling with amazement at the little boats with chimneys, little houses, and small animals. He had an innocent and kind expression on his face, as he was lifting them in the sun, looking at them from all sides, smiling to himself. Happiness is not fleeting and transient. The entire summer he was happy, carving this miniature world of his, and now, all lined up in a row like soldiers were admired.

Suddenly I sensed the departure from this place squeezing my heart, feeling the severance in my soul. I looked around the island. The hot sun was smoldering the sand, the trees, and the rocks; a few birds were flying sluggishly overhead, and the sea was somewhat agitated. From afar, I could see the fishermen returning from their fishing expeditions, and nature was elated. A new day was arriving, exulting the soul and the heart. I approached Mark, as he was admiring his creations, sitting on the sand by the water, caressing them with astonishment, as a mother caresses her newborn. How content he looked; how free and liberated from the shackles of human consciousness. He raised his head.

"Did you finish your work?" he asked, looking at my eyes with a gratified smile, which glowed throughout his face.

"My work will never end, Mark. I will continue until the ink is drained from my pen, and I have no more to give. But even then, my soul will exclaim at the sight of the chains surrounding it, until I release it," I said with persuasion, and my words hit my heart to its deepest domain.

He looked far away into the sea, at the mountain, at the seagulls flying low over our heads. He turned to me with a gloomy and desolate gaze, which revealed the heart-breaking reality.

"When are we leaving?" he inquired, as he got up to stretched his legs.

"In three days," I said, and started walking toward the mountain. The pine branches were clashing with my hair, and I could smell the resin levitating from them. It was the first time since I arrived at this island that I felt so inimitable, so wonderful, and so free.

After breakfast, I went outside, and I sat down on a rock under a tree, gazing at my surroundings. The century-old trees, the blue sky and down there, among the rocks and the trees the blue sea, calm and inviting, were exulting my senses, and my brain was fighting my ephemeral thoughts. For a few weeks here, my thoughts went on a rampage; they would abandon my head, scattering all over; but they would assemble again, piling up on top of the pages. I discharged and empty my brain; now I felt lighter. I agonized over the time I spent here. My thoughts were chasing me, and I felt impelled and provoked to let them loose. I was compelled and obliged to write; to inducing my brain to the extent that had nothing more to give. I squeezed it until nothing more was extricated. For now, my demons were defeated and expelled, and new ones were replacing my desolate brain. I had a lot of work to do when I got back to the city: my responsibilities to the organization, and my hunger for the fight, which I had cultivated inside me so meticulously, were growing.

I was ready.

*

THE last morning at the island was cool. A few clouds were piled up over the mountain, and a cool breeze was streaming down. The water was agitated and turbulent. The white cups on the blue sea were moving toward the shore with a sound that only the sea could produce. The ferry would arrive at eleven-thirty; we didn't have a lot of time. We picked up the suitcases on impulse, and we started toward the wharf, walking on the cool sand. I don't remember if we spoke at all. I was just looking at the disturbed water which the ferry was leaving behind it, and we hurry to get there on time. Mark was staying at the island for a few more days before he went back to his village. We placed the suitcases on the ground, and I extended my hand.

"I'll write, Mark," I said, wanting to believe that and convince myself.

"I'll write to you too, Mr. Daniel," he said with a considerably more conviction than my attempted persuasion. I felt inadequate and deficient in front of this man, having spent so much time together. My dishonesty was troubling me, and it was disturbing and unsettling. Those fraudulent words which I uttered to my friend. *Was I truly going to write to him?* I was thinking as I waved goodbye. How critical was it to him whether I wrote or not? Was it of any great consequence or any great magnitude the fact that he would receive a letter from me as soon as I arrived at the city?

*

I was heavy-hearted contemplating my departure from that place. The house of Andreas embraced me again with contentment. I stayed only overnight. The room was the way I left it. The bed across from the open window, the wardrobe against the opposite wall, the small table in the corner, and the smell of the sea and the meadows still lingering throughout, piercing my senses. I lazed on the bed and picked up a book. I could not concentrate. *I'll write to you too* the phrase was coming back to me. I wanted to say more, but I couldn't. He was a nobleman, simple, modest, and uncomplicated. He had that innocence which defined a humble and unassuming heart. The heart of a man who went through a great deal in his life; the man who suffered immensely from the dishonesty and cruelty of society.

The large wooden clock on the wall chimed three times. The same chimes which I heard a few weeks ago, when later that morning I met Mark at the wharf, looking motionless at the deep sea.

I was given a ride to the town, where I would catch the train for the city. Andreas left me at the train station. It was late evening, as the town square was deserted, and a dark veil was placed upon it; only the lights of the train platform illuminated an otherwise deserted station. Two dogs were working the ground looking for food, moving in slow motion extending their noses, smelling and leaking the ground as if it were a bone, euthanasia for their appetite. I went inside the station. The ticket booth was empty. A lonely soul was sleeping on a bench. Maps were hanging on the walls and photographs, portraying the town's decades past. The old station hadn't changed much; situated there at the edge of the square, resting next to the river, with a few buggies outside, and people standing on the street frozen in time.

The night was harmonious and pleasant. I couldn't sleep, being eager from the anticipation, yearning for my return to the city. I went outside on the train platform. The small river next to the station was raging slowly downstream, jumping over the pebbles, creating the kind of sound which has not been refashioned yet by any musical instrument. The town was immersed deeply into an inscrutable sleep. Its lights went out slowly, one after the other as if it were an order from high above to sink it into a profound and peaceful sleep. Only the red lantern of the train station was lit, which was hanging from a pole over the trucks. A dog's bark was heard, and it didn't stop until it got very tiring; but the fatigue and exhaustion reduced it to make little sounds, determined to keep the village awake.

The perceived sound of an owl was heard in the distance, as the water of the river next to the station was taking a tumble among rocks, with a distinct and conspicuous sound. It was quiet all around with the stillness and muteness of the dead.

*

THE horizon was immersed into a deep orange color, as the sun struggled to make the climb from behind the eastern mountain. It was a cool pleasant morning, with a light breeze emerging from the west. The roosters of the town were awakened some time ago, announcing the arrival of a new day. The day birds gathered at the edge of the river bathing, playfully chasing each other. The village square was bustling now with activity, as the villagers opened their doors, stepped out over their threshold, and wiped their eyes to welcomed the new day.

The train raved its engines, and with a jolt and a bounce, rolled slowly on the trucks gaining speed. I was sitting by the window in a desolate coach, looking at the images which were passing me by in a hurry. The train slithered, like a snake, on the steel tracks with a constant metallic clatter. The wildflowers at the side of the train cars were gesturing my departure, in the sudden wind generated by the momentum and the speed of the train. The trees were passing by reminiscent of soldiers in a parade.

The coach door opened, and a man with a bundle under his arm entered. He bowed his head, conceding to my presence, granting me and wishing me a good morning in a low deep voice. He sat a few sits away from me, placing his bundle on the empty seat next to him. He took a newspaper from his coat pocket and opened it. He started reading the paper with a great deal of concentration. From time to time, he would shake his head and murmured something inaudibly. He seemed like a farmer; anguish was smeared on his face, capturing the distress and agony mounting inside him. I was quite familiar with the plight of the farmers. They were losing their land, or at least part of it, to the government, and there was nothing they could do except complain and grumble. My father had already lost part of his land to a new highway. It was severed into two pieces, with a future highway running in the middle. Cultivating the land in such a state was difficult for the farmers; pasturing the animals was equally as difficult. They were left to their own devices. The isolation and solitude, which the farmers felt, abandoned by their government, were flaunting inside their hearts. The Ministry of Agriculture, along with the ministry of Public Works, were falsely encouraging the farmers, indeed insisting, that this was progress. The prosperity was waiting at their threshold, as their products and livestock would arrive at the markets much sooner. They further insisted that the market was wide opened across Europe, and their products would reach the consumers far and wide. It wasn't true, however, because many European countries refused to deal with this oppressive and inhumane dictatorial regime, as the government was finding itself isolated by the hour.

The farmer finished reading his paper and got up. He passed by me again, he bowed his head slightly and returned with a cup of coffee.

"There is hot coffee in the canteen," he said, going back to his seat. He was sipping his coffee gazing outside the window. He seemed to have a lot on his mind; his lips would be moving from time to time as if he were praying to an invisible high power. He had a desiccated thin face, his eyes were deep inside their sockets, his nose was pointed and bony, and his arms were long and reedy. I got up, and I approached him. I extended my hand, and he took it to a cordial and friendly handshake. He had a strong commanding grip.

"I'm Daniel," I said, looking straight at his tired and gloomy eyes, the result of many sleepless nights.

"I'm Elias," he said, and a smile wrapped his face which traveled very quickly and disappeared. He seemed distressed with a great deal of anguish painting his face.

"Are you traveling to the city?" I asked.

"Yes, I'm going straight into the wolf's mouth," he said, and he smiled again briefly.

"The wolf's mouth?" I asked mystified.

"I lost half of my land; the progress has taken it away."

"They call it progress; we call it *a state of seizing, a heist.*"

"My great grandfather had settled there many years ago, and this land belonged to my family for generations. Now I'm losing a good chunk of it." His wet eyes looked away through the window; his gaze drifted across the fields.

"I had news from my father; he also lost part of our land to a new highway. Many farmers are facing the same predicament."

Elias shook his head in revulsion and disgust. "We're all in the same boat," he said, "we'll sink and we're all going to go down together."

This was not a prophetic or forewarning articulation; it was a reality. The frustration of the farmers was escalating, given the government's claims and mandates, and there was no sympathy coming from the capital.

CHAPTER XI

Two years had elapsed since I enrolled at the university in this maltreated and assaulted city. Although its bruises were felt at every step and at everyone, no one spoke about it openly. People didn't even talk about other dictatorships, other wars, other revolutions, which had polluted countries with a stench of corpses, which would never go away. Those were the years of yearning for life, freedom, and contentment, clearly endured by the sort of people who had suffered imprisonment, exile, and torture.

In the shadows of all the people who went through it, of whom some of them did not walk out, sat that *Yellow Building*. It was dawning. Its shadow was long, as that building's silhouette was sitting in the glooms and obscurity of murder and deceit, treachery, torment, and anguish. Correlations were the blemishes of destiny, once I thought; if that were true, then our destiny was accidental. No, there were no correlations. We were marionettes of our subconscious yearnings. Since I was a child, I yearned for freedom. I realized early enough, that my yearning for freedom was not accidental. It was brewing inside me since infancy, defying any physical laws. Personal freedom comes from within. These, as best I could recall, were not diminutive believes or assurances --since they were weighed with an honest hand-- but rather yearnings, desires, and passions. On one side stood the soul yearning for freedom; on the other, my ultimate demise and my mortality; but the merit of the soul is immeasurable.

*

I returned to the hotel after a long walk on University Avenue. As soon as the front desk clerk saw me, gestured at me to approach the desk. He announced to me that there was a man here querying about me.

"Made inquiries about me?" I ask anxious and disturbed.

"Yes, he came up to the desk, looked at me for a few seconds wedging and cramming his eyes as he was zooming on me, and he asked if you were here," said the clerk with a distinguished and concerned gaze.

"Did he say what he wanted of me?" I asked fretfully and with concern.

"No, he said that he would come back. He looked like a police officer in civilian clothes." The clerk looked at me and said with trepidation. "Are you involved in anything illegal or subversive?" I didn't grant him the pleasure of an honest answer. Instead, I turned to the newspaper on the desk.

"No, of course not," I said, reading the newspaper headlines.

"You need to be careful who you associate with, Daniel. What you read, what you say, the air you breathe," he said with apprehension.

He was an old man, with wrinkles around his eyes and face. His burned from the sun face was thin and rigid. His eyes, deep inside their sockets, had that piercing and intensity stare when they looked deep into my eyes as if they wanted to penetrate my entire being. His hands looked as if he hadn't spent his entire life behind a desk. Hard, sunburned, and solid his forearms were hanging low, and his veins were protruding over the surface of his skin, indicating that he had a hard life. His thin tall torso was slightly bent, his bones were projecting from under his shirt, signaling his age. He was a kind, disquieted, and reassuring man, soft-spoken and mindful. I thanked him, picked up the newspaper, and walked towards the stairs.

"Daniel, there was also a young lady that passed by asking for you." I stopped and turned around.

"Did she say anything?" I asked anxiously.

"She just said to give her a call."

I ran up the narrow staircase, unlocked my room, and went straight to the phone.

CHAPTER XII

A RIDGE OF CLOUDS raced across the sky, while lightning could be seen from behind the mountains. I should have proceeded to dash and take shelter from the approaching rainstorm, but as the officer's words were beginning to sink in, my hands and my entire body were quivering, while my mind was pursuing my body's trembling. Gazing upwards, I noticed the storm spattering darkened veils of water from between the clouds as if the sky had opened up its cataracts, tarnishing out the moon, and covering the entire city in darkness. I tried to quicken my pace, but consumed by panic and nervousness -- from the dreadful and horrifying words of the officer -- I walked with ponderous and dreary legs, pursued and hunted by sheets of rain. I took refuge under an awning of a store, trying to gather and assemble my thoughts, determined to adopt a plan. A thrust of resounding thunder rumbled nearby, and I felt the vibration under my feet. Moments later, the feeble current of the lighting system of the city, which had defined and illuminated the surroundings up until now, diminished and faded away. The street lamps on the submerged sidewalks flickered, then eclipsed. The embodiment of anybody resembling human souls was absent from the entire city. The darkness of the blackout spread and covered the entire city, along with a rotten smell rising from the sewers. The night became unyielding and impenetrable, as the rain bombarded and overwhelmed the city, obscuring it with its dark veil.

As the capricious and erratic rain slowed down, I was able to leave my shelter and head toward Avgy's place. I accelerated my pace in fear of the rain resuming its downpour. I reached the apartment building almost out of breath. I rang the bell waiting for a response. The soft voice of Avgy came on the intercom and I was allowed in. The humidity inside the building was unbearable, as the heat, accelerated by the moisture in the air, making breathing very strenuous and demanding. I climbed the stairs to the second floor and knocked on the door. Avgy was dressed in shorts and a T-shirt. Her hair was falling upon her shoulders, while her eyes had a sparkle, illuminating her entire face, irradiated by her suntan. My clothes were drenched, and water was dripping down from my hair covering my forehead. After her insistence on taking my clothes off to dry, I put on a T-shirt and a pair of jeans she offered me. I sat down close to the air-conditioning, and she offered me a glass of white wine; she sat across from me on the sofa scrutinizing my face.

"What happened to you? Where were you?" she inquired concerned.

"I'm coming back from the Yellow Building, where I was questioned by the chief," I said, while the memories of the interrogation came back to me.

"What did they want? Why did they question you?"

I took a deep breath, and my eyes fell on the floor. I opened my mouth to say something, but I was left wordless. What did they want? Why did they question me? Why do they question anybody who was asked to scale the threshold and venture inside that repulsive building? I collected my thoughts and recounted the hours I spent with the chief of police in the interrogation room. "He asked me about my family, where I come from, my father's activities, and my thoughts about the government," I said, thinking about my father, and the fact that he was never involved in politics or any organization, political or social.

"Daniel, whatever thoughts you may have about the government, you understand, you'll never be able to express them," Avgy said asserting, that those deep thoughts were never to be revealed to a police officer of a totalitarian right-wing regime.

"He also questioned me about my studies at the university, if I have any connections with the students' subversive – as he put it – organization on campus and my activities outside the university."

"What did you say?"

"Of course, I denied any involvement in any organization. He went on to ask me about people I don't know and people I know. What they are doing, what courses they're taking, and any connections to anti-government subversive organizations."

"Did he mention any names affiliated with us?"

"He asked me about Michael to which I replied that he's a fellow student at the university who I know from a distance and our seminars."

"I think they are digging very deep this time. I'm sure they asked Michael the same questions, but they must have a lot more information about him to detain him for so long."

"I was detained for two and a half hours, Avgy; he strained my brain, attempting to extricate cordial and painful information out of me. I thought I was going to go mad after a while."

"Was he exasperated with your answers?"

"Yes, he was, demanding explanations and actualities."

"Did you give any?"

"False or unrelated events which were not incriminating."

"Did he say anything about Michael, when he'll be released, and where he's detained?"

"No. I may have heard his screams if he were still there. The building smelled of malt. The walls and floors were dirty and marked with holes and scratches. I felt imprisoned, and the idea of spending even one more hour there sickened and frightened me."

"That's where Michael spends his days and nights, sleepless, pestering, agonizing moments."

"At some point, the officer went out, closed the door, and he left me alone for half an hour. I was not sure why he went out, or what he was doing during that time, but it was half an hour of hell," I said, bending my head over my legs closing my eyes. I stayed silent for some time, reflecting.

"Are you okay, Daniel?" Avgy asked, kneeling in front of me, placing her hand on my head kissing me.

"Avgy, they have infiltrated and discovered our organization. A lot more people will be guided by their fate to pass the threshold of that building, doomed and hopeless, and only a few will be let out. The screams and voices coming from all directions were waking up inside me with a startling and terrifying sense of insecurity, fear, and uncertainty. He had a smirk on his face every time a scream pierced and penetrated the air, as he would look at me with an intimidating stare. He was holding a baton in one hand, and he would hit his left palm with it, as he was waiting for my answers. Another officer knocked on the door, and he went out briefly to talk to him. It was a frightening experience," I declared apprehensively, wiping my face and hair with a towel.

"That *Friday* was an ill-fated and predestined day, which has shown its face time and again in the *Yellow Building*, on the streets of the city, on the islands, on people's psyche," Avgy proclaimed, surveying my wet face.

*

DIM daylight was rupturing the darkness when I finally stopped reading the books which were buried under my mattress. I stood in front of the window, consumed by anxiety, looking outside as a caged animal looks toward freedom. All my objections, my scepticisms, and apprehensions seemed irrelevant and trivial. I was conquered by fatigue, repentance, and fear, but I felt I was powerless, and I needed to leave my room. I put on my coat and ran down the narrow staircase. I stepped out of the front door; it had started to rain again. The sky was dissolving into the slow arrival of light, that seemed to be coming from the depths of the sky before fading away behind the rain. The street was almost deserted, but in the corner stood a desolate outline figure of a man with white hair, dressed in a rather old, large for his size, black overalls. He raised his hands trying in vain to catch raindrops, laughing to himself. As I walked past him, he looked at me and smiled grimly. His eyes were the color of blue, like the sky which was at that point obstructed by the clouds.

"Good morning," I thought I heard him say.

I tried to cling to the wish that strange man uttered, and I slowed down my pace, hoping that it wouldn't be too early and that Avgy was already awake. My feet and legs were hurting from the long walk and the tension,

I felt all over my body. There was light rain now falling from the sky; the water was running down from my head, stigmatizing my face and forehead. My clothing was wet. It was a warm morning, however, with light fog covering the streets and buildings. The overpowering humidity was mixing with the heat. The sun was up by now but hidden behind the clouds. I was dripping wet when I reached Avgy's building. The rain was beginning to settle, and I had the good fortune of finding the doorman stationed at the entrance. He was the caretaker of the building and – from what I heard from Avgy – a secret romantic and hidden Casanova. He had come out to watch the spectacle of the rain and the fog covering the city, broom in hand, wearing a yellow raincoat with the hood up covering his grey hair.

"God's crying," he said, admiring the covered from the dark clouds sky, offering me a preview of his brittle and diluted sense of humor.

The autumn of that year was unusually very warm and by now, the weakened leaves of the trees were hanging on for dear life, as the rain and the light wind were battering them, assaulting and antagonizing the creations of spring, aggressively. The distant memory of my interrogation with the chief of police inhibited my spirits again, discouraging and daunting my efforts toward the organization and my studies. But perhaps life had decided to allow me a retreat, as an incentive to my melodramatic anguishes, so that I could begin to sprout and flourish my ambitions. The interrogation was detrimental, damaging my efforts toward my exertions and my endeavors, impairing my self-esteem, mutilating my mind, and ravaging my being. But none of that would put a damper on my exploits, and what I had to undertake, without relinquishing my values and beliefs.

CHAPTER XIII

The letter from my parents, which I read and reread until I knew it by heart, brushed aside all the doubts and apprehensions I had, which were left in me from all the carnages of animals in the small town. The uneasiness and trepidation fashioned by the alleged killer of those animals created an uproar in the town, and there were many questions soliciting answers. Speculations and suppositions were expressed by the villagers, whose animals were slaughtered perversely, demanding answers from the authorities. Being engrossed in that letter, my father's concerns and fretfulness were echoing in my head, as I was contemplating actions that my father should take. The police had detained a few suspects, but they were released due to the absence of evidence. In the midst of all this, the government was systematically persisting on the annex and appropriation of properties, for the new extension of the highway. Was it a coincidence, that their animals were slaughtered in the middle of this government proposal? Spreading fear and terror to the villagers of this small northern town?

A police inspector had visited my father, asking questions about the circumstances surrounding the episodes which took place – all and all five of his animals were killed – asking him if he had any foes, which would result in this gruesome and revolting outcome. He asked him if he were indebted financially to anybody, which was an absurd proposition, since the animals were killed perhaps by a deranged killer, and the responsibility of the authorities was to find and prosecute the perpetrator.

In his letter, my father pointed to the fact that he missed me, and that after losing my brother at such a young age, he put all his hopes and faith on me, to support him and assist him to take care of the animals and the land. But he did not count on the fact, that the universities were in the cities, and if I intended to receive higher education, I would have to go away from home. I was well aware of the reality that both my parents were conscious of the fact, that education was very important to me, and that it was elemental for me to pursue my aspirations and ambitions, as I did not incline to end up in the village, plowing the land and tending to the animals. They were perceptive to that. It was a hard life my parents were enduring, dwelling in a small village with no amenities or services, which the city folk enjoyed. That made it even more difficult for them to function amid transitory days, in that desolate and dismal place which they chose to raise a family.

I was able to envision both my parents, sitting by the fire at night after all the chores were carried out; having dinner by themselves, talking about this and that, exploring their misfortunes, surveying their brain to come up with solutions – which by the way might have been unattainable under the circumstances – looking forward to what kind of life they were anticipating after they retired. The political situation was oppressive. The plans of the government to arbitrarily take a portion of their land away for a new highway were deplorable. Their animals were killed who knows by who, and the prices of their harvest kept on hitting bottom. All these worries and ambiguities put a damper in their heart and their pocketbook. In my despair and desolation, I did wish I were there to help them figure out and consider their life, their exertions and tribulations and assist them. The internal forever conflict, which went around and around my head, had no elucidation toward any possible solution to the woes of my parents. There was no departure from such human condition unless something changed fundamentally; and the change might be gradual or even unattainable, but the effort, nevertheless, was there.

*

ARISTOTLE claimed that *we are social creatures,* and indeed we are. Although our actions and behaviors define us as social creatures, however, our physiognomies and circumstances define our human existence. The human condition is a condition that we contemplate from many different perspectives, such as the positive or negative aspects of our lives. These aspects define our human condition. The human condition is also defined by the internal and external struggles we endure, along with our emotions which are products of our existence. Although the word *condition* may suggest that it's an ailment, perhaps, which all humans carry with them since birth or an anathema which may define the fate of humanity, it is simply based on our behaviors and actions we paraded during our ephemeral and transitory stay on this planet. What we do in between our arrival to this earth and our departure, defines us as humans, and what we fashion is sustained persistently for generations. Internal and external struggles are products of our existence, along with our emotions which also define the human condition.

*

Such was the life of the elderly in the village, who had no more strength left to work the land or take care of their animals; and if they had no successors or offspring to take over their responsibilities, they suffered the consequences of being incapacitated and forlorn, with no funds and no prospects to take care of themselves. Would I be able to assist my parents after I graduate, or should I persuade them to sell the land and the animals and come along with me to whichever city I would find employment in?

Our future was fickle and impulsive; not so much financially as it were politically. The country had been isolated, and there was an incursion of international protests to pressure the government to release political prisoners and improve human rights. The sun didn't look very bright over that unpredictable political situation; it didn't look very bright over the imprisoned people who opposed the regime, or even over the possibility that I might end up on an island or in a prison, because of my political activities and beliefs. But I believed. I believed that the human spirit could not be imprisoned and chained, tolerating and enduring the inhumane treatment and handling of the citizens by the government. The human spirit was intended to thrive, create and guide, instead of dying uncultivated and raw. What would our forefathers think of today's state of affairs?

CHAPTER XIV

The clouds spattered down from the sky that Saturday morning, inundating the entire city with sweltering mist and humidity, which made the thermometers exude sweat. At noon, the temperature was already glancing at mid-thirties Celsius. With books in my sack and many thoughts spinning around my head, I set off for the national library to meet Avgy. The sweat was scraping my forehead and spine. The library was – and remains – one of many places in the city, where the nineteenth-century architecture had not yet been served their eviction notice. A double, curved stone staircase at either side of this extraordinary building, led up to a big veranda decorated by six pillars at the front. Between the two staircases, there was a patch of green grass, with a few evergreens growing, obstructing part of the facade of the building. A statue was stationed in the middle, among the evergreens. This neoclassical building was built at the end of the nineteenth century, as the last neoclassical trilogy of the city, which included the Academy and the University. The two smaller structures attached at either side of the main structure, were of the same architecture, with three long windows on each, which made the entire unit look very symmetrical. A network of reading rooms and open spaces were placed strategically throughout the floors of the library, giving a comfortable and serene feeling to the reader. Allowing my consent to the blades of the fans, which swirled above my head, my exaltation was immense due to the high temperatures and humidity.

Avgy had claimed a cubical on the first floor, bending over an open book anticipating my arrival. I approached her and placed my hand on her smooth and silky hair. She raised her head granting me a smile. I sat across from her; she bent over and she kissed me on the lips. Her kiss burned me; I felt dizzy and light-headed with the sudden rush of blood to my brain. I held that kiss on my lips for a long time, as I passed my fingers over them again and again, feeling her warm skin on them. I held her warm soft hand, looking at her straight in her undiluted eyes. She had a comfortable and relaxed smile on her face, and her whole essence glowed. We didn't talk. We were just exploring each other's faces. She had on a plain yellow T-shirt and jeans, and her hair was tied back in a ponytail. Her knee touched mine, and an exhilarating feeling transfixed my entire body and senses. I raised my hand and placed it on hers; her warmth tantalized me, and I kissed it looking at her eyes. I took my books out of my bag, but my eyes never left hers; they were still pinned on those brilliant eyes of hers, and I couldn't let them go. I did not open my books. I had no desire to study. I had never felt this feeling before. This overwhelming feeling, which occupied my heart with ecstasy. It jumped and skipped a bit, and caught up with my blood, which carried it to my brain, and filled me with happiness and frenzy. It was at the café that I met her for the first time when Ari introduced her to me some time ago. I could not stop thinking how beautiful she was and how gentle her eyes and her entire being were.

I smiled and I let her hand free.

"Have you read the news this morning?" I probed her, opening the newspaper. "Catastrophic outcome, as a result of an anti-government demonstration. Four dead and nine injured; the battleground was Kent State University in Ohio. What a horrific and dreadful massacre of students by the Ohio National Guards," I said.

"Yes, sadly, I glanced at the article at a newsstand. It's inconceivable. How can one allow deadly shootings like these to take place on university grounds?" Avgy pleaded exasperated with disgust.

"Unarmed students, nonetheless."

"What was that they were demonstrating for?"

"They were simply demonstrating the invasion and the bombings of Cambodia by the US forces. Nixon is trying to contain communism in that region. It's appalling and repulsive what they're doing in Cambodia, killing innocent women and children."

"Is it any different Daniel, from the appalling situation we have here? At least they're allowed to demonstrate, although they're killing them for that right; as for us here, we don't even have that right," Avgy said with repugnance.

"Have you seen the pictures?"

"No, not yet."

"Here," I said, and turned the paper to face her, "a heartbreaking picture of a woman over the dead body of a student."

"My God, that's a dreadful scene," Avgy said, looking at the picture, "how awful. Those must have been very horrifying moments for the students."

They were, indeed. A poem by Yannis Ritsos' *Epitaphios* came to mind.

My son, little heart of my heart,
Little bird of my poor courtyard,
My wasteland's blossom,
How did your eyes close without seeing that I weep,
Without stirring, without hearing the bitter words I speak to you?
My bird, who used to bring me water in your hand,
How can your eyes not see that I beat my breast and tremble like a reed?

Avgy continued reading the newspaper article, as I opened my book, trying to concentrate; but my brain was gone, and it was not coming back. I was thinking of the events at Kent State, I was thinking of Michael, and my mind was jumping hither and thither, trying to settle down, to become peaceful again and reconcile the events. Could that happen here? I was thinking. Was it possible that the police and the army could be as detestable and hateful as to shoot at the students, demonstrating peacefully without weapons? Is it possible that as we read what happened at Kent State, we could be reading our fate, perhaps?

I closed my book again and looked at Avgy who was still reading the newspaper.

"Avgy, I was thinking about Michael; his news is heart-rending and agonizing," I said, looking at her brilliant eyes as she raised them from the newspaper, holding my hand.

"I wonder how he's doing at that island. I wish I could visit him," she said and squeezed my hand affectionately.

"I'm not sure if we can. Besides, it won't be a good idea. They're looking for co-operatives, and we could be a target," I said, and bitterness filled my heart. Fear, anger, resentment, and shame engulfed my senses. *He's our brother, and we have the obligation and compulsion to visit him*, I thought, as doubts and misgivings were sharing my fears. I had been too cynical even to suggest that. Fear had overpowered me until indignation settled in: I must reconsider.

*

As my mind wandered to the island where Michael was held, to Kent State, and back to the island, my thoughts meandered around my brain, envisioning the number of men and women murdered every day, as a consequence of their ideals and beliefs. Where were we headed as a society, approaching the abyss of destruction, as we buried our young children, disrupting families, distorting our society's fabric, bearing the burden of civilization under oppression, which was laid upon us? Powerful nations invade feeble nations, overthrowing governments, tormenting and preventing societies from acquiring a political system that is according to their socio-economic epitomes and principles. A renowned 19th-century German philosopher said that *the oppressed are allowed once every few years to decide which particular representatives of the oppressing class are to represent and repress them.* But even if Carl Marx hadn't said that we as a society had witnessed it, coming to pass in many places, as the oppression upon people took different forms over the years, in order to conceal the appalling and diabolical exploits of the oppressors.

*

THE night was falling heavily upon the city, and the rain was beating on the pavement and buildings, with such an extraordinary force. The clouds were spewing their entrails downward. The sound and the force of the wind were relentless and inexorable. It was almost late evening when we left the library, wrapped in our thoughts. Avgy glanced up in the sky, as the streets were transformed into rivers of water. She looked at me with disappointment. "How are we going to get home?"

"It will stop soon enough. These clouds are moving quickly," I said, with conviction glancing at the sky.

"Since when you became an expert on weather predictions, Daniel?" she said laughing.

"Living in the village has educational side effects as well."

We stayed undercover for some time until the rain eased. When it lightened up and the rain started to diminutively slow down, we started running. But midway home it started again, and we were drenched to the bone, as our clothes were saturated from the rain. We reached Avgy's apartment soaked to the skin and out of breath. We found the entrance to the building, and we rushed in to escape from the downpour. We went up to her apartment, contemplating how to dry our clothes and our bodies. Avgy suggested that we take our clothes off, and place them next to the heat vents to dry.

The rain and the wind were relentlessly beating the windows. Lightning could be seen now and then among the buildings across the street. Thunder would follow, sometimes closer sometimes further away, which would shake and rattle the window pane. The few candles Avgy lit were flickering on top of the coffee table, while shadows were wavering on the opposite walls. The pictures on the walls had adopted their own life, and in that semi-dark environment, the figures on the paintings seemed to be moving back and forth creating a sense of eeriness with a ghostly impression. We were sitting on the carpet on the floor with a glass of wine, anticipating the next thunder and how close it will hit. The soft unobtrusiveness in the room was interrupted by the episodic and intervallic rain, ravaging the world outside. Avgy moved closer to me and put her arms around my neck. She bent over and gave me a soft kiss on the lips. I extended my arms and got hold of her body. Slowly I placed her on the carpet, looking at her eyes. Laying there with her hair around her face, and her bright eyes looking at me, I could not resist any longer. I approached her face, and my lips touched hers. She emitted a small sound that came from deep inside her. My heart skipped a beat, as my lips were moving around her lips, her neck, and her shoulders. A flame was burning inside me, and I could not stop it. My lips didn't want to leave hers, as I was transported into a different world, elated and enraptured, full of ecstasy and anticipation. The lights went out, as darkness blanketed the neighborhood. I let myself lay next to her, holding her tied against my body.

Early morning came, and we were still on the carpet, with a blanket over us, and a pillow under my head. With her lips half-open, Avgy was sleeping peacefully next to me, breathing quietly. I bent over and gave her a soft kiss on the forehead. She opened her eyes and smiled with an angelic expression covering her face. She extended her hand and touched my face, caressing it with warmth and affection. Outside the sun was struggling to show its face among the few clouds still lingering around.

"Good morning," she said with a sleepy voice as she was trying to get up. "I'll make breakfast."

"Maybe some coffee first. I'm dying for a cup of coffee," I said, offering my hand to help her get up.

"OK. Coffee it is," she said and got up. She went into the kitchen and she came back with two cups of coffee. "The lights are back on again," she said, "it was a wild night, last night, with the rain and the wind," she declared, placing the cups on the coffee table.

"But you slept like an angel. Nothing seemed to bother you," I said, as I moved closer to my coffee and I took a sip.

"Not true. I sleep very lightly. The floor was not very comfortable and the carpet was itching my body," she said, sitting next to me placing her hand on my thigh.

"I thought it was quite comfortable on the floor." I laughed as I said that because I was also awfully uncomfortable all night.

"You were quite noisy," she said, pinching my thigh.

"Was I?"

"Yes, you were," she said, and she laughed. "When I was small," she resumed, "my brother and I used to sleep next to the fireplace in the winter, whenever my parents were in a good mood and allowed us to be natty. We lived in a small town outside the city with my grandmother. All night I could hear my grandmother from the living room snoring."

"Did you hear any animals howling last night?" I said, and I laughed.

"I thought I heard animals howling last night in a very close proximity, within this room," she said, sharing a smile, and kissed me on the cheek.

"My snoring wasn't that bad," I said with a smile, "was it?"

"I'd rather not say. But I *will* say that I was not sure if it was you or the thunder and the wind outside quivering this room."

*

NOON was closing in when the metro train left us at Victoria station close to Stephan's apartment, where he was waiting for us. We got a phone call late that morning, as Avgy and I were having breakfast, waiting for our clothes to dry. He was arrested and beaten up badly by the police. He was left heavily injured at the steps of the police station. He managed to walk to his apartment, where he gave us a call. I could hear the pain in his voice and the anguish, trying to breathe, suspecting that he had one or two broken ribs.

He was thrown out on the street, bloody and disoriented. His face and chest were so severely bruised, that he sat on the steps of the police station to catch his breath to recover from the dizziness and pain he felt. Passersby were avoiding eye contact with Stephan, either because of shame, because of trepidation, or because they were petrified, offering help to anyone injured sitting outside a police station, fearing the consequences by the police, of being, perhaps, collaborators or simply human. Stephan wasn't sure if what he felt was shame, indignity, or humiliation, sensing that the passersby were apathetic to his condition. His sense of pride, however, was very strong, knowing very well that he was brave, a freedom fighter, and not some kind of a charlatan or imposter. Michael had the same fate, but his fate went even further. I was convinced he was mistreated and victimized as badly as Stephan, but his ordeal continued all the way to the island, and I was certain it still went on.

So, it was with some apprehension that I observed Stephan, from the shelter of my spectacles. The lenses of my glasses betrayed nothing of the concentration with which he watched for my response to his present condition. He knew that if his eyes or his face were to betray any knowledge, any recollection of our pact as an organization in the event that he had talked, then he would have no option but to turn on his heel and walk away – although that would have been impossible under his current condition. The awkwardness would be too great to ignore, for not only was there the question of what he might have said to the police officer and what they did to him but the shame of him being interrogated and mishandled. The shame of which might have well destroyed a man and his dignity, as well as other lives and the organization itself, if he had talked. But there was also the shamelessness of his disgrace if that was indeed all it was.

To my relief, the sight of his seemed to kindle no spark in my gloomy eyes. His massive body was brutalized and maltreated; he was missing half of his clothing, and what was left on him was discolored from blood. The sleeveless vest was open to his chest, and around his waist, he was wearing his usual leather belt, which was undone. I was watching him, shifting my weight between my legs, knowing and convincing myself that he had not talked. A secret's worth depends on the people from whom it must be kept.

When we reached his apartment, the doctor was already there occupying himself with repairs on Stephan. One can hear his painful groans and moaning, filling the room as if he were an injured animal desperately trying to overcome the anguish of pain. His face was bloody, and he had scratches on his arms; he was covered in bandages, dressings, and slings; Mary was sitting next to him, assisting the doctor. It was very hard to look at his face, which carried a bruise with a bloody nose and mouth, while the doctor desperately trying to stop the bleeding and bandage him. His bloody mouth, which was missing a tooth, was deformed, as he attempted a smile as soon as he saw us.

"How are you feeling Stephan?" I inquired.

"Better than ever," he uttered with a painful smile.

"Stop pretending damn it. You look like shit, Stephan. You don't look alright. Is your head spinning? Are you hearing voices?" I said with annoyance as my stomach was churning.

"I'm sure I can hear disputing sounds as if a penguin was trying to play the violin," Stephan said with a painful smirk on his face, which quickly traveled away.

"Don't worry Daniel, I have seen worse than his injuries, since that horrible *Friday*. Many young people have come to me with worse injuries," the doctor insisted, reassuring the rest of us, that this was a normal occurrence among the visitors at the *Yellow Building* since it was kicked off that awful *Friday*.

"So, the person who has chiseled you a new face is none other than a police officer; I see you move about in the highest circles," I said humorously. "How are you on confessions, Stephan?"

"The last four years have been a great deal of practice for me, and many things got lost in the way. No word uttered," Stephan said earnestly, clinching to his chest with pain.

We escorted the doctor to the door and thanked him profusely for his good provision and delivery, and a good overhaul of Stephan. Of course, there was no obligation and commitment on the part of Stephan, as the doctor was not expecting anything gratefully. When we went back to the bedroom, Stephan was sitting up having a glass of brandy. Eventually, the pain, the brandy, and the exhaustion had finally sent him to sleep. Mary was stroking his hair, while his face had a painful smile painted on it.

CHAPTER XV

The stairwell was a pit of darkness. Flashes of lightning hemorrhaged through the cracks of the front door, illuminating the silhouette of the steps for a brief moment. Fumbling my way onward presumptuously, I found the first step by tripping over it, and I initiated my climb; embracing the banister, I slowly climbed the stairs. Soon enough the steps yielded to a plane-level surface, and I realized I had reached the first floor. Holding on to the banister, I climbed the stairs to the loft of the old house.

Before Avgy's father was arrested, he purchased this old house thinking, perhaps, he would renovate it and offer it to his daughter after she graduated from university. Unfortunately, his plans went adrift and didn't turn out the way he anticipated. He was arrested shortly after the purchase of the house, and now it was sitting there vacant and fragmented. Avgy offered to hide Jason in that house until things calmed down. The police had searched heaven and earth to find him, but they were not aware of this hiding place, and they hadn't come near it. Avgy and sometimes Ari frequently visited Jason to bring him food, water, and newspapers and converse with him. There had been a very active period for the police the last few months, going after students, members of various unions, anti-government organizations, and ordinary citizens, who the police had suspected and labeled as having leftish appetites. The police interests in those groups of people had alarmed many residences of the city who had dubious and disputed political past, as far as the police chief was concerned.

It came as a shock to all of us when the police went to Jason's house to arrest him; but fortunately, he was not at home. He was informed of the police's arrival at his house. He immediately contacted Ari and Avgy, to ask for assistance and discuss his next move. Avgy suggested her father's old house for his hiding place, which was not occupied, and which was sitting vacant in a very inconspicuous neighborhood of the city. The house did not have electricity, and in the winter, it got awfully cold.

Upon arriving at the loft of this old house, I could hear shuffling, and I sensed that Jason was in one of the rooms. It was hopelessly dark, and I had to feel my way around. Fortunately, the windows of the rooms were bringing some light in from the lamp posts outside, which shone on the hallway just enough to find the room where Jason was hiding. I found him sitting on a mattress on the floor, with a book in his hands, having difficulty reading, as his eyes were battling the weak light entering the room from the street. He had been here in this room for two weeks, without any prospect yet of getting out. When he saw me, he got up, and he put his weak arms around me to a welcoming embrace.

"My brother, you came. How is this miserable and dismal world doing outside? Any more arrests?" he said, as he sat down again on the mattress.

"The dismal world outside is still the same: terrifying, panicky, depressing, and desolate."

"Any news from Stephan and Michael?" he inquired, wrapping his arms around his raised legs.

"No news from anybody yet," I replied, as I move closer to the small window.

"Move away from the window, Daniel. You never know who's watching the house," he said, and one could sense the distress and dread in his voice, being terrified of being discovered.

"I brought you some food and a few books. At least you can read during the day," I said, and I sat on the mattress next to him.

"Yes, thank you," he said, as sadness covered his voice.

My anger was accelerating by the minute, as I was watching him sitting on a mattress on the floor in the darkness, sad and with no immediate prospects. He hadn't gone to school for weeks, and his work was mounding. He was a fugitive from the authorities and was on the run protecting his cause. The foundation which he built, along with so many others who had died or were dying in the hands of the army and the police, he was now protecting. The ideology of survival, freedom, and integrity as a basic concept, defined the ideal state or objective of the philosophy and principles of the person. Jason's humanism was based on the values of human inevitabilities, stipulations, and aspirations, as a conceptual platform. Spending time alone in this abandoned house -- isolated from the rest of the world -- Jason was considered an outcast by the police, but a champion among his mates. His humanism was by nature progressive; his beliefs, which would develop and upgrade the desired state of the human being over time, gave him the strength to endure the isolation and seclusion. My first thought on waking up this morning was to tell Jason about the latest developments of our organization and the resolutions taken, regarding many issues including the upcoming demonstrations. Jason was a classmate of mine, who devoted his free time and his talent to the invention of wonderfully ingenious contraptions. His mind worked constantly, and I was afraid he would not survive isolation in that abandoned house for too long.

CHAPTER XVI

A DEEP DREAMLESS NIGHT and the prospect of seeing Avgy again that evening persuaded me that somehow the affections and fondness she had shown lately, were very engaging and reassuring. I had a vision of her all day yesterday, which must have been pure coincidence. I rarely forget my dreams, but last night the dreams didn't come. Anticipating my meeting with Avgy again, it was enough to abandon myself into a deep sleep.

The sun had started its descent on its way to the western mountains when I left my apartment. It was a pleasant evening; the shadows were getting longer, and the breeze coming from the south was gentle and warm. I walked toward the railway station where I would find my way to Avgy's apartment building. The streets were active and demanding, the sidewalks filled with people, and the shops were still exploiting the late evening. The cafés were busy with commanding and contented patrons, and the tables and the umbrellas on the sidewalks were an inviting place for an evening beverage. I unbuttoned my jacket allowing the welcome breeze to hit my chest. At the railway station, I turn into a small cobblestone street, where I would find her apartment building. I rang the bell, and her voice came through the intercom. I took the staircase to her floor, and knocked on the door. She stood at the threshold smiling, put her arms around me, and kissed me.

Her apartment was warm, and the air condition was working in half of its capacity. She took me by the hand, and she guided me to her bedroom.

Two candles were burning on the night tables. The bed was dressed with white sheets. She hugged me again and kissed me, drawing me toward the bed. I placed her softly on the bed, allowing her body to lay on the silky white sheets, while her arms were still around my neck, and I kissed her again. The next few moments were full of anticipation and wonder, as I watched her undress. Her soft and suntanned skin came into view. I followed the lines of her body from her succulent luscious lips to her neckline, her breasts, her belly, and down to her painted toenails.

Avgy's naked body was stretched out on the white sheets, which shone like sluiced silk. My hands slid over her lips, her neck, and her breasts. Her silky-smooth polished body, glowed in the weak light of the candles, was trembling and quivering under my touch. Her flawless legs were resting firmly on the bed, as her arms were pushing my body toward her. I let my hands explore her belly, while my tongue was traversing it with ecstasy. My tongue followed the contour of her body, back up to her neck and lips. Her brilliant eyes looked up to the ceiling, her eyelids shuddered as I gently charged her, entering her body between her trembling and bronze from suntan thighs. Her legs hugged my back, and her hands embraced me so tightly, causing me to lose my ability to breathe. The same hands which had held mine on Academy Street during our walk, after our first dinner some time ago, now clutched the sweat-veneered buttocks of mine, her nails mining into them, as they guided me toward her with frantic and eager animal desire.

I was panting.

I couldn't breathe.

While my body was touching hers, I held her hand, as we laid there on the bed still, after the marvels and sensations of love. Curiosities had been extinguished, as the spectacles of lovemaking were preceding the serenity and the tranquillity of the room; we were enjoying the esprit de corps of each other. My mind was wandering to the furthest points of the earth, searching for a more tranquil, more serene place than the one I was in. The sounds from the road were invading the stillness of the room, as the darkness was taking over, giving more authority to the candles to shine, portraying mobile and trembling shadows on the walls and ceiling. As she laid there, I turned to face Avgy, caressing her thighs, passing my fingers over her belly, breasts, and face. Sweat was forming on her forehead, and her silky body was warm and calm which looked almost translucent and undisturbed. She looked thoughtful and sad, as a tear stigmatize her high-cheek-bone face.

"What's the matter?"

"I'm sad, Daniel. I'm sad for Michael, I'm sad for Jason, for Stephan and I'm sad for us," she said, whipping the tears from her face.

"You look sorrowful and mournful; unhappy and grief-struck. Life has its turns, and we accept them. We grief for our friends, their misfortunes and sufferings, but we know that's what they've chosen, and that's the road they've taken. They need our support, not our tears," I suggested, wiping the tears off her soft and velvety face.

"My heart breaks thinking of Michael; what he's going through, the pain Stephan endured at the hands of the officers in that *Yellow Building* and Jason's loneliness in that dark forsaken house," she said, and sat up. She put her arms around her raised legs.

"Would you feel better if we went to see Michael?" I asked her, empathizing with her, feeling her pain.

"I don't know. It may be dangerous for us," she said, and she rested her head on her knees.

Silence covered the room; I could hear her deep breathing, as the trembling shadows from the candles were dancing on the ceiling and walls.

"Why are you sad for us?" I probed her alarmed.

"I don't know what the future holds for us, Daniel; I don't know where we will end up. This is not a peaceful and unruffled environment for us, to make plans for the future. We are at a state of war with our government."

She looked past the walls of the room, beyond the city, far away. Her mind was jumping the mountains, cutting through clouds; she was sad and thoughtful, reduced to a frightened little girl, facing a precipice in front of her.

Where is our future? What do we expect? I thought. Did we have any?

Was there a future beyond the colonels? We knew our immediate future; we calculated and measured it, and it suited us. Where was the other future? Could we have predicted what would come beyond the present? And if it did come, would it be what we had expected? My eyes could not see beyond my struggle; my heart could not jump ahead and guide me. I had one path at the moment; the one that would lead me to my emancipation. I was captive and confined within my skin; my soul was crying for deliverance, and my whole being was immersed in my agony.

We are in a state of war, Avgy's last words pierced my heart, and my brain was trying to process this inconceivable and sad state of affairs. I got up to splash my face. The cold water calmed me down a little, as my brain was clearing up, sorting through my thoughts. This conflict between the government and its people was seen as a universal and ancestral aspect of human nature, or it could have been an outcome of specific socio-economic or ecological circumstances. Probing this struggle between the government and its people, one might insist that it was on an uneven platform. The destruction and the mortality were heavily on the populous side, rather than on the government side. Warfare is referred to as a common activity between two groups – in this case, the government and the people – although common activities didn't exist here. One side used everything in its power to fight the enemy; using regular military forces which were characterized by violence, aggression, destruction, and mortality, primarily directed to the other unarmed side: the people. Such was the situation as grave as it seemed, and only the people were extraordinarily hurt.

CHAPTER XVII

Despite my love for literature and philosophy from a very young age, there were times in my childhood that I dreamed of becoming a shepherd, like my deceased brother and the old shepherd I met on the mountain. The root of my ambition, apart from the marvelous simplicity with which one sees things at the age of eight, rested in the skillful mastering of the fife by my brother, the angelic expression he possessed while playing the fife, and the obedience of the sheep to him. But my dreams of being a shepherd were diminished and were pulverized into a mere reflection. What contributed to this, was the discovery of literature, the art of the narrative, and the virtuosity of creative writing.

Even though I was negligent and had left behind my aspirations of becoming a shepherd, I had a yearning for my town, my parents, and the astonishing nature surrounding my village. My nostalgia and musing for shepherdship, however, was still hovering inside me as an apparition that refused to leave. My reminiscence brought back profound and prodigious memories of my youth. And now, as I was sitting in the train approaching my village, I gazed at the mountains, the river, the fields, and the animals, accepting what the earth was offering them. I felt a serene and placid sensation, in anticipation of seen my parents again, and stare at the sky at night, as I used to do from the hill across from my house when I was a boy.

The window in my room commanded such a fine view of the hills and the river. The fact was that even when seated at my desk, I had only to crane my head a little to catch a glimpse of the mountain and the meadows. Their presence beyond my front yard seemed to me a mocking reminder of what I had lost since my departure to the big city. Yet, even to revisit those memories, was to be assailed by a wave of guilt; to yearn after that earlier life, seemed not just ungrateful, but disloyal to my senses. Whenever my thoughts stayed across the river, I would constantly remind myself of my good fortune in being where I was, receiving all that nature could offer me: the river, the mountains, the hills, and the meadows, consenting to its beauty. Nor was gratitude hard to summon, for to be mindful of my luck, I had only to think of the fate that would otherwise have been mine. Instead of sitting in this room, I would have found myself in a different place or perhaps meeting the fate my brother had. Such indeed was the lot to which I had resigned myself when I revisited my room. In my sleep in this very room with the window open to the salubrious and refreshing breeze, with its smells coming from the fields, I used to dream of nymphs climbing down from the stars on the glimmers of their wavering light, dancing in their silvery ensemble, chanting to the ecstasy of nature. Or was it the adulation of nature and the splendor of our existence?

When I reached the house, my mother was drawing water from the well. As soon as she saw me, she let the bucket fall back in the well full of water with a big splash, and she ran toward me. She had aged a great deal, and her gray now hair was blowing in the wind, giving her an aristocratic and refined look. I began to wonder whether I was growing too fast or my mother was getting older. I looked around the yard, reminiscing my early days on the farm, and everything was the way I left it. Realizing, perhaps, that my parents were getting older, and they didn't have the vigor or the vitality to continue taking care of the yard, the animals, or the fields or making any improvements to their lives. I felt I neglected them not being here helping them with the chores and tasks of everyday life, as they were getting older and they needed a helping hand.

I sat at the kitchen table at my usual spot, as my mother made tea. She brought out some cookies she had made earlier and fresh bread from the oven. The entire kitchen smelled of savory and fresh-baked bread, and my nostrils were filled with the aroma the oven was exhuming. She reached in the cabinet and took out a container with homemade cheese she had made and cut a large piece, putting it on a plate. The tomatoes were large and inflamed, the fresh onions, cucumbers, and peppers from the garden -- portraying their true colors and shapes -- smelled as if they were still in the ground. She made a large salad which I hadn't had since I left home. How amazing it was to return to my home and felt like I never left. The kitchen looked the same except for a few fascinations and gadgets hanging on the walls, or new contraptions and devices placed on the counter.

"How's dad doing?" I inquired with concern, as I was told in a letter that he had some health issues.

"He's getting better and stronger. But he won't be able to do his job for much longer," my mother responded, detecting something hidden in her answer. Was she trying to tell me that the time had come for them to leave everything behind, sell the whole lot and get out of the farming business?

"Why don't you sell everything, and come to the city? Dad will be much happier there, and you will make new friends. It's a big city, and you won't be bored," I said, thinking that perhaps she insinuated it in her reply.

"I'm not sure if your father would like that. He's used to this place here, the small town, the animals, his friends. I think it will be very difficult for him to adjust to a new life in the city. As for me, I'm getting older, and I can't take care of the house, the garden, the chickens, and everything I'm occupied with all day. It would be a great change for me." I gathered she craved a fundamental change in her life, without the chores and the responsibilities she was in charge of at the moment.

"I don't think I will be coming back to the village mom after I graduate, but I can't leave you both here alone and without support. Think about it, and discuss it with dad. You may be able to convince him to change his mind. I'm not trying to evade my responsibilities, you understand."

"He's troubled now with the killings of the animals, Daniel; then, the government is taking away a large portion of our property with minimum compensation. But the fact is that no one is here to help him with his work, and that is heartbreaking. I can't watch him anymore struggling with the land and the animals all day long. He's getting older, and his health is failing him."

"That's an incentive mother, for both of you, to get out of all this and enjoy your life. Come to the city."

"He's a good man, Daniel, but he does go on and on about everything that's happening here and around the country. The oppression and subjugation coming from the government, the fear and apprehension that we all feel, have put a damper on our spirits, and we're afraid even to get out of the house."

"The same apprehension and uneasiness we feel in the city, mother. A friend is hiding in some abandoned house; another friend is exiled; I was interrogated by the police. People are terrified and nervous to even talk with neighbors in front of their houses. Police and army vehicles are all over the city; it has become a police state."

"How do you manage with all this uproar and chaos?"

"People manage; they work, some of them, they have time for their families and friends, and dare to organize; that's their only hope, anticipating change."

"But how do *you* manage, Daniel? Are you careful?"

"Yes, I am, mother; but I cannot stand lethargic and dormant, expecting for the change to arrive somehow. We have to work, and that's a big job for anyone."

"Just be mindful of yourself, your studies, and the reason you're in the city. Things will change. Our country has seen and endured a lot of turbulence over the years, but we always persist and manage to survive and carry on with our lives. We will keep on going with this one too. But you must be hungry," she said, bringing a bottle of wine and two glasses from the cupboard. I poured wine for both of us, and I filled my plate with the salad my mother prepared. I stayed quiet for a while, staring at the plate in front of me, sipping the wine reflectively.

"You look preoccupied," my mother said, examining my face.

"It must be the heat, mother. It penetrates the brain and it slows it down," I said smiling, and I bent over to kiss her.

"There must be something else. Is there anything worrying you?" she said, contemplating my face.

"No, just thinking."

"About what?"

"About the political situation, the plight of the people, the injustice, my friends. It has been very difficult for all of us under the circumstances, especially in the city."

My mother nodded gloomily and turned her attention to her salad. She was a very subtle and discreet person, amidst everything that was going on. She didn't particularly live in the past, and she hardly mentioned her childhood, her upbringing, and the poverty she went through as a child. Her hidden resentment for their current situation, which was as natural as breathing, and the sadness that seeped from my mother's face, was the real aspect of her soul. As a child, which did not have to understand something to feel it, I understood my mother's face, and what she was portrayed with all her emotions been out in the open. Life had changed dramatically for a lot of people, and I wondered if it would ever get back to normal.

"Tell me, Daniel," my mother said with interest, "how are your studies going?"

"I'm working hard getting ready for my graduate studies," I said looking at her, and my stoic face did not reveal what I was going to say next. "But I must tell you: I'm involved in an anti-government organization at the university. A lot has happened since that ill-fated *Friday*. People are taken to the police headquarters, only to be interrogated and tortured. They're sent to the islands, where they're tortured or killed. I've heard of torturing techniques which only the Nazis and the CIA used to interrogate people and make them talk."

"Who told you that?" she inquired concerned.

"People talk, mother. There are accounts from those who have survived the tortures. A fellow student, and friend, has been on the island for a long time, and another friend has disappeared. I must see an end to this apocalyptic situation, and put a stop to the unethical actions of the government. The remnants of what is left and the demise of our society, have left us wandering without any prospects for the future. We are consigning our lives to the government. The end-game is near," I said, as I raised my glass and took a sip of my wine. That's what I was waiting for: the *endgame*. Man is a strange creature; if we didn't like something, we fought to change it. Once that was done, we looked for something else to change. It was a perpetual, never-ending war within, which went on until death came to end it all.

"When there is war or an oppressive government like ours, things happen, which is very difficult to explain, Daniel. People die every day in their hands, and life is getting challenging, and it's becoming more and more difficult to bear, as the economic situation gets worse," she said surprisingly because I had no idea that my mother's thinking was taking that direction.

"The economy of the country is as bad as the political situation," I said, pointing to the suffocating and smothering world out there.

"It will take a long time to bring things back to normal after the government falls and that yellow building closes down for good," she said, letting her gaze stroll outside where the chickens were picking the ground, and the goat was on its two back legs, feeding on the olive tree.

"Yes, it's true; of the people who walked into that yellow building, many of them never came out," she said, and our eyes met briefly. She was aware of that legendary *Yellow Building* and its reputation. I supposed its standing had traveled beyond the limits of the capital.

I went outside. The breeze from the mountains was a welcoming relief, as the heat and humidity were stifling me, making it difficult to breathe. The shadows were getting longer, as the sun had already reached its zenith, and it was now dumpling down further and further away, into the depths of the western mountain. I was always fond of this time of day when the heat was still lingering, the shadows were getting longer, as the soft warm breeze was caressing my face. This was the time of the day I would hear the bells of the sheep, as they strolled down and through the river and up again into the fields for their nightly feed.

It was early evening when my father finally arrived, after spending the entire day with the animals and the crops. He looked extremely tired and run down. His clothes were worn-out, dirty, and muddy, his hands green from earth dirt, and his face had a tiresome and exasperating expression. His eyes, always bright and inquisitive, were now fatigued, shattered, and drained, with dark lines underneath them. His body bent over a little, as he looked like he was going to fall forward at any moment. When he saw me, he was revitalized; his face illuminated and he opened his arms to welcome me, while his whole face brightened up, as his eyes closed slightly to a wonderful smile. The kind of smile you can only see in exulted and jovial parents' eyes. His entire face brightened up, and the exhilaration and contentment spilled over to his entire being. He went to wash up and change clothes. My mother had the table ready; he approached her from behind and gave her a warm kiss. I was sure I had seen them kiss before, but that moment was an exclusive moment. He showed affection and closeness; and as years take over our bodies and new problems take over our lives, the affection and earnestness never leave a person.

My parents had new issues to deal with, new decisions to make, and they were approaching all this with absolute and complete apprehension. Although he was happy to see me, certainly, there were worries crafted all over my father's face and voice. They had reached, my parents, a crucial and decisive moment in their lives, as they had to make major and foremost decisions about their future. Take a look at their prospects: how to spend the rest of their lives, as loneliness had overtaken them, and had befallen upon them with my absence? It was certainly clear that my father could not work the fields any longer and take care of the animals. It was clear that the years of laboring over everything had taken a toll on them, stigmatizing and denouncing not only their body, their face, but also their spirit. Not the least of all the reasons, why my parents so often found themselves slipping into a state of melancholy, was that they had not yet been able to find a way of being properly useful to themselves. Now, just as a wave of despair was beginning to build, my parents were startled out of their despondency by my arrival and my short stay at the house.

My father was a good family man, always bestowing and providing for his family, making sure that we as kids had everything we needed for our education and the development of a good character, which was very important to him. They were heartbroken, to say the least when I left home to go to the city for my studies; they were heartbroken with the political situation, the turn of events with the killings of the animals, and the expropriation of their land by the government; they were heartbroken when we lost my brother. I was unwilling to summon up my brother's last days and his death, not because it quivered and disturb my soul, but because I didn't want to call to mind the sadness that sheltered and concealed my parents' heart from that day on; but I did not forget him. Reluctantly, summoning up memories to ponder and recall my brother's life, I mused over the remnants of him often, and he always remained in my memory.

Unforgettable memories engraved my brain, as I recalled my youth and summoned up events and incidents: the brilliant sunshine, the astonishing mountains and meadows, the old shepherd, my brother and later his death, and the nights I spend on the hill counting the stars. My youth was remarkable, and the memories were carried over to my later years, with font reminiscences, celebrating the wonderful years I spend at my village.

At this point, my parents were reaching sixty, and their bodies couldn't take any longer the abuse they were submitting it to. My father asked me about my studies; he said that he was very proud of me and what I had accomplished. He asked me about life in the big city. I tried as hard as I could to paint a rosy picture of the city, the life there, its people, and the opportunities anybody would have, pledging to an attainable good life for their final years. I was trying apparently to convince him to come to his senses and move away from the village. He had a stubborn bone in his body, and I was sure it would take a lot more to convince him of my idea.

*

I stayed in the village for a week. I called on places which I used to spend an enormous amount of time in my youth. Some of the trees got taller, others died or were blown down by the wind. The goats always reached for the lower branches which they could nibble on, standing on their back legs; that was why the lower branches of many trees were bare. I went to the place where I had met the old shepherd playing his fife, but he was not there. Another younger shepherd was sitting at the same spot. I wanted to ask him about the old man but I hesitated. Maybe he was dead or gone to another place, or maybe he gave up altogether this harsh and punitive life on the mountains, spending day and night minding his herd, playing the fife. I went to the river where my brother told me that he was dying, and the place where he laid down before my father came to take him home in his arms. I visited an old childhood friend from school, who was by now married and had two children of his own. Life had not changed much in this small town, as people were going on with their lives, not asking for a lot or demanding anything unattainable or frivolous.

Before I left my village, my father promised me that he would think about relocating to the city. He was apprehensive about transplanting his life at that age, but he gave me his word that he would seriously consider it. I was hoping for that. I left home with a clear consciousness, that eventually my parents would get out of this unpleasant and horrendous situation, move to the city, and enjoy whatever was left of their troubled and austere life.

CHAPTER XVIII

INVOKING UP IMAGES OF Avgy while sitting on the train, I spent nearly the entire trip back to the city daydreaming of her. Envisioning her naked body under my fingers, I could almost relish, with my senses and my mind, her sweet aroma. I surprised myself recalling with radar-like accuracy, every delineation, every curve of her body, the soft touch of her lips on mine and those pale thighs, so smooth they were almost feather like, which ran in parallel up until they met at a junction, which my childhood friend called: *passageway to ecstasy*.

"You've got your head in a haze young man, is there anything the matter?" said the conductor. As I looked up, he had a smile on his face, shifting from foot to foot keeping his balance, as the train was rolling down the tracks quietly. "Your ticket please," he said again, extending his hand. I pulled the ticket out of my pocket and handed it to him. After studying the ticket, he drilled a hole on it and gave it back to me. I put it back in my pocket, and I looked at my watch the myriad time, realizing to my dismay that there was plenty of time before I could see and touch Avgy. I tried to read, but Dylan Thomas' poems propelled me back to my previous thoughts about Avgy. I knew Avgy now for a few years, and we were much acquainted with each other. We discussed even renting a place, and moving in together, as soon as we finish our studies.

I was captivated and charmed the first time I saw her. She gave me those forbidden books, which I concealed and buried under my mattress; she told me about her father who had been in prison, about the organization, and Stephan, Michael, and Jason.

*

In her apartment now, Avgy was walking toward the hall closet, which contained her long-forgotten apparel, determined to organize it and sort it out. She passed by her father's room with the door solemnly and ritualistically closed. She stopped momentarily, lifting her hand to knock on the door when a thought like a lightning flashed in front of her. The room was vacant, and her father had been in jail for some time. She opened the door slowly, unaccustomed to not nocking first and unacquainted for not calling her dad from the hallway. The curtains were drawn, and the room had a somber and an absence feeling; compounded by the light darkness, covering the walls and the contents of the room, concealed any apparent feelings and sadness which might have spilled over the years. The lack of light was obscuring the essence of the room, sheltering and enfolding the happy times she recalled she had with her father when she was much younger and indeed fortunate enough that she did, evoking amiable feelings.

She scanned the room from side to side, the bed, the dresser, the pictures on the wall, the closed closet. She took a few paces toward a picture portraying her alongside her father when she was twelve years old. She had a charming blue dress on and a hat, clinching to her father, squeezing his neck with an innocent and adorable smile on her face. As she came closer, she noticed that her father had a broad and blissful smile on his face, looking at her, while the beach behind them was saturated with bathers, among numerous umbrellas and beach chairs. Tears came to her eyes, and she wiped them with the back of her hand. With a solemn and subdued look on her face, she walked around the room touching and patting her father's things, smelling her father's aroma, and staring at the empty bed where her father slept, converging her feelings, summoned by memories long gone. She approached the night table which had her father's diary on it. She attempted to open it, but immediately she closed it and put it back.

She walked to the closet and opened the door. Her father's clothes were suspended as if they were washed and placed in their hangers just the day before. She unhooked a shirt, and placed it against her face, attempting to smell her father's scent, sensing remorsefully his evident absence. She passed her hand gently throughout the clothes as if she were stroking the grass of the lawn in a park. She had a pensive and meditative look on her face, as she was doing this, reminiscent of the years' past. She missed her father, and she hardly saw him anymore, as she was aloud only a few times a year to visit him. She was terrified on the mere thought that he would not survive, not be able to endure the entire jail sentence. She closed the closet door. She walked around the room deliberately, stopping by the window and opening the blinds. The summer sun spattered its rays inside the room through the windowpane, and the new light made the room brilliant, giving as much to it as to Avgy a new outlook. She walked toward the door wistfully and exiting she closed the door behind her.

*

THE visit to her father in prison a few months ago was a horrifying and ghastly experience. The heart couldn't take the disappointment and disenchantment she felt, as she walked into the compound, seen the horrific conditions which the prisoners lived in and which were widely visible. She walked into the office, where she was submitted to a body search by a female officer before she was allowed into the interview room, where the inmates converge with their lawyers and their friends and relations. It was a small room, with a table in the middle of it, with scratches and holes and two chairs on either side of the table. She sat down apprehensively, looking about and through the small window at the door, toward the narrow hallway from where her father would be guided in. The paint on the walls and ceiling was chipped. There was graffiti decorating the walls with various colors, enhancing the unsightliness of the surroundings. A single light bulb at the end of a wire was hanging from the ceiling, while grime and numerous cracks were marking the floor, which was dirty as if it were never swept or washed.

The atmosphere was depressing and demoralizing, listening to the sounds of the prison, dampening the spirit, inhibiting the soul, diminishing any human dignity, which might have survived among those prison walls. One could hear inmates shouting, yelling, talking loudly, or banking on the walls and gates. There was a guard outside the interview room, who looked as if he were twenty or twenty-two years old. He was armed with a semi-automatic machine gun, looking suspiciously around him, as another guard was guiding her father to the interview room. The guard stepped aside and opened the door. Her father stopped momentarily at the threshold and looked at her with a smile, which was neither a happy one nor one that indicated relief. His eyes were sad with black circles around them, his clothing was out of place and dirty, and he was unshaved. He walked with a slight limp, which added years to his age. His hair was uncut falling over his shoulders and eyes. He approached her and hugged her. "I'm very happy to see you. This is a horrible place," he whispered in her ear. The guard closed the door and remained standing outside, keeping an eye on the goings-on in the room through the small window. Her eyes were wet and her heart was beating faster than the drums of a sub-Saharan African tribe. She extended her hands forward, reaching over the table, and held her father's hand in hers, looking at his eyes. They talked about the horrific life in prison, the appalling mistreatment of the inmates, the repulsive food they were given, and the frequent interrogation by the master, which were sometimes turning into violent hostilities. The short time they allowed the inmates for these visits was ill at ease, uncomfortable and distressing, as the guard always kept an eye on them at all times. She left the prison with a heavy heart and with less hope for her father than when she first came.

*

WITHOUT forgetting her mission, which was in her mind since that morning, she approached the hall closet with her clothes in it. She had planned to go through some of her neglected and disremembered clothes, to give away to the deprived and poverty-stricken. Along with a heap of her shirts and trousers -- something she had long given up for lost -- came tumbling out her father's clothes. Those were the clothes that her father wore when he attended her high school graduation six years ago. She smiled as she reached for them, with a sense of reminiscence and memories of the past. This was beyond praise, it seemed like a sign, an omen of good things to come. Forgetting all about the mission that had brought her to this venture, she started examining her father's clothes, smelling them, placing them on her face, on her lips, and began to weep a silent sob. It was these clothes, as much as her father's smell hovering over them, that she remembered; he would put on his shirt and trousers and go out to dinner with her, and she was so blissful and exulted.

For more than four years now, ever since the ultimate arrest of her father, who had been the only person in her life who cared immensely for her, Avgy's heart had been filled with intuitive and prophetic menacing. He, that the awakening was at hand, had told her to watch carefully for any signs of fragility or vulnerability of the government, which was sure to be manifested in the unlikeliest places and the most improbable forms. Signs which would give evidence of weakness on the part of the government and its allies, which would pave the road to the uprising, and consequently for the eminent liberation and emancipation of the nation. He had promised her that he would return soon and asked her to keep her mind open and her senses watchful so that the signs would not elude her when they were revealed – yet, now, despite her best efforts, she could not believe in the evidence of her senses.

The time was near.

*

SUCH were my thoughts, as the train was roaming down the trucks, and the soft sound of metal on metal was putting me to sleep. It started to rain, and the fog that was spreading around the fields and the mountains, was like a soft blanket covering the earth, giving it an imposing and majestic appearance. One could hardly see the peaks of the mountains, which looked like the top part of the mountains were cut off, as the emergence of the clouds was closing up to the trees, losing an inch every time I looked. The wind picked up as well, throwing the raindrops around, bouncing on the windowpane of the train. The launch of winter was harsh, the rain was cold, and the snow was in its way any day now. The few birds that remained, were sheltered among tree branches and caverns. It was delightful to spend Christmas with my parents in the village. The smell of burning wood in the air, the smoke coming up from every chimney in the small town, and the smell of Christmas baking was drifting in the air.

As the imposing rain continued falling with incredible force, the train approached the station, it slowed down, exhuming steam from its engines, shunting from track to track. The hiss and grind of its locomotive descended to a statelier register as it approached the station. As soon as it had lurched to a stop, I pulled my valise from the luggage rack above my seat and departed the train. The station was astoundingly overcrowded with Christmas travelers, and I could hardly walk among the swarm of people carrying suitcases and babies in their arms. I found my way outside in the wet and busy street, with myriads of people hastening with umbrellas to get away from the rain. There was no thunder or lightning; just rain falling upon the city quietly and orderly.

CHAPTER XIX

After I left the train station, I went to connect with Ari. We discussed my next mission, one of a number of them which I executed on behalf of the organization. If his remarks and declarations meant to convey and grant me courage for the mission, they failed miserably. I regarded and scrutinized the plight of people's everyday lives. I observed the dilemmas and the daily troubles of human skeletons on the streets of the city, who suffered and teetered and grieved in the corners of their neighborhoods, and my heart hemorrhaged. It was perhaps obvious to me, that the perceived and apparent stricken presence of the calamity which had engulfed the people of this country, was testimony to the ethical nothingness of the universe of the generals, who had destroyed any human dignity and propriety with extreme brutality.

That same afternoon, after I left the train station and visited Ari, promising that I would keep him up to date with my activities, I went along to see the administrator of a pharmaceutical company for a job prospect. The building had seen better days and now, emaciated in filthy floors and flaked paint on the walls was blemished by the years gone by. The office administrator was a jolly and jovial older man, sank in his domain cheerfully. His lips were growing a half-smoked cigarette, which seemed to be shared with the rest of his face. His breathing, which most likely sounded more like a snore rather than normal breathing, was hard to tell whether he was asleep or awake. His greasy hair, which was falling over his forehead and with his hoggish eyes popping out of their sockets, he seemed like a naughty and rascally little boy. It seemed as if his suit was procured from a flea market for a song and a dance, but he was fortunate because his flamboyant shirt made up for it. Exploring the interior of the building with stolen glances, it seemed that not much was happening, other than the odd mouse or spider climbing the walls and rafters, and it was apparent that not much business was taking place here.

With an apologetic gesture, he indicated his embarrassment over the condition of the building. "We're trying our best to keep the building livable. We are in the process of renovating it," he said, and he looked away into oblivion.

The atmosphere was getting awkward and ill at ease, and to break the ice I mentioned the name of the woman who recommended me for that vacant position as if I were referring to some old friend of the family.

"Yes, I remember her when she was young. She was quite good-looking," he remarked. "Although I'm not what I used to be," he continued, "I can now comment on her looks comfortably; she's gone on the heavier side. I was very good-looking in my youth. Women would go out of their way to be seen with me. But women are not like that anymore. What can I do you for, young man?"

I presented to him my case as a student who was looking for employment in the pharmaceutical industry. After chattering for five minutes, he dragged himself to a filing cabinet and picked up a folder.

"Let me see…there is a sales administrator position available as of now. This position is requisitioned by another office in the city," he said examining the file, placing and replacing his spectacles.

"Can you tell me more about it?" I asked as I didn't have the slightest idea about the pharmaceutical business.

"I've spoken to the secretary of that office occasionally on the phone. The fact is that most of the business goes through that office."

"Would you happen to have the address of the office?"

"According to the requisition, the address is…3…1…7 University Avenue, although I can't read her numbers very well, the woman I've spoken to on the phone. As you very well know, women are no good at math. But they're good for…"

"May I see?" I interrupted.

"Of course," he said, offering me the folder.

I took the folder and looked at the requisition. The numbers were perfectly legible. The street number was 211. It shocked me to think of the accounting practices going on in that office.

.CHAPTER XX

R ECENTLY THE NEGLECTED, DISCARDED, manic, and impoverished people -- as I observed them on the sidewalks and alleys of the city -- were left on the streets to die without any prospect of improved living conditions for them. Auspiciously, their harsh life on the streets had lasted only for a very short time, as their punitive existence took a toll on them. They were pledged longevity, neither by the government nor by society, and consequently, they were left to their own devices to care for themselves in the cold of winter, the heat of summer, or the abrasive life they endured. As neglected as one could be in an affluent society such as this, these people, who had many medical and psychological issues, were living their neglected lives on the streets with no medication, food, or shelter. According to recent reports, their lifeless bodies were taken away shortly after dark, making their last voyage to the communal grave in an open carriage.

Such were my thoughts going through my head, when I followed the road toward Avgy's apartment, where the high-rise buildings, mansions, boutiques, bistros, and shops skirted the boulevard under the soft lights of the street lamps. My footsteps were echoing on the pavement, as the noise from the street fused into the litany of sounds of music coming from a bar.

*

NEGLECTED by ordinary thoughts, I began my new career, however unplanned, as a sales representative with a lot of vigor, vitality, and enthusiasm. I had visited the main office of the pharmaceutical company on 211

University Avenue, where I had my entrance interview. Unfamiliar with these kinds of procedures, I felt somewhat nervous, anxious, and unsettled, as the questions about my past, my family, and my university life all came into light, trying to search through my deserted memory. I was not sure if I were dishonest with my answers or cryptic and obscure about my past and my activities. Nevertheless, I went through this ordeal, and I secured the job. Having studied the entire job folder, my functions covered visits to potential customers on pre-arranged appointments. I was not keen on the job, and I didn't relish it as I should have had.

As a deprived and meager student, which was a class of its own, I earned most of my way through school, which was something that I would relish for the rest of my life. I learned the truths about pharmaceutical companies: they were promoting their costly products ahead of inexpensive generic and good quality medicine. I also learned how to dance around questions, without avoiding them, and how I should never leave the customer without a signature on the dotted line. This kind of dishonesty, as much as the assertiveness and forcefulness that took place to secure a signature, took a lot out of me. I was not sure if I was going to do it for a long time, or until I finished school, or until I found another more enjoyable and amiable job. I would walk into each pharmacy or clinic with an aggressive attitude which was contrasting with my personality. The acting was well-rehearsed, as part of my brain was left at the side of the street, so as not to thrust myself into insanity. Pretending, smiling constantly, and throwing around compliments and civilities, was not my specialty. I was not sure if I were believable with my rhetoric or the customers needed inventory, or to put it insipidly, in need of kickbacks. My job was to convince them to buy my products, and that was exactly what I attempted to do, despite my reservations about the ethical aspects of it.

The pharmaceutical industry had been blemished and marked, with unwanted and undesirable criticisms by the public. The industry had been lobbying all levels of government for years and had spent more money on marketing their products than researching new medicine. It had offered astonishing amounts of money as kickbacks to doctors and pharmacists to promote their products. And because of the favoritism that the government had shown toward the industry, and because of the importance of its products to public health -- since the government made extraordinary purchases of its products -- the industry should have had become a public utility.

I brought a good deal of business to the company, and I was valued and esteemed as one of their best employees. At the end of each month, someone would have the fortuity to claim the best results and the best employee record, while the rest were dreaming for that moment. I was fortunate enough or privileged, if that's how I considered my providence, to meet the criteria for the *award* of good kismet, as the gift offered was a one-time bonus. At times I was terrified from the simple thought that perhaps I was crafted for that kind of work, which unnerved me considerably and threw me into disarray. I was contemplating incorporating my work with my organization undertakings, but I was very careful with the person sitting across from me at the table. My organizational activities and my duties as an oppressed citizen and student were very important to me, and that thought never left my mind. My freedom was hanging in the balance if it hadn't already tipped over, and my dignity was suffering as a result of it.

CHAPTER XXI

In an attempt to redirect my thoughts, the next morning, as the Sunday bells tolled and the devoted and faithful proceeded to church for Sunday worship, I set out for another place of worship; I went to pay my respects to the museum, which as of late, new findings had been exhumed and unearthed from the aged old soil of the city. The city was enormously deep. Setting foot on this city, one could sense a surreptitious and mystifying force, diverging affectionately and tenderly through one's veins. One intuitively could sense one's soul to begin to swell and intensify. But this obscurity and ambiguity had become ever deeper and richer, since the discovery of the treasures of this ancient civilization, which until then was buried beneath its soil.

After I visited the museum, I left the city, and I took a bus eastward which led me to the sea. I got off the bus near a cemetery, where I observed a coffin carried by friends and relatives of the diseased, in an ancient procession, as it seemed. I avoided looking at the coffin, as the sight of it would frighten me. That dreadful day in my early years, as you remember, I observed my brother being buried, as my parents were clinched to the coffin refusing to let it go. I quicken my pace passing by the procession, as I was overcome by fear. There were vineyards and fruit trees beyond the cemetery, and I was engulfed in my thoughts. I walked leisurely, observing the vintage which had begun already. The grapes drooped heavily touching the ground. The smell of the fruit trees overwhelmed my senses, immersing my entire being into a state of bliss; I submitted myself to its fragrance.

An old man riding his donkey came by; he saw me, and he stopped as I was watching the men and women harvesting. "What are you contemplating about young man?" I turned, and I saw the old man on the back of his donkey looking at me smiling.

"This is a magical time of the year," I said, offering my hand. "I'm Daniel." "I'm Uncle Theodore," the old man said and shook my hand. "This is harvest time," he continued, passing his glare over the fields, "and Christmas time for us the farmers; we harvest what nature offered us and what we are grinding away all summer long; one and one make two! You seem like a nice young man," he said, and reached into his basket which was covered with fig leaves, and retrieved two pears and a few figs, and offered them to me. "Take this fruit, so you can taste their honey. Are you from the city?"

"Yes, I am; I came to marvel the miracle and spectacle of harvest."

"It is indeed a miracle; the wonder of nature, which emerges out of the earth, the trees, and the vines."

"What do you produce uncle Theodore?" I asked.

"Oh, my boy, I used to have many acres of vineyards, but I can't work no more. I'm left now with a couple of acres of fruit trees. That's all."

"My father has a farm up north and a herd of sheep."

"You're a country boy, too. So, what are you doing in the city?"

"I'm attending university."

"Oh yes, the students in our days are going through a lot."

"Everybody is going through a lot these days, Uncle Theodore," I said, and been nervous, continuing this conversation, I changed the subject. "Do you sell your fruit?"

"Yes, I take them to the market, but I go around the neighborhoods alone with my donkey and I sell the rest," the old man said, giving an endearing and lovable slap to the donkey's behind.

Uncle Theodore had white hair, a long pointing beard, large gluttonous lips, and a thick and red from the sun neck; his eyes were brown. It would have eaten plenty in his life, that large body of his, drunk plenty, love plenty; but not yet satiated.

I thanked the old man as he was handing me the fruit. I submerged my teeth into the juicy and sweet fruit, engrossed in the aroma that exhumed.

I walked among orchards and vineyards, smelling their aroma, tasting their fruits, while numerous birds, flying around, landing on trees, were having a taste of the fruit as well. The sun had climbed, the sky was clear, and the earth was dry. A few clouds were drifting across the sky. The wind was calm, bringing gently the smells of the sea and those of the earth into my nostrils, in a combined symphony of smells. I opened my shirt letting the wind caress my chest, as my hair was blowing softly in the breeze. On one side there was a mountain, covered completely with pine trees, while a few houses were bursting out among them. On the other side, there was a small hill which was enfolded with grapevines, all placed carefully in order one next to each other, while on top of the hill there were five desolate pine trees. Above it, the blue sky was enhancing the numerous colors of the surroundings, giving it a bright and elusive look, as if it were a nineteenth-century painting. A shepherd was taking his herd for a walk along the dry river bed, while the sounds of the birds, the ships arriving at the harbor, and the traffic on the road running alongside the river, were adding to the ambiance of this picturesque countryside. The few colorful farmhouses placed hither and thither submerged in the vineyards, were giving the alien visitor a sense of refuge and sanctuary.

I had walked a fair distance, looking at the farmers harvesting the grapes and the fruit from the pear and fig trees, leaving behind, still hanging on the vines, a few grapes for the poor. That was customary since ancient times, to leave something behind to be harvested by the most unfortunate. The shadows were curled up now under the trees; it was almost noon. As I was walking, enjoying the world, having my mind tacked to my struggles, the smells of fresh bread were hitting my nostrils; I felt hungry. My nostrils trailed the wind, and I followed the smells; leaped over a trench, jumped over a fence, I got into a vineyard, and I caught a glimpse of a low shack underneath an old olive tree. The smoke was climbing up in the sky along with those exceptional smells. A swiftly moving, long nose, a skeletal, undernourished old woman was bending and striving over a built kind of tandoor furnace, baking bread. Next to her, there was a big dog, black and furry with its front paws resting on the tandoor; its gluttonous mouth was opened, exposing a mouthful of teeth. As it heard my footfalls, it dashed at me barking. The old woman turned, as she saw the young newcomer, she rattled; her eyes were small, and they were brilliant in front of the fire. She was happy to see a man in her loneliness; she stopped with a baker's trowel in her hand.

"Welcome," she said, "are you hungry? Where are you coming from?"

"From the city."

"Are you hungry?" she asked me again, and she laughed. My nostrils were moving faster than the dog's nostrils.

"Yes, I'm hungry; and forgive my forwardness." The old woman was hard of hearing; she didn't hear me.

"What?" she said, "speak louder."

"I'm hungry my good woman. Forgive me."

"Why should I forgive you? There is no indignity being hungry or thirsty, young man. All these come from God. Come then, don't be ashamed," she said, smiling again as her only tooth came into view. "Here you will find bread, fresh cheese, olives, and wine to drink." She picked up a loaf of bread, which she had placed next to the furnace a little while ago, among the others. "Here, this is the loaf we keep for visitors. It's not mine; it's yours. Sit down and eat."

I sat on the ground, resting my back on the old trunk of the olive tree. The old woman offered me olives, cheese, and a cup of white wine. I started eating; the bread was delicious, fresh out of the oven, still warm. I calmed down, pacified and thankful for the old woman's offerings. I was eating and drinking the wine, and I felt that the body and the soul united and became one. I was devouring the bread, consuming the wine, and I was blissful and contented, because both of them, body and soul, were nourished. The old woman, taking a break, leaned against the furnace looking at me.

"You were hungry," she said, "eat some more. You're a young man. You have a long and laborious road ahead of you; plenty of burdens and frets; you need to get strong to persevere and keep hold of your life." She cut another piece of bread, gave me more cheese and wine, and came and sat next to me. "Where are you headed?"

"I'm chasing my devils."

"Where? Speak properly."

"I don't know, my good lady; I'm chasing my devils, my battles."

The old woman looked at me with an angry look, and she grimaced her toothless mouth.

"Why? You're a young man. Enjoy your life. These things are not for you, yet."

I kept quiet. The old woman shook her head, and her mantilla slipped from her thin white hair. She quickly adjusted it over her head and wrapped it around her neck.

"You're looking for yourself?" she asked, and suddenly I felt her genuine question piercing my inner soul. *Yes, I'm looking for myself* I thought, but I didn't dare utter it loudly. She looked at me again, she got up, she stood in front of me. "Oh, you adverse and fateful young man; you won't find yourself in the vineyards and the mountains; it's inside you. You have to look deep down inside yourself, in your thoughts, your dreams; that's where it is. You look in vain all around. Every footprint on the sand, every breath you take, every word you utter, it's all you. That's where you'll find it."

The old woman was speaking and as she was speaking, she was getting more agitated. But she said what she had to say, and she calmed down. She touched my shoulder. "Forgive me, my young man. I had a son charming like you; one morning his brain moved; he opened the door, and he went away. He said he was looking for himself. And now, I bake this bread, but who am I going to feed? My children? My grandchildren? I'm alone, deserted, living a solitary life. But …" she said, and she stopped, as she wiped her eyes, "for years," she resumed, "for years, I would raise my hands to God and shout: 'Why was I born? I had a son but you took him away. Why?' I yelled and yelled but he didn't hear me. One night I had a dream. He came to my dream and said 'scream and yell if you want all you like; I'm deaf'. Since then, I stopped yelling."

I got up, and I shook the old woman's bony hand; she looked at me with a tear marking her face. "Don't you have eyes, my son? Can't you see the sun, the vineyards, the sea, the women? Go and open your eyes. Haven't you ever read the bible? God doesn't want prayers. He wants you to get married and have children."

"Goodbye, my good woman. God may repay you for the bread you fed me," I said, as I walked away, back into the vineyard, and toward the fence.

The men and women were still harvesting the grapes and the fruit; the heat of the sun was now piercing my skull, and the warm breeze coming from the south was hitting my open chest. *Look at the sun, the vineyards, the sea, the women,* were the last words the old woman uttered, which disturbed and inconvenienced my brain. Such were my observations and thoughts, as I walked slowly on the unpaved dirt road, dipped in my thoughts, hoping for salvation from my notions. The deep blue of the sea was now visible in front of me, among the immersed green colors of the pine trees and maples. The white caps of the water were visible, moving in a peculiar direction, which seemed to be sideways in contrast with the position and outline of the shore. The sea was illuminated; the sun was caressing it. On top of it, white and blue butterflies: the fishing boats, and above them the feathery fishermen: the seagulls. The mountains of the island across the way were clearly and noticeably visible, with white splashes decorating the foggy bluish-gray color of them, which seemed to be dwellings of the islanders. The few ferries which had arrived at the harbor already were busy loading and unloading passengers and provisions. A few sunbathers were laying on the white sand, sunbathing under the scorching sun. On the right by the sea and at the side of the mountain, was the cemetery decorated by the numerous white crosses all in a row.

*

I arrived back in the city in the early evening. The sun was traversing the sky downwards, the merchants had packed up their carts and went home, and the evening ramblers were already out for their nightly stride. A few overloaded patrons were staggering out of tavernas with happy faces and smiles, and with bright out-of-focus eyes. My experience today at the vineyards of the small town I visited was overwhelming. There was indeed life beyond the city limits, and the people were engulfed within nature. They were one with it, and as the sun climbed the sky in the morning and descended at night behind the western mountains, people lived their lives peacefully and with as much dignity, as the government had allowed them. The ferries continued their trips back and forth to and from the islands, the farmers waited for their crops to mature, and the fisherman brought their daily catch to the market.

Was that happiness and contentment which these people felt? Was that what life should be? And if it were, did the political situation help them feel free, to live their lives with dignity? Was that freedom for them? Were they afraid to speak their minds, read what they liked, talk with anyone they wished, and go where their freedom would command them? Many questions remained unanswered. The people were oppressed, feeling the weight of their beliefs upon their shoulders, unable to complain to ease their pain or even speak out their grievances. Many had relations and friends in jail or exile. Many were grieving their dead, having fallen victims to the government or the police for their ideologies and convictions. Practical life elements were as prominent as theoretical ones. One should not go through life without having both the practical and the theoretical elements, which constituted life. They were essential elements, as part of a system of ideas, which aspired both to enlighten the world and to change it. Did that mean that one must sacrifice one's life for their ideals and beliefs? And if that were true, then how many had to die? How many had to sacrifice their lives, so they may achieve normality and gain their dignity back? Was it not the right of a person to be valued and be respected for their own sake, and to be treated ethically? Wasn't dignity of great significance in terms of morality, ethics, law, and politics, as an extension of the Enlightenment-era concepts of inherent absolute and immutable rights?

Being submerged in my thoughts, I hadn't realized that I walked to Avgy's place without even feeling tired. I hadn't seen Avgy for a few days, and my anticipation was immense. I had developed great feelings for her, and I intuitively even thought that I was in love with her. I was infatuated and enchanted by her presence, with all my feelings spilling over my heart and soul, and I always had her in my mind. Her childlike and innocent face, was like a phantom in front of me incessantly, seen her talking, walking, studying, or just looking at me.

I greeted the doorman as I walked into the building. He was a quiet man sitting in front of his desk, reading a newspaper. He returned my greeting, and I proceeded to take the stairs. She answered the door, and she smiled, and her entire face shone as she saw me. I put my arms around her, and her warm slim body filled my embrace. I could smell her aroma evaporating from her body and hair, promoting my senses to exaltation, intensifying my feelings and my love for her. I told her about my outing to the vineyards of the eastern region of the province, and how inviting it was to be there among the fruit trees and vines, full of fruit. I offered her a pear and figs which uncle Theodore had given me. We were sitting in the living room talking when there was a knock on the door. It was Stephan.

CHAPTER XXII

I hadn't received any news from my parents for a long time, and I began to fret. The life of the farmers in the village was not as leisurely and laidback; I was aware of the fact that taking care of the animals and the land, was a chore that was not very amiable, in such a harsh environment. They worked very hard during their years at the farm, buying and selling animals, cultivating the land, and raising kids at the same time. Upon returning to the hotel, there was an envelope waiting for me at the front desk from my parents. I sat at a chair in the lobby and opened it.

My dear Daniel,

I'm sitting under the vine sunshade writing to you. I hope my letter finds you in good health. It has been a while since my last letter to you and as you know, there are certain issues and concerns which your father and I have encountered and tried to cope with and play against. Your father's health is improving, but I cannot say the same for our land situation, trying to fight the government and the ministry of agriculture. This battle is now over. They have given us some money, which is not compatible and consistent with that of the price of the land. They have moved ahead with the annexation of the land, and already big machinery has moved into neighboring properties, and started excavating for the highway extension. I'm not sure if this is a curse or a blessing; we are losing quite a big portion of our property, which has divided our land now and will be sitting at either side of the highway. I'm not sure how your father is going to work the two pieces of land, and how much he has to travel crossing the highway to achieve that.

The authorities here are very close to laying charges against the suspect they caught, who's alleged to be the perpetrator who killed the animals; there'll be making an announcement shortly. It has been a strange and peculiar year, to say the least, with all the goings-on in this town. Our goat had four offspring, and we have new hatchlings running around the yard. I pray I don't step on them, as they are so tiny. My health is good, thank the universe for that. As for the weather, it has been raining but now it's quite dry. When are you coming to visit? Are you still working at a pharmaceutical company?

Call it a New Year's resolution and good news for you. Your father and I have decided to move to the city close to you. All the animals and the land –and now the two pieces of land – will be sold, and we will purchase an apartment wherever we decide to settle down, as we are learning that there many suburbs in the city.

Be well, write back, and let me know of your plans for the summer.

Your loving mother

I folded the letter and put it in my inside coat pocket. Although their move to the city had been my idea for some time now, I began to have my doubts. The political situation was dire, very unstable, and the uprising and unrest were on the verge of erupting at any time. Life in the city was indeed precarious, very intense, and unsafe, to say the least. I should have insisted that they bought an apartment in town, so they weren't uprooted to a strange, unfamiliar, and threatening place. I had a lot of difficulties trying to convince them to come to the city with me, but now that it was becoming reality, I reassessed it and re-evaluated it, and it might not have been such a good idea. I didn't want them to be caught up in the unrest, get them mixed up with the organization, or divulge to them details about my activities. The situation was getting very grave and somber here in the capital, and the students, as well as the citizens, were well organized; they were in our side as were the unions and farmers. There were talks about big-scale demonstrations, but I was not sure how this was going to transpire and materialize, given the restrictions the government had imposed on gatherings of large groups of people. There would be massive arrests, scores of people would get hurt or worse, and many more would be sent to prison or exile. But the determination not only of the students but also of the populous was abundant, and no matter how many lives would be lost or how many more would be incarcerated, the objective was to bring the police state down. There was enormous support from the outside. Some foreign organizations were willing to finance the insurrection. There were many more organizations inside the country, which worked very hard and intensely to recruit and finance such an undertaking.

People had been sacrificed throughout past centuries for various causes; either to change or to rewrite history. Religious wars had more victims than any other war or conflict in the history of the world. Then, there were revolutions, uprisings, hostilities, wars which had changed the path of history, as recently as a decade and a half ago; and there had been more since. There had been six years of martial law; restrictions of fundamental freedoms; unethical and unlawful arrests and imprisonment, and oppression of education and daily life. The future of the country was uncertain, and once a proud nation, it had become now disgraced and reprehensible; such a nation could not tolerate, by any means, the shackles which had been put around the hands and feet of the cities and towns and indeed its people. Friends, relatives, neighbors, and strangers had died at the hands of the police. That couldn't go on. Democracy should be obliged to prevail, and freedom should be the only option for the people. *Freedom or Death* was the mantra of our forefathers. *Freedom or Death* was our mantra then.

PART II

CHAPTER XXIII

"Greek historiographers and journalists *have hypothesized about a 'Generals' Coup'; a coup that would have been deployed at [king] Constantine's request under the pretext of combatting communist subversion," wikia. org* reported at the eve of the coup d'état which took place 21 April 1967. Was it a forewarning, an intuition, an omen, or a natural flow of events, which brought the city and indeed the country to a standstill, in the early hours of that morning?

The 1960s was a time of prodigious and excessive paranoia and distrust, among the right-wing functions and the army. The actuality of communism permeated the political life in the West; Greece was no different. The anti-communist obsession was also real, and the viciousness and the ferocity of the political rhetoric were unquestionably poisoning the political spectrum. Elections were due to take place on 28 May 1967; the thought of a left-wing lining government had made some people as well as the colonels anxious and panicky.

Many conservative *National Radical Union* politicians feared that the policies of a left-wing Centrist government would lead to a constitutional crisis. As it turned out, the constitutional crisis originate neither from the political parties, nor from the Palace, but the middle-rank army patchiest. There were fears that the country will turn left, reclining over to the Soviet Union, getting away from the conceivable dependence and reliance on the West, the United States, and the NATO alliance. One such politician proposed that *"in case of such an anomaly, the king should declare martial law, as the monarchist constitution permitted him."* The king was receptive and sympathetic to that idea, having his plans. According to U.S. diplomat John Day, Washington also worried that certain left-wing politicians might play a powerful role in the next government. Moreover, according to two American diplomats Robert Keely and John Owens, who were present in Athens during those events – along with the U.S. Sixth Fleet -- King Constantine asked the U.S. Ambassador Phil Talbot, what the American attitude would be, to an extra-parliamentary solution, given the conceivable problem. To that, the embassy responded negatively in principle, indicating, that, *"the U.S. reaction to such move cannot be determined in principle,"* adding, however, *"the U.S. response to such attempt cannot be determined in advance, but would depend on circumstances at the time."* The king categorically denied that when he was asked, although the evidence was present. The sixth fleet and the CIA were also in the country, during the dreadful events of that tragic and ill-fated *Friday*.

The planning and the execution of the coup, known as *Operation Prometheus,* swung into action in the early hours of April 21, which was led by a group of right-wing colonels and high-ranking officers, who established the military dictatorship known as the *Regime of Colonels.* In the early hours of that ill-fated early *Friday* morning, tanks were placed in planned and calculated positions, gaining complete control of the city, using elements of surprise and confusion. Small mobile and tactical units arrested leading politicians, including the Prime Minister, members of parliament, and citizens suspected of left-wing sympathies.

The years that followed the atrocious and ruthless coup, were years of deprivation, despair, suffering, and terror. The junta stuck severely to reigns and decrees of the military dictatorship, by carrying out executions, murders, torture, and the restrictions of fundamental freedoms and liberties. That brutal dictatorship lasted until 24 July 1974, and one of its downfalls was the failed response to the Turkish invasion of Cyprus by the Athens regime, along with the uprising of university students in which hundreds had been killed.

The king having initially gone along with the coup, to maintain some sort of unanimity in the country, according to his thinking, was not very happy with the outcome. His remarks to the US ambassador Phil Talbot *"...a bunch of incredibly stupid ultra-right-wing bastards, having gained control of tanks, have brought disaster to Greece."* His words were sardonic and contemptuous, considering his initial pledge to and covenant with the plan. In retaliation, the king attempted to stage his own counter-coup eight months later, which failed, and he was forced to flee to Rome.

The White House Situation Room informed President Lyndon B. Johnson about the early morning military coup in Greece at 12:30 am (EST) in Washington DC, in the early hours of the morning of 21 April 1967.

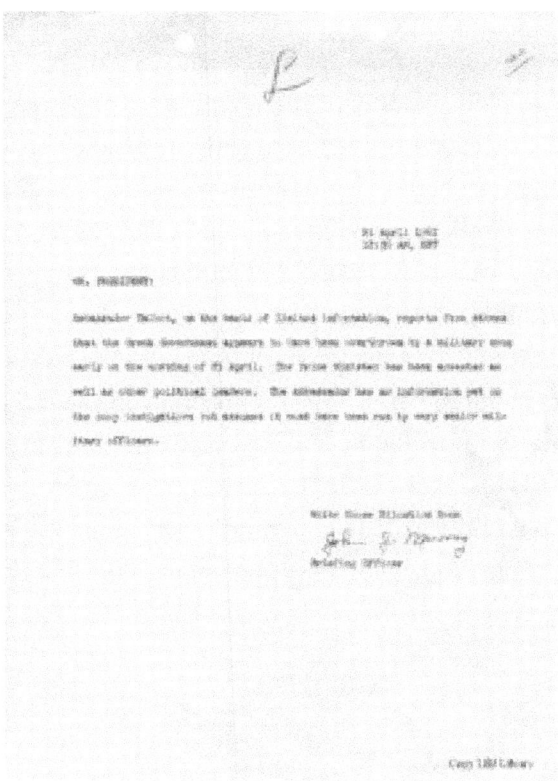

In Washington meanwhile, details emerged throughout the day about the overthrow of the government. While the Prime Minister, as well as other political leaders, were arrested, King Constantine seemed to remain in power. This led some to question whether the King was involved and embroiled in the coup. The same day at 6:30 p.m. President Johnson received updated information about the situation in Greece. In that memorandum, National Security Advisor Walt Rostow explained that rather than being involved in the coup, King Constantine had the new leadership forced upon him. There were initial rumors of a possible counter-coup, but over the next several days and weeks, the new regime established power in the country.

The CIA, however, was not too absent from the scene either—and as the embassy staffers had suggested—a possible diabolical secret CIA operation was in the works, to encourage the candidacy of moderate pro-Western elements, to strengthen the anti-leftist forces at the polls. As a result, after the January 1967 *country team* meeting, Ambassador Phillips Talbot was briefed of the outcome of the meeting, and in turn, he recommended to Washington a CIA covert operation to support candidates in a few swing districts. As one very high U.S. administrator official commented: *"maybe we should let the Greeks try a military dictatorship."* However, high ranking Greek military officers, entrusted and encouraged by these sorts of remarks by the U.S. administration as well as by the U.S. Embassy and the CIA, conspired to pave the road to a military coup with the blessing of the U.S., which brought about the disastrous events of the ill-fated *Friday*. The U.S. took a kin predetermined interest in suppressing Socialism in Europe and around the world and had a C.I.A. operative, named John Maury, who was in consultation with the colonels, supporting the junta leaders. American Vice President Spiro Agnew praised the junta as *"the best thing to happen to Greece since Pericles ruled ancient Athens."*

MEMORANDUM

THE WHITE HOUSE
WASHINGTON

~~SECRET~~

MEMORANDUM FOR THE PRESIDENT   April 21, 1967

SUBJECT: The Greek Situation as of 6:30 p.m.

As the day's events become clearer, it looks more and more as if a small group of middle and lower grade officers triggered the coup and forced it on the King and the High Command. The King told Phil Talbot a couple of hours ago: "Incredibly stupid ultra-rightwing bastards, having gained control of tanks, have brought disaster to Greece." We had earlier thought the King probably was in on the coup all along, but his interview with Talbot sounds like the real thing.

He also asked: (a) whether there's any possibility we could land Marines if necessary to help him and his generals reassert their control over the armed forces; (b) whether we could urge the new government to take his orders; (c) whether Sixth Fleet helicopters could evacuate his family if necessary.

The line now being worked out in State--Secretary Rusk will focus on it shortly--is to continue saying nothing publicly but to use our influence privately to help the King get on top of this government. But we want him to know that this is his job and that we aren't going to move the Marines in to bail him out. We still don't know enough about how the forces line up to take sides publicly; a mis-step could encourage dissatisfied military to strike back, and the fighting could get out of hand.

Since the situation is far less clear than we had originally thought, I think we will do best to avoid all public comment tomorrow unless the situation is radically different in the morning.

W. W. Rostow

DECLASSIFIED
E.O. 12958, Sec. 3.6
NLJ 97-14
By ___ NARA Date 10-14-97

CHAPTER XXIV

ORDINARILY, THERE WERE NO second chances in life, except to feel repentance. On occasion, fate got mislaid in the uproar of the predicaments of society and failed to recall, disregarding her schedules. The three fates, -- or *Moirai* as they were called in Greek mythology-- Clotho (Spinner), Lachesis (Alloter), and Atropos (Inflexible), were three goddesses who determined human destinies, or the span of a person's life in particular and the allotment of misery and suffering. These three fates were personified as three very old women, who spin the threads of human destiny, dispensing it and then cutting the thread, thus determining the individual's moment of death. Stephan was a victim of fate, and who was later forgotten by fate herself, and was left alone into the oblivion of destiny. He was summoned by the police an erstwhile ago, and there wasn't a word from him until he appeared one day at Avgy's doorstep. Alive. When a knock came at the door, Avgy and I had just finished breakfast. Silence covered the room, as we were looking at each other, not knowing how to respond. A second knock came. Resolutely and decisively, I got up to answer the door. Stephan was hardly standing on his feet in the hallway, holding the side of his body with a sad grimace of pain painting his face. The scars on his face were visible, as a result of the mistreatment he received during his stay at the police headquarters at the *Yellow Building*. He had a black eye, and his nose was out of disjointed. He was walking with a limp, and his clothes were dirty and smelly. He came in and sat on the couch.

"Stephan, you're back," Avgy said, receiving him by the arm to help him sit down.

"I was vacationing at the headquarters," he said with a smile, which turned into a painful grimace and quickly disappeared.

"What did they do to you?" Avgy asked with concern, looking at his injuries and the dry blood and dirt covering his face.

"Nothing unusual. We all get the same treatment. They're fair that way."

Avgy went to the kitchen and put the kettle on for tea. She returned with a wet cloth and set to wipe Stephan's face with it.

"How's your sight?" she asked, as she was wiping dirt or blood around his eyes and nose.

"A little hazy and fuzzy, but it will be OK," he said with a painful grimace, as Avgy was wiping his face. "They ask questions with a blow to the face. They don't wait for the answer; it's a preemptive action, which brings about fear and anxiety," Stephan said, looking at his bloody hands.

"What kind of questions did they ask you?" I asked.

"It's still unclear what they wanted from me. They didn't ask me about the organization or any of you. They asked me about my father's activities years ago, and my activities at the university. They were questioning the newspapers I read and people I see and talk to."

"Did they ask you about Jason?"

"Yes, they wanted to know where he's hiding. They asked me repeatedly, as my answers were hesitant and cautious. They broke my nose during that exchange."

"Would you like some tea, Stephan?" Avgy asked, as she put down the cloth and got up to go to the kitchen.

"Yes, please," Stephan said and cracked a painful smile. He reclined, stretched out on the couch, and closed his eyes with a frown.

"Maybe they were just probing information from you," I said, but I'm not sure he heard me, as the pain of his body swept over him.

Taking advantage of Stephan's deep sleep on the couch, I went outside. The street was quiet; a few passersby were hurrying home, as the night was coming slowly, and the street lights were emerging one after the other. I can count the times I walked down this street, storming my mind with inexplicable and perplexing thoughts about my life, what happened to Jason, Stephan, and Michael, and the homemade bombs exploding now and then around the city. There had been no casualties, but it was indeed a signal to the establishment on the brutal and inhumane way they were regarding people and the callous regards to the constitution and liberties. The only thing different about that time was that Stephan was back, animated and breathing; the hope was that we would pay a visit to Michael at the island and that Jason would come out of hiding soon.

The most alarming thought, however, was the fact that the political and economic situations had not changed, contrary to the government's claims that the life of the citizens had improved immensely since they seized power. In most cases, there were more people incarcerated and exiled than ever before, a lot more people had been arrested, tortured, and murdered, which had created a sense of trepidation and uncertainty around the country. The propaganda machine, of that illegitimate and unlawful government, was working day and night, retaliating against the alleged subversives, spreading false information, intelligence and deception through the newspapers, radio, and television, that those people were traitors, collaborators, and enemy of the state, and had to be defeated. Because of the overburden and erudition of that machine, people were always cautious of their conversations, their engagements, and even their thoughts.

In rapid succession, three military trucks passed by, driving at a high speed, chockfull with armed soldiers. There was an explosion somewhere in the city, and they were rushing to investigate the incident. If I had ever nursed a hope that these explosions should happen while the soldiers were present, it was always an afterthought. I was more unsettled by the fact that the *subversives* were risking their lives, setting up such bombs –homemade nevertheless -- than the aftermath of the explosions. What aggrieved me mostly, of course, was the fact that those bombs did nothing so far to unsettle the government, although the international community was condemning not the bombers but the government and the harsh treatment of its people. But for me, these condemnations were a constant strain to admire. I rapidly run out of compliments and imaginative interpretations.

Hard-pressed to keep on bustling over the condemnations by foreign bodies, I couldn't help but suggest timidly -- because abstract expressionism had hit such a dead-end in recent years -- they should rather try approximating the damage this government had triggered to its people.

Nevertheless, even Stephan, who had such pain tolerance and who had such a gift for it, could have sustained his efforts for only so long, without doing something to make his life a little more livable for him, as he demonstrated during his stay at the *Yellow Building*. One can only envision conceivably what went on within the four walls of his cell, as well as in the interrogation room. What was going on in Jason's mind, being closed up in that loft for weeks, with the only thought that if he got out chances were, he would be apprehended? Or Michael's situation at the island away in exile? How many times was he awaken to be taken away from his cell for execution? And how many times did he come back undamaged but with a little grayer hair on his head?

I had impetuous and impulsive hopes, when I first rushed into the activities of the organization, discerning and intellectualizing the outcome of each endeavor.

When I returned to Avgy's apartment, Stephan was sitting up drinking tea. He had taken a shower, and he was wrapped in a light blanket to dry.

"Did you find out anything about the explosion?" Avgy inquired with apprehension and concern.

"A bomb exploded close to the national museum, but no fatalities have been reported. The police and the army are investigating. I doubt they will find out anything. The executors of these bombings have become very systematic, disciplined, and methodical," I said with conviction.

"We had our incidents as well," Avgy said, reflecting on our own organization's activities during the past years. Consequently, several other dissident and rebellious organizations had resulted in similar bloodless bombings. "The attempts and challenges," she resumed, "are to cause damage to the infrastructure, government buildings, and military installations, foreign and domestic, rather than causing human casualties."

CHAPTER XXV

I PLOWED MY BRAIN with tongue, picked up my tools, and sat down to write a letter to my parents.

Dear parents,

I know you doubt me on this, but I did try very hard to persuade you to come to the city, having a passionate attachment to you both. But I had never experienced my feelings for my country, as an exercise that I was obliged to rehearse like scales on the piano. The harder I tried, the more aware I became that my very effort was an outrage. Surely, all this painfulness I felt for my cause here in the city, that in the end I simply parroted, should have come knocking at the door uninvited. Hence, it was not just your situation that depressed me or the fact that I was increasingly more immersed and focused on my political subversive activities, rather than on you; I depressed me; I was guilty of emotional neglect.

It must have been this overarching commitment to you, to what is really an abstraction, to one's parents, right or wrong, that can be even fiercer than the commitment to you as explicit, and that can consequently keep me devoted to you when as individuals they disappoint. On my part, it was this broad covenant with parents-in-theory, which I may have failed to make and to which I was unable to resort when I finally tested your maternal and paternal ties to a perfect mathematical limit on my staying in the city. In fact, when my head cleared, I remembered my parents and felt ungrateful. I have been unable to hold your hand as you held mine. Yet, offered the clasp of a living son, I crushed it.

The point is, I don't know what exactly I'd predicted would happen to me when I returned to the city after my Christmas visit. I hadn't foreknown much exactly. I wanted what I could not imagine: you, being here in the center of all these activities and incidents in the city. I wanted to be truthful; I wanted to be pragmatic. I wanted a door to open and a whole new landscape to expand before me that I had never known was out there. I wanted nothing short of a revelation, and revelation by its nature cannot be anticipated; it promises that, to which we are not yet aware of. But if I extracted one lesson from my brother's death, it was that expectations are dangerous when they are both high and unformed as was then my age.

Your Loving Son,
Daniel

I revisited, wrote, and rewrote this letter to my parents many times, trying to expose how I felt about them moving to the city, under the current circumstances. The truth was that I wanted them here with me, but not with the turmoil and chaos that was now engulfing the capital. I tried again to persuade them to stay in town and buy an apartment there, rather than moving to this disarray and turmoil. It was a very delicate and fascinating escapade, trying to persuade them again for what they wanted to do in the first place.

They managed to sell the properties and the animals for a very substantial profit. Financially they were in a very good place, which would enable them to acquisition a very comfortable apartment in the middle of the town, and have an undemanding retirement.

In the end, of course, we finalized the inevitable: they would buy an apartment in town, and I would stay in the city to complete my graduate studies. Although this agreement was pretty raw, it was the best deal for them. But then again, desperate people would often choose short-term relief in exchange for long-term losses. I don't mean that I regretted the deal we made; it was for their safety, though in terms of substance it was badly timed. Staying in town, they would be in their element, with friends and relatives, close to nature; something they have known most of their lives. They have worked hard throughout their lifetime; raising children, taking care of the animals and the fields, and battling the government for their land and their survival. I had no more to give them. My last proposal was my final attempt. They wouldn't have been happy in the city with the latest developments and what was more to come. They had lived a peaceful life in the village, not much of destruction, or upheaval. I felt a lot of guilt for the letter I wrote to them, for my standing as their son, and for the fact that I could not be there to stand by them and help them. Was there a time in one's life that said, *"this is the end; I have nothing more to give or to do with my parents; I'm breaking my link with them, and I carry on my own life."* I imagined there wasn't; the link was always there, and we always felt responsible for our parents especially in their later years. Not so much financially, as they would be well off to live the rest of their lives comfortably, but mostly emotionally. They wanted one or two grandchildren on their lap, and at Easter time to turn a lamp on the spit with their family; witness birthdays, baptisms, and Christmas. People didn't need much to be happy, especially older people. They yearned for their family to be close by, they wanted to raise a glass of wine with them, and have a meal together now and then.

How much had I missed these small indulgences and luxuries myself, during the time of my staying in the city! But I had gotten myself into a different and diverse world and at times, I felt that there was no room for anything else. Thinking of my eminent and resolute position within the organization and within my mind, I could not have done any more than what I had done already. I could have stayed in the village, be a shepherd, plowing the fields every spring and harvest every fall; neglecting my intellectual thirst, unable to call to mind my needs and desires. I would have sat under a pine tree in the heat of the day with my herd around me, playing the fife, and at night, I would be staring at the sky. I wouldn't have had a concern about the political situation, disregarding my own beliefs. Life would have been effortless and undemanding, with uncomplicated thoughts going through my mind. Was I trying to defend and rationalize my position and my way of thinking? Was I vindicating myself of my actions ostensibly?

CHAPTER XXVI

As I meandered the corner from the kitchen into the living room that morning, the sun, coming through the window, was flooding the room, and its warmth permeated my entire body. I sat on the couch with a cup of coffee, and my face was tackling the sun undiluted and in full strength. I decided, that the notion that I was resistant and invulnerable to nonsense and rubbish, was taking root. I'd always made it a policy—which I flatter myself with sometimes—to confront and play against the rumors and deceptive news we read in the papers daily. Fabricated and deceitful information was streaming down into newspapers, television, and radio across the country, endeavoring to alter and transform people's views about what was going on. In the news this morning it was announced that the islands—which were used by right-wing governments to lock up subversives and enemies of the system—were almost empty. There were not exiles, and there were no political prisoners according to the authorities. The ones who were in prison were traitors and mutineers, the authorities insisted, who went against the good of society and against the efforts and attempts of the government to improve the lives of the citizens. But my policy of misgivings and distrust towards the authorities had kept my approach and ideology intact, and my methods integral and undamaged.

The colonels regarded salvation from socialisms—as absurd as it may seem—as an act of consciousness and desire for nobler and worthier life. But they mocked and belittled people for their beliefs and their obstinate defiance toward specific discontents and frustrations. Because to fail to embrace the yearning for democracy and freedom, betrayed a weakness of character. I never took this longing for freedom and democracy ever for granted and ever so seriously. One must exert hard and employ rationality, fearlessness, and bravery to not only attain these basic freedoms but also to ensure that they were kept unscathed and sheltered. The yearning made me greedy; like an addict devouring his sweets, I wanted more. It was not true that neither of us could compete with the military muscle of the government. The hint of indignation and resentment towards the authorities had given me monstrous strength to overcome any feebleness and fragility, in order to combat the evil forces, which had oppressed the nation and its people for years. And how we sheltered and groomed ourselves for the prospect of such rebellion, was an indication of the determination we devised, to seize and conquer what belonged to us and what was our absolute right, being ill from impenetrable and incomprehensible conditions we had endured. For years I had been waiting for that intervening urge to burst and spill over my senses. The urge that was triggered by the inhumane and cold-hearted state of affairs, which pulled me off the fence into the combat zone of society: I had to contest. Over the years, the aversion and loathing for the ruling body grew more compelling and formidable. Once I had habituated to mounting to my challenge, believing that I was enslaved and that I was not independent and free; gradually my trepidation and anxiety capsized and inverted.

*

I had often hypothesized that one might trace most people on a scale of the roughest kind, which would determine their position on it and every other aspect of their lives, related as to how much they were willing to fight in this world as opposed to giving up. I think since Jason had reached that extreme possibility of choice, he despised and detested being self-imprisoned in his city, and wanted out. Any sense of spiritual memory, might have contributed to his decision to leave his place of hiding, and face the consequences of been apprehended, arrested, or even jailed. Jason seemed incensed that idleness and lethargy on his part were counterproductive, and he needed to get back to his former activities. It was not public exoneration that he truly craved. Sitting there in the dark, in that cold house in the attic, recording every minute in his mind, the undeserved and excessive isolation, he was enduring as a result of the discriminatory position he was in.

Later that evening, as I was walking towards Jason's hiding place, I mumbled to myself that everything would be alright, although I had no way of knowing. I was stricken by the thought, however, that it may not be a good idea yet to flaunt but I was overcome with contempt. I must confess the emotion I felt, by which I fastened my feelings, was pushing me toward a critical threshold, which was revulsion and aversion. Loathing the time Jason had spent at that dark and cold house, the loneliness he felt, and the distress and discontent about any prospects for his future as a student and as a beleaguered and demoralized citizen. Jason was a very idealistic man, with a great deal of stance towards the future of this country and the outcome of his venerated principles.

*

I reached the house with my heart hanging from my lips, and tired from the long walk. I ascended the stairs to the loft. It was as dark as the devil's quarters, and only the dim light from the street lamps coming through the windows was illuminating the hallway and the room where Jason was hiding. I stood at the threshold of the door looking at him, sitting on the mattress in that muted room, and trying to make up his vaguely visible frame, contributed by the darkness in the room. I felt a sense of admiration and wonder for Jason, sitting there patiently, in the dark in that cold house. He was covered in a blanket that was falling from his shoulders, and his bright eyes were lit up by the dim light coming from the street. He stayed silent, presumably looking at me, trying to make up my form.

"Hi Jason, it's me, Daniel," I said and walked towards him.

"Hi Daniel; thank you for coming. Come, and sit down," he said, making room for me on the mattress.

"How are you feeling? Is the loneliness tormenting you, persecuted by your thirst for freedom?" I said, sitting on the mattress next to him.

"I have my moments, Daniel; sitting here in the dark for two weeks, with nobody to talk to; but I feel free, only in spirit. The rest, body and heart, are still besieged."

"Not for too long. We'll take our chances, and we'll get you out of here."

"Even so, Daniel, my heart will still be besieged and blockaded. I'm surrounded by books and memories and hope. The body suffers; the heart agonizes; the soul tolerates and waits."

"The moment I rested my eyes on you tonight, Jason, at once I noticed how peaceful and serene your face was; the calmness, undisturbed, radiated across the room. Your eyes were laid on me comfortably with a smile; your temples were vibrating, and your lips were moving. Don't be ashamed Jason, we all know your secret: you are ready. Your mind is well-defined and transparent. And quietly, without feeling it, like the fruit which is hanging ripen from the tree, my thoughts were hanging from my mind. My thirst for the cause came back even stronger, exhuming strength from you; it came back even more intensely, persuasive and compelling."

"I remember," Jason said, "I remember, always, as I encounter and come across agony, I fight, I become desperate and I scream. But when the time comes to feed the hunger of the struggle, coherence, and harmony feel my heart; silence. And slowly, without effort sometimes in my sleep, sometimes on the street and having my mind wandering somewhere else, I feel and I welcome deliverance in my soul; then I assemble my strength. Similarly, the tree is fighting a secret fight: the rain, the cold, the wind; and one day, quietly under the emissions and the glimmers of the sun, the tree appears full of blossoms; then I calm down my heart, as I look at the flourished meadows; as such, I sit quietly at night at the seashore of my secret island and gaze at the sky. I'm ready."

"Tonight, I'll get you out of here."

"It's time," Jason said, and if there were light in the room, one could have seen that brilliant intensity covering his face.

"We'll take our chances; you can't stay here any longer. We have to make a move."

Jason looked at me, and he formed a bitter smile. He touched my hand,

and he looked away into the darkness. The apparitions had disappeared; had gone away, and only silence took possession of the room. Apparitions, which had come and gone, in the stillness of the night; those which tormented the soul, afflicting pain and discontent, and which would leave one only with memories of the past, provoking and enticing the spirit. On one side the brain, on the other the soul and in the middle the heart; the body stands there like a whisper, a remark in reserve; which one was going to win? Which one would come out triumphantly and declare victory? The soul said: *"I will die for them, for my beliefs."* The brain said: *"I have to think about it and decide; I need to make plans have dispositions, schemes."* The heart said: *"let's fight to the end."* But the body said: *"I'm tired."* I'd need light, air to breathe, sidewalk to stroll on, and smell the odors of the city; I'd want to get married, have children, have a decent job, go to the café and talk to people; enjoy the sun, perhaps a vacation or a trip to faraway lands. The spirit said: *"you need to march; you need to climb the mountains with a rifle in hand; you need to fight."*

The agony escalated inside Jason, and turmoil exploded all over his body. The time he had spent in this forsaken house, was not enough. His brothers and sisters were enduring that every day. He should endure that with them. The stillness was deafening, and the heartbeat, echoing against the walls, was biting fast.

A police siren was heard coming from the street below, and I could feel the tightness of Jason's hand squeezing mine. Feeling embarrassed, I supposed, he let my hand go, and he got up. He walked to the other side of the room, and he stood facing the wall. Many thoughts were circling his head: his adverse staying at this house, which was detrimental to his mental health and the essence of his soul; his struggle for freedom, the hostile and antagonistic state of being, and his friends in jail or exile, tormented his soul; the sad state of affairs for the country, indeed.

"I have to get back to my struggle, my battle," he said, and he turned around to face me.

"You will, Jason; but first, we have to make sure that you're safe."

"Daniel, my spirit is decaying, my soul is decaying; I walk around the rooms, up and down the stairs; I approach the window, and I peek outside; my mind turns around like a windmill in a hurricane," he said, and he wiped a tear from his face. Jason's turmoil was hurting him deep inside. He looked like a caged animal.

"We're leaving tonight, Jason."

"How are the streets?" he asked.

"Very quiet. It will be a breeze to get out. We'll walk to my place."

He turned, looked at me, and his mouth formed a smile. "I'm ready," he said and walked toward the door.

I got up, and put my arm on his shoulder.

"Let's go, Jason," I said, and he led the way. He headed down the stairs as if he were taking charge of his life, guided by his determination. His soul and spirit won. He would fight; he was determined.

*

THE night was cold, and it started to rain when we stepped outside. The rain was hitting our face, and the wind was blowing relentlessly. There was something eerie in the air tonight; the streets glared from the rain, the sounds of the rain and the wind sounded like fairies singing from afar, and our shadows, sometimes in front of us other times trailing us, were dark like tar in that dejected and dismal night. The street was deserted. It must have been around ten o'clock when we turned the corner toward my place. Another police car raced down the street, and my heart skipped a bit. I looked at Jason; his face was very calm. He looked in the direction of the cruiser, and he laughed silently.

"Little do they know that the fugitives of the city are walking the streets at night. Do they know that?" he said, laughing again gesturing with his hand.

We swiftly turned the corner, and we quicken our pace. The back roads were quieter and more deserted. The rain had eased by now, and only the paddles on the sidewalk were glittering, twinkling our way. He was going to stay with me for the night until we decided whether he was going to go back home or be a homeless person for a while. We reached my hotel, and by chance, the old bony man was not behind his desk. The lobby was empty. We hurried up the narrow staircase to my room. I locked the door behind me and sat on the couch.

"Here we are," I said, "we've made it."

"Yes, we did," he said and smiled with relief. "I will take a shower, then we'll talk."

He went into the bathroom to take a shower. I can hear the hot water running, and I felt reassured and pleased that Jason was out of hiding, dismissing any notions of his alleged freedom, getting rid of any thoughts and impulses that maybe it wasn't a good idea for Jason to come out of hiding so soon. He came back into the room, wiping his hair dry, and sat on the armchair.

"Thank you for providing for me, Daniel, during this infuriating time I spent in hiding. My self-esteem was retreating, and I was terrified I would give up," Jason said, as he wiped his face with the towel.

"It was my duty, Jason," I said with a smile. He shook his head and looked at me smiling.

"I appreciate that, Daniel. I'm thankful to you, to Avgy, to Ari who helped me during that difficult time."

"You can stay here tonight. We can figure out tomorrow what we're going to do," I said.

"I need to go back to my studies. Two weeks have been a very long time away from the university."

"We can figure this out, too."

He got up, and he approached the window. The night was cold and windy, and the trees on the street were fluctuating, shifting from side to side and in all directions from the wind. The sounds from outside were penetrating the room, sounding sometimes like a whistle, while other times like a freight train going through the room. The traffic was light, and a few pedestrians on the sidewalks were wrapped up with scarfs, trying to have a steady pace, as the wind was pushing them backward and askew. Sirens can be heard from far away fading into the distance, as a police car with flashing lights raced down the street. Jason turned around to face me.

"Do you think the time has come, Daniel?" he said, piercing me with his deep eyes.

"Time?" I asked.

"Yes," he said, "time, for the final challenge. We have one shot at it; we must do it right," he said, and his eyes, bright and dark, became even brighter.

"Yes, it's time. It's time to escalate our actions for the final show-down."

"Are we ready?" Jason asked.

"We are, as much as we could be. We cannot prolong it any longer."

"We must fight for our freedom and our education," he said, looking at me standing in front of the window.

"Please, stay away from the window. You never know who may be on the street prying on us."

Jason smiled, and he came and sat on the chair. "Yes, the time will come when setting bombs and holding meetings will not be enough anymore. We must fight for our shortcomings, for the truths, for our decency and honor, for our integrity, for the bread of the people," he said.

"Yes, for our bread, for our education," he looked at me, as his lips were stretched to a smile, "for our freedom. The three most eminent and essential elements of an absolute society."

The three integral and fundamental elements of an all-inclusive and accomplished society. If one kept half an eye on the news internationally, one couldn't fail to notice mentions of our struggles for democracy and freedom, since that political upheaval was ushered upon us, changing the fabric of our society. Fundamental rights were escorted and marshaled away into prisons and holding cells.

*

LOOKING back at the uprising in France in May 1968, one couldn't fail to recall the civil unrest that took place, paralyzing the country politically and economically; punctuated by major demonstrations and general strikes. Most universities and factories were occupied by dreamers, optimists, and visionary students. Workers were challenging the government; they were demanding traditional institutions reverting to moral values and order. They protested against capitalism, consumerism, and American imperialism. Eleven million workers went on strike across the country – more than twenty-two percent of the total population of France – for two weeks, with the reinforcement and collaboration of students and trade unions. The protests reached such a critical point, that the fear of civil war or insurrection was imminent. The president secretly fled the country to a French military base in Germany for a few hours, as the strikes and the unrest were unfolding. The wildcat strikes and the student occupation of university campuses across the country were met with forceful and powerful confrontations by university administrators and the police. Upon the return of the president, the National Assembly was dissolved, and parliamentary elections were called to resolve this extraordinary situation unfolding across the country. The unrest in France in 1968 affected French society to its core for decades afterward. It is considered to this day as a cultural, social, and moral turning point in the history of the country. That movement succeeded *"as a social revolution not as a political one,"* as Alain Geismar pointed out.

"This is our inspiration and our brilliance, Daniel. We discern and recognize it; it can be done; it's been proven. What we need is the will and the determination of the people to achieve it," Jason said, pointing towards the window, or the entire striven city.

"We're going to need more organization and a lot more discipline. The student syndicate has been broken by the regime. We cannot even hold our elections at the university level. The junta is imposing non-elected students as union leaders in the national students' union, and our hands are tied," I said, with frustration and revulsion.

"Our supporters and affiliates are numerous, so we're not doing so badly," Jason said with a smile.

"No, we're not, as long as we keep the momentum, and our plans unbroken and intact."

Jason got up, held his head with both hands, closed his eyes, and a sad look covered his face as if he were to reveal a foreign and unconventional thought.

"Daniel, the anticipation and eagerness I sensed during my time in hiding, have given me a new perspective in my existence. Life is very fragile and precious. We cannot discard it. There are only a few basic fundamental essentials we have, and we must preserve them. I feel that this entire city is a prison, and we're wandering among its bounds as inmates. We have lost our freedom, Daniel," he said, wiping his forehead with the towel.

Jason was right.

"We cannot look at it only from that perspective, Jason. We're here to fight, and we're doing it. Although our road looks like the road to Golgotha, it's not unattainable. Some of us will be crucified, some of us will be jailed while others will survive, as luck would have it; but also, democracy and freedom will survive with us," I said, reinforcing Jason's thought.

"The man Christ took the road to Golgotha and died. He died for his beliefs and his ideals."

"Yes, as did Socrates. But we have a different Golgotha to climb. We don't have Roman soldiers who are dragging us to the crosses. We don't have the wrath of the natural elements as we're trying to cross our desert and climb our mountains, as Moses did. But we're not expecting God to feed us manna, either, or provide us with sustenance or life instructions. We have to make it alone. We must preserve what we have, to be able to reclaim and salvage what we've lost. Only we can do that."

*

WINTER came, and the earth was cold. Many trees were naked, and they were also cold, but the pine and the olive trees reserved their coats winter and summer. The destitute and deprived people were naked too, and they were cold like the naked trees.

The morning was bright and calm. The sun was coming out behind the buildings with such brilliance and anticipation, that only a February morning could be longed for. The shadows of the buildings were long, as the light was navigating among them, to strike the street and houses with the warmth which was so desired after a cold and rainy night. The morning noise on the street was getting livelier, as the merchants were announcing their commodities, and the traffic was picking up momentum. It was still winter; February was a short cold month, which could be disheartening and gloomy. I opened the window to get some fresh air into the room. The cold morning breeze was affecting my movements, as the hair stood up at the back of my neck, and my naked feet were cold on the floor.

"Good morning Jason," I said, as I turned and looked at him still on the couch stretched out peacefully, lessening his stress, diminishing the effects of the dreams from the night before.

"Good morning Daniel."

"Did you sleep well?"

"Yes, I did," he said, and he sat up.

"I made coffee; would you like some?"

"Yes, please. My dreams from last night are still disturbing me, hassling my brain."

"Here, the coffee will do you good," I said, offering him a cup.

"It's nice to wake up in the light, in a warm room. I've forgotten what this luxury feels like, which we take for granted," Jason said, taking a sip of the warm coffee, turning his gaze toward the window.

Lazily, I hauled myself into the bathroom, dragging my feet. I washed up and dressed quickly, as we were trailing time from behind. Ari was waiting for us at the café. Jason and I traced a back alley to take us to Ari's café, away from the main street and the flood of policemen and army personnel. As we arrived at the café, we learned that the junta had drafted a dozen more law students, taking them away from their studies, interrupting their lives. So far, eighty-eight law students had been drafted by the army, which was aiming to dismantle the syndicate of the students who had been identified by the authorities as *subversive youths*. It was a law that the government passed some time ago, to forcibly draft those so-called *subversive* students. It was terrible precedence that the government was setting. No student, *subversive* or not, was keen and eager to abandon their studies and join the army. Of course, it was common knowledge that the purpose of that law was not to simply enlist the students, but merely to break their solidarity, as the government was carrying on this unlawful practice against the freedom of expression of the students.

*

ON Wednesday 21 February 1973, there was a first massive public engagement against the junta, which started with the law students. It was the frustration and infuriation of the students, as well as of the public, after so many years of academic and social oppression. On that day, the law students went on strike; they barricaded themselves inside the buildings of the Law School of the university in the center of the city, demanding repeal of the law, which took them away from their studies and forcibly drafting them. The police were ordered to intervene, and many students were reportedly subjected to police brutality. The anti-dictatorial student movement was growing among the youth, and the police utilized brutal methods to confront the threat. Furthermore, these student uprisings were also heavily influenced by the youth movements around the world in the 1960s, notably by the events in May 1968 in France.

CHAPTER XXVII

Dusk fell almost stealthily on the city, as the sun had fallen behind the western mountains, and a cold breeze was blowing from the north; a shroud of orange light glided from the sky, compelling the shadows to dissolve. A blanket of an absolute uncanny light covered the city, giving new colors to everything underneath that mantle. It was seven o'clock when I left my hotel room, to meet Avgy at the restaurant where we would have dinner. I walked amidst a crowd of people in that cold, dark and windy downtown, fastening my pace, meandering among them, all bundled up, trying to find my destination on time.

The events at the law school at the university were in my mind. So many students were hurt, so many were jailed, and so many were sent to the border to serve in the army. But their battle was not over. Our battle was not over. It hadn't begun yet.

She was walking down the street wrapped in a banjo. Her scarf was floating in the wind, hovering over her left shoulder. She looked exceptionally beautiful, as her hair was fluttering around her face from the wind. She approached me, and offered her lips to mine; I draped my hands around her and kissed her. She had an innocent and kind smile, enfolding and wrapping her face, which radiated so intensely, enveloping her entire being. Her zeal and passion she had shown about life, her dedication to the *cause,* and the love and enthusiasm she had revealed towards all-natural things, instinctively were virtues and attributes which she possessed, routed deep inside her heart and soul. I have seen her cry, and I have seen her laugh, and every time she showed a sort of spontaneous emotion, exposing it with the same demeanor and with the same sensation and sentiment. Her concerns about her father's incarceration, and now his poor health, had allowed her an agonizing and fretful existence that was unsettling. The fear of something happening to her father was demoralizing and dispiriting; he was getting old; he didn't have the strength and potency to survive any longer the mistreatment, unethicality, and prejudice in prison; prejudice toward his *cause* and principles. There was no justice; there was no fairness; there were no courts except the fabricated and sardonic military ones; mock trials and predetermined verdicts. Avgy was caring about the burden of her father's actions and of her own. But she was optimistic about the outcome of all this. Optimism is based on the humanity, solidarity, and camaraderie of society. She deeply believed in the social order, even though it was demoralizing, as the current political and socio-economic situation had disheartened a lot of people.

Holding her hand, we entered the restaurant. The waiter showed us to a table by the window; we sat down, ordering a bottle of wine.

"You look so beautiful," I said, extending my hand to shelter hers in mine.

"Thank you; you don't look too bad yourself either," she said with a smile, which revealed her white perfect teeth. "I saw Ari at the café this morning. He gave me the latest from the events at the law school."

"Yes, I was there in the morning when all that was going on. A lot of students were hurt, many were arrested," I said with deep remorse and emotion. "What came to mind," I carried on, "was the suicide of the geology student in 1970 in Matteotti square in Genoa Italy, who set himself ablaze, as an act of protest against the junta. A similar kind of protest we see here; the future of the students is not certain; their lives and their prospects are at stake."

We allowed silence to take over, as the hustle and bustle inside and outside the restaurant were successfully interrupting that moment. The music was playing softly in the background, as the forks were hitting the plates in response to the adverse gluttony overtaking the patrons. The waiter brought the wine, and I filled our glasses. I raised my glass.

"Avgy, we must remember the tears, the pain, the struggle of people to be free from the shackles of tyranny. Easter means the passage from darkness to light; from persecution and tyranny to freedom; but this particular Easter will go even further; we will celebrate the passage from death to immortality," I said, and I empty my glass. Avgy looked at me with a skeptical look and smiled a bitter smile.

"*'From death to immortality'* heavy words, Daniel. You speak of death again. Your words, like double edge sword, pierced my heart. If there is an anathema hanging over you, speak freely."

"Death will come, Avgy; there isn't another way to conquer freedom: immortality to our words and actions."

"Does that comfort you, Daniel?"

"Yes, it does; but I'm thinking of you, too, hoping that you would be alive so you can mourn me and weep for me."

"Oh, Daniel…"

"Sometimes, I so long to die," I said interrupting, "so I can be free; I'm even desperate for it."

"Why? It will never make sense to me."

"I know how disappointed you would be, all of you. It would seem easier to slip away into the oblivion of freedom."

"I would never be disappointed in you."

"Really? I always assumed it was a chronic state as far as I was concerned."

"You mistook me, Daniel. I'm dismayed by your theory, not you. I know you are a good man, longing for freedom, but not without faults, but a worthy man all the same."

Avgy sent me a sympathetic and understanding look, and she looked down at the table. Her bitter smile still lingered at her lips, remained as a reminder of how desperately we needed this victory. She shook her head and remained silent.

"Daniel, I was thinking," Avgy said, breaking the silence, "we should go and see Michael. It has been a long time since we had any news from him. Now that Jason is out of hiding and Stephan is healing, Michael is the only one in my mind, besides my father, of course," she suggested, and her gaze flew somewhere indeterminate and unfixed.

"We need to locate where he's held, and find out the process of visiting him," I advocated, thinking that perhaps it would be a very difficult course of action, considering the hostile environment within the *Yellow Building*.

"I'm sure we can get that information from the police headquarters," she said, and a grimace of disgust formed her face.

"Hopefully they will allow us to visit Michael, despite the charges against him," I pointed out, somewhat worried that they might not allow visitors to the island.

"I hope they do."

"How dreadful it must be for Michael, being away onto some deserted island, not knowing what the next hour will bring. The abuse and maltreatment they endure in such places: mock executions, kept in isolation for days and days without a glimpse of the sun, or tied up in sacks with cats and thrown into the sea. As you said once: *'they pushed a friend off the train, they locked his coffin, and oh, what an irony, not even free in the eternity … a proper place for a free man to die.'*"

"I see you memorized my poem," I said smiling rather proudly, hearing my words coming out of her lips.

"Also, my favorite: *'We cannot measure freedom. It's not land to measure it by the meter; it's not the endless sea to measure it by the mile; it's a heartbeat.'* That's what Michael and Jason and my father and you and me and so many others are musing and envisioning. One cannot restraint and muzzle freedom; it cannot be quantified and appraised."

I looked at her bright eyes, and my heart was filled with contentment. I remembered when I wrote that poem. It was the inspiration of Mark, who exhumed his freedom and inventiveness so perfectly, sitting on a rock, carving his imaginary reflections; it was also the mountains, the sea, the endless sandy beach, which exhaled freedom; it was exhumed and unearthed from the bottom of the sea, from deep down the bowels of the earth; from the rocky slopes of the mountains; the warm salty air, and the long-traveled waves, which carried their weight from Africa.

"You're smiling! Do you feel proud of your creations?" she asked with a smile.

"Yes, I do. But I feel that words are not enough. I wrote plenty, yes; I spilled my heart and soul on paper, and now all my inspiration, my thoughts, and agonies are sitting in my desk drawer. I have an obligation and duty to go beyond that; I must materialize every word I've written; I ought to." I took a deep breath, and I bent over taking a hold of her hand. "Avgy," I said looking at her eyes, "there is no time for words anymore. We can spend all our lives writing and reciting all we want. We may fantasize and daydream until we have no more to give; life is more than that. We must engage, and fight for what we are here for on this earth: the ephemeral has no place in our lives any longer."

"You're doing it, Daniel; your heart and soul are now in the movement. You're crusading ahead."

"I feel my heart lighter, fluffier, now, more manageable, because of the effort I've given to find and tell my sorrow; I've illuminated my fight, and for the first time I could distinguish the faces inside my chaos. Mystic each face seemed to me, sometimes, and other times, it seemed as if all the faces were in synthesis, in a fusion of light, calling me to take me away."

I looked outside; the square was bustling with people. The lights were on, and the sky over the parliament building was dark. My thoughts were flying out, soaring and hovering over my head, which had no end. Like birds, my words came back to me, harassing me and torturing me to bring them alive, to explore them and define them.

"You're in deep thought, Daniel, what is the matter?"

"I was far away, Avgy, forgive me."

"I'm glad I brought you back. I didn't want to have dinner alone," she said and laughed.

"Have you had any news from your father?" I inquired with apprehension, trying to come back from my unexpected trip.

"Yes, we spoke on the phone. I said that I'd go to see him soon. He's the same; he can't wait to get out."

"How's his health?"

"The same. Sometimes it flares up, he has pains in his chest, but then they go away. The doctor monitors him. His medication changed, and he's waiting to see some improvement."

"We should go together to visit him. He would like to see another person from the outside world. It'll give him continuity and endurance."

"Yes, we should do that, and also visit Michael."

"That would require greater undertakings and exploits. Visiting exiles in the island is dangerous and certainly attention-grabbing."

"You mean for us? Do you think they will *mark* us?"

"It's possible, but what else can they do, that they haven't done already?"

"Book us."

"That's also possible."

"The yellow building doesn't solely have the reputation of torture and murder. There are a lot more gruesome activities that are taking place on the islands. One can't imagine the horror these people go through, before their unconceivable death. They're asked to drink the soapy water after they've shaved. What more atrocious and hideous acts one may do, to demoralize and hurt people? Not much."

Horrific revelations by survivors, affirmations that raised the hair at the back of one's neck. What kind of thoughts would go through the minds of the executioners of such acts? Unless they had been conditioned and indoctrinated. All senses and feelings were gone. The desensitizing of feelings damaged the persona of the soldier or the policeman who was involved in torture and murder. They were not facing another human being, but the enemy.

We finished our dinner, and the waiter cleared the table. We order cappuccino and cognac.

"I feel having something sweet," I said, looking in the direction of the fridge with the sweets displayed behind the glass, which looked enticing and alluring.

"You're having it already," she said smiling.

"I need something to sink my teeth in."

"Well?" she said, looking at me smiling.

We left the restaurant and walked in silence with her arm tucked in mine. The streets were so quiet, that it seemed as if the capital itself, in its stillness, were holding its breath. It was late, of course, and most people were in bed by now. Avgy couldn't recall the last time she had been out so late during the week.

I walked her to her building and waited as she fished in her handbag for her keys, all the while saying nothing. Avgy looked up, and open her arms to hug me. I took a step forward and dropped a kiss on her lips, light and fleeting. Her mouth was pleasantly warm, contrasting with the cool nightly air.

"Thank you," she whispered, "I mean, that is, thank you for tonight. I very much enjoyed it."

"Thank you Avgy; I did as well."

"Are you taking the trolley home? Are they still running this time of night?"

"I'd rather walk. Remember what I said about your father. You are a good nurse, you will make it, and he will recover, I'm sure."

"Thank you, Daniel; good night then."

"Good night."

She let herself in, as I listened to her departing footsteps.

CHAPTER XXVIII

"Never before in my life had I felt seduced, trapped, and caught up in an environment so volatile and dangerous," Mary explained, "the way they carried out, watching the law students demonstrate, defying the police, exploring the alcoves of the soul. I had never known such pleasure before, as I did yesterday with contentment, watching those students challenging and daring the authorities, disregarding everything, including arrest or even injury or death. This skirmish yesterday taught me, that rebelling against the authorities in such a way, for the cause we all believe in, to gather my tools, get the courage to do my part, and live more intensely; it gave me the courage I had lost."

Mary along with Lisa had joined the organization a few years back when they were both electrical engineering students at the Polytechnic. They had shown a great deal of dedication and fervor in the cause; they had been involved in a few risky and critical missions, assigned by the organization. Their demeanor was impulsive and passionate and had dedicated many hours recruiting and encouraging potential insurgents and students to join.

During our weekly meeting, Mary and Lisa outlined the mechanics and methods, with which they would build the radio station. Currently, they were searching for an AM frequency, which to launch the station without any interference. They outlined a list of building materials they needed, such as a megaohm register, capacitors, electronics breadboard, operational amplifier, speakers, wire, and other necessary material. An antenna had to be built, and find a secure place to install it. The preferred location for the broadcast was at the university, utilizing the electronics lab.

The success of our rebellion depended partly on the success of the radio station and the methods and means with which to reach as many people as possible, within a wide area. Stephan suggested that they should be broadcasting live with speakers around the campus, placed in deliberate and tactical locations. They should be asking the public to join them, giving them planned locations of gathering, suggesting what to wear, how to protect themselves from tear gas, and other means, which the police use to disperse the crowds. Their slogan should be broadcasted over the radio and displayed on large signs, placed all over the university campus. Many medical students had been drafted by the organization, to be standing by, responding to any emergency crisis.

*

MARY's words brushed aside all the doubts and uncertainties I had up until then. At dawn, after I spent the whole night wide awake, engrossed in her words and the voices I heard behind them, I left the hotel. I dressed quietly and in a slow pace, and I left a note for Avgy at the front desk. When I stepped out of the lobby into the street, the shadows were long, and the early morning light immersed everything into its magical colors. The small paddles left on the sidewalks from the early morning rain were glittering. I buttoned up my jacket and set off briskly toward the metro. Warm air was coming out of the tunnel of the station, as I descended onto the platform. I purchased a ticket and got into a carriage occupied by and crammed with early workers and drudges, carrying their lunch wrapped in newspaper. I claimed my place standing by the door, trying to breathe, as the odors and fumes from the tunnel were entering the carriage. Traveling through the bowels of the city to the end of the line, I had a long trip ahead of me. As the train remerged into the light again, it seemed as if I were discovering a new place. Dawn was breaking, and orange light was propelling from among the clouds, spraying its color over the fronts of shops, houses, and apartment buildings. That early winter morning was cold, covered with a blanket of clouds, hanging low over the city. The streets looked busy with the morning rush, as the pedestrians, bundled up, were finding their way to work. The wind had picked up, blowing through trees and alleys, giving a sense of late winter blues.

The train arrived at the station opening its doors, as the urgency of the passengers to disembark, trailed any sense of politeness, spilling onto the platform. I climbed up the stairs to the street, and I felt the cool breeze brazing my face, as I heard the clattering of the train leaving the station. I walked briskly toward my destination, which was a few blocks up the gradient. By the time I ended my journey, I was out of breath.

The bookstore, which Lisa had suggested, was behind a building on an alley, sandwiched between a warehouse and a bicycle repair shop. That was the place where many disenchanted and disillusioned Athenians would come -- sent or recommended by trustworthy and cautious sources -- to find rare books banned by the government. All literary, legendary, and cultural banned books, were hidden in the basement of that store, which only the store clerk had access to. Prodigious and inspired minds, who were looking for the lost and prohibited written word, would get referrals to that place. From ancient philosophy and drama to the nineteenth-century political theorists, to twentieth-century literary works were inaccessible. The consequences were grave if one were caught in the aftermath of possessing such a book. Ray Bradbury's *Fahrenheit 451* came to mind, in which a futuristic American society had outlawed all books, thus burning any books found at a temperature of 451 degrees Fahrenheit. Censoring literature and destroying knowledge, was also the concern during the McCarthy era in the United States, where there was a real threat of book burning. But this ceremonial burning of books did not escape the dictator Metaxa; one of the first actions of his dictatorship, only twelve days after the abolition of democracy, on 4 August 1936, was to perform massive book burnings in several Greek cities. As an imitation of similar actions in Nazi Germany, hundreds of leftists, communists, Marxists, and pro-democracy books by both Greek and foreign writers were set on fire in medieval-like ceremonies. The current Athenian government was not as intrepid as to begin burning books, however, it was as depraved and ruthless as if they had accomplished that already. Prohibiting the reading of such books was as debauched and dissolute as preventing and disallowing the mind to accelerate into new heights. Stifling the intellect and psyche by banning books, was as if cutting through the heart of society.

As I left the bookstore and returned to the metro, holding the bag with the books I had purchased, I pictured Avgy visiting the bookstore, walking down the same road, looking at the same buildings with the same porticos being altered from the rhythm of time. I could almost see her walking down the street, with that air which she exhumed, contemplating her life, and the happiness which was almost borrowed and only as long as we could feel it inside us.

*

WHEN I got back to the hotel, there was a message from Avgy waiting for me at the front desk. She said she wanted to see me. I went to my room, and I called her on the phone. She answered with a grim voice which provoked so many thoughts in my head. She indicated that she had news from her father, and then she fell into an impregnable silence. After a long pause, she said that her father was not feeling well, and he was hospitalized. She asked me if I would accompany her to the hospital. I hang up the phone, and I got ready to go and meet her. She sounded very distressed and confused, as her father had certain health issues which surfaced every so often.

I went to her apartment to pick her up, and we walked to the metro. She was silent the entire trip and seemed preoccupied with her thoughts. Contemplating, perhaps, losing her father, if these incidents persisted, or she was perhaps reminiscing the pleasant times she had with him, the intimate conversations, and the wonderful dinners they had shared with a bottle of wine. She could not bear losing him. Her mother had died when she was an adolescent, and her father was the one who stood by her through the difficult years, after her mother's death. Even though she was ready to start her own life, now as a mature woman, her father was the pillar of her existence. He worked very hard to ensure that Avgy acquired a good education, as she never missed anything important in her life. He was there for her during the difficult times, as she was there for him during his incarceration. He had spent a few years in prison, and his health was failing him and deteriorating. Avgy hoped that with the change in government, all the political prisoners would be freed, yearning for her father's release as well; and that couldn't come soon enough.

A cold breeze gashed through the streets, as the resolute sun seized colorful reflections from the rooftops, spreading its long shadows along the streets and the park. We left the hospital heavy-hearted, as her father's condition was not improving. The doctors didn't know how long he would be in the hospital, having no idea yet what kind of treatment he needed. He had lost a lot of weight during his imprisonment, and his hair was even greyer, according to Avgy. He looked as though he woke up from a dream, and I couldn't make out whether he was seeing us or not. His mistreatment and neglect in prison, as with all the political prisoners, had taken a toll on him. Malnutrition and ill-treatment battered their souls, being confined into a cell, not been able to relish the sun or feel the warm breeze of late morning. Since that ill-fated *Friday,* many souls had been lost, and many more had rotted in prisons and desolate and isolated islands. But there was only one thing that kept some of them alive, having suffered, enduring the torture and mistreatment: the search for justice. The body might tolerate the agony and the pain to a great extent, but the soul of the free-spirited man could be deeply and permanently injured from the grief and the anguish.

CHAPTER XXIX

I WAS ONLY SIX years old, but I still remember the day my mother took me to the cemetery, where my brother's bones were resting. It was noon in late summer, just before the schools opened. We walked among tombstones and freshly dug craves, trapped under a hot sun, which was reflecting its heat off the white marble of the graves. There was an eerie stillness about it; the cemetery was empty of creatures of this world, while its permanent inhabitants were buried deep in the ground. My mother was holding my hand, squeezing my tiny fingers in her strong grip, as I was trying to make sense of the fact that she was delivering a notebook and a pencil to my brother, placing them on top of his grave. This inexplicable act was going around and around my little head, trying to make sense of it. I was only six or seven years old then, grieving my brother's death, left alone to battle the demons of my young age. He wasn't there any longer to offer me his books, his advice, or to explain to me whatever was bothering my unripe mind. I would need him now more than ever to elucidate and justify to me the mysteries of death. Why did he have to leave me and go so incredibly far away from where I could not reach him?

Such was my young then intellect, bothered by unexplained and arcane thoughts of a six or seven-year-old mind. Later on in life, I realized and figured out what death was all about. The mysteries of death, which troubled my young mind then, had disappeared. Death was real and in actuality. Contrary to the Phoenix legend, it did not give birth to life. It was death and not parallel or adjacent to life; it was simply the absence of life. We merely return to dust.

These thoughts were replaced by other mysteries, to inconvenience and disturb my adult mind. More ephemeral thoughts; thoughts which disturbed me so deeply, rooted in my brain, trying to explain, to vindicate me. Why is such wariness and mistrust coming from the regime? I could make out hundreds and hundreds of human faces scattered around prisons, being dejected, taken away from society, and locked up because of their beliefs. Michael came to mind, as I searched in the domain of my brain to find out a reason for his imprisonment and what was going to become of him. My brain knew how far away he was and where he was, but I could not reach him; I could not comfort him and speak with him. Did he need a notebook and a pencil? Could he still write? Did he have all his limbs functioning? Is he in the right mind or have they taken that away from him as well? I should go to see him; I should conquer my fears and go and comfort him, and speak with him. I had an obligation.

I made my decision.

*

OUR trip to the small harbor at Sounion, on our way to visit Michael, was full of anticipation and expectation. Homer's Odyssey came to mind. The story recounted that, as the Greek commanders sailed back from Troy, after its destruction, the helmsman of the ship of King Menelaus of Sparta died at his post, while rounding *Holly Sounion, Cape of Athens*. It was a tragedy for the king, as he lost one of his best friends and companions. King Menelaus then overcame by grief, as he mourned his friend's death. To give him full funeral honors to show his sorrow and woes, he veered the ship towards Sounion and performed an elaborate funeral which included cremation on a funeral pyre on the beach.

As we reach the little harbor, there was a small fishing boat docked there with two officers waiting. We were asked to identify ourselves, and by conforming to their request, we produced our identification cards. After a short examination of our credentials, we were allowed to board the boat. We sat on a bench across from the officer sitting at the controls, as the other officer sat to the left of us, examining us with an inquisitive and enigmatic look. They wore their grey policeman uniforms, and their guns were visible, hanging from their waistbelts. They didn't speak, although with the sound of the engine and the wind we couldn't hear anything anyway. The trip to the long desolate island was short. We disembarked the boat, and we were escorted to the officers' quarters, where we were questioned about the purpose of our visit, our relationship to the prisoner, and other subjective and intimate questions. We were asked if we were law students at the university or if we were involved in any subversive activities. I supposed after the law students' demonstrations, they were vigilant and suspicious enough to ask us that. As the interrogation ended, we were shown to a room where we waited for Michael. It seemed to me that the minutes on the clock on the wall were passing at a slow pace as if they were hours, dragging their feet. The striking impression though was that all around there was stillness and silence. It was still winter, and spring wouldn't have arrived for another month, although the flowers were blooming outside the offices, and the sun was hot and imposing. Looking outside the window at the yard and as far as I could see, where the land met the sea, it was deserted. A few sea birds flew in front of the window, disturbing the silence with the usual screeching sound they produced. Two fishing boats could be seen on the horizon, returning to their posts, as the sun was climbing the sky, dispersing its heat without remorse.

The door opened, and a man who resembled Michael—or used to resemble Michael before his exile—came in, led by a guard. When the guard exited the room and closed the door behind him, Avgy got up from her chair and embraced Michael who was standing in front of the door, stoic with his glare into oblivion. I shook hands with him, and held him close to my heart, as he opened his mouth to utter with difficulty and anguish a few words: "thank you for coming." A tear traversed Avgy's face. Michael looked very thin and tired as if he hadn't slept for days. His clothes were clean, and he was shaven. I wondered what he did with the soap water after he shaved his face! Life in exile was relentless and severe. It took a portion out of one's life, as the days and months went by with no end to maltreatment and oppression. They were allowed to go outside only one hour a day—or sometimes none -- spending most of their time in seclusion.

In 586 B.C. thousands of Jews were deported from Judah into exile by Nebuchadnezzar king of Chaldeans. They were forced to forge a new national identity and new religion. They referred to themselves as *bene gola;* a characterization that connoted *children of exile*. Yahweh – the self-existent one, and the creator of the universe, as the Hebrews believed – gave the Jews a promise that they would be protected for life. That promise however was misplaced and vanished. He failed to protect them from the devastating exile they endured. That calamity, which was a form of cognitive discord and dissension, could have precipitated the most profound desolation and despair, or the most profound departure and deviation from a worldview. For the Jews in Judah, it did both. The deportation and the exile of the Jews from their land were no different from the exile and the isolation of thousands of people in this country during the seven-year ordeal since that ominous *Friday*.

We spend half an hour with Michael, which was barely enough to ask questions or being able to penetrate and figure out his state of mind. He did not seem in high spirits, but he looked fairly healthy physically, although that did not reveal anything about his mind. There was no telling what a mind could endure, although it couldn't have been very healthy, considering the circumstances and conditions at the island. We left heavy-hearted, escorted by the two officers they brought us there. Our pledge to Michael was that we would do everything possible and conceivable to attain his freedom. No matter how strong the person seemed to be, no one could endure the living conditions, the torture, and the physical and mental abuse imposed on the prisoners. The unethicality and the injustice were intolerable. No one had given them any promise that they would be protected for life—as did Yahweh to the Jews -- only the constitution did that, and that institution, to a great extent, did not exist any longer.

Afterward, I thought about the horrific marks and wounds that covered his face and arms, and I felt enticed to inquire about them, dreading that perhaps the guards might have something to do with them. But there was a look in the eyes of Michael that made me think it was better not to bring up the subject. Perhaps he would tell us one day when he felt the time was right. Despite the mistreatment and appalling conditions at the prison, I was glad he was alive. He endured a lot, and he had witnessed even more, and his soul was wounded with discontent and revulsion, but his spirit was still alive. His words pierced my brain; after what he had gone through, he still had that flame inside him. He spoke of the guards and the interrogators and how he was mistreated by them.

"Renounce your treacherous and traitorous ideas," shouted the interrogator, "and I will set you free. Renounce your disloyal and deceitful red book, and I will torture you no more."

"You have no authority or power, but to kill my flesh," Michael declared to the interrogator. "My soul and spirit you cannot touch; my voice, you cannot silence and drown; they are immortal. My soul and spirit will remain untouched and unscathed forever; they will reach the heights of the sky, as I climb my ladder to reach higher grounds; the other, my voice, will remain on this earth for centuries to shout and cry for justice."

Michael was a disciple and advocate of truth and justice. I was convinced, he believed all that he said to the interrogator, with all his heart and soul. He wasn't afraid of death; death would put the body away to decay in the ground; but his soul and spirit would be forever eternal, enduring this perpetual world that was uninterrupted and everlasting.

CHAPTER XXX

The sun emerged from behind the mountain, coming into sight like a bite of fire, repealing the night, revoking any rights that the mighty darkness might have had; it knocked on the doors of the city and a clatter and commotion elevated from the houses which were lifting in the sky. The city was awakened. The sun handed out light to the minds of the people, to mull over the overnight dreams they had and put them aside.

Being dead to the world, Avgy was still asleep, immersed in the world of dreams; her mind was flooded with thoughts as she was struggling against her will to wake up. Her eyes were fluttering, trying to soothe her mind and wake her up. Gradually and leisurely her senses were galvanized, setting off her brain; she could hear the noises coming from the street and felt the sun on her open chest. She opened her eyes triumphantly to the day's euphoria. She got off the bed and went to splash her face. The cold water caressed and molested her face, and she opened her eyes. She cracked the window open, and the morning sounds poured into the room. The morning breeze invaded her half-naked body, as it was mixing with the heat of the sun engulfing the room. The phone rang. She was staggered and stunned; somebody was calling her that early morning, and she wasn't even completely awake yet. She stayed on the phone for a few minutes. The drowsy and lethargic expression she had since she woke up, had now changed to an alert expression with all her wits about her, uttering words like: *"what happened,"* and *"is he OK,"* *"where is he now,"* and *"oh my God."* She hung up the phone and she buried her face in her hands in a silent sob. She dressed quickly and picked up the phone; she was crying.

"Hello, Daniel?"

"Good morning Avgy, what is the matter?"

"Daniel, my father is back in the hospital in a very serious condition," she said and started to sob.

"What is the problem this time?"

"I don't know yet. He was delirious all night, and he had a pain in his chest. His head was hurting and he was vomiting. Will you come with me to the hospital? I'm afraid Daniel, this time maybe it."

"Yes, I'll come. I'll get dressed, and I'll meet you at the metro," I said. I hung up the phone, and I rushed to get dressed.

The metro was very hectic and full of activity with rush-hour travelers. We squeezed inside the train, standing up in front of the door. Many different smells were coming from all directions: the perspiration of passengers, cheap cologne fragrances coming from women, and bad breath. I was glad when we reached our station. We poured onto the platform with hundreds of other passengers, and we rushed for the escalators to take us to the street. We walked hurriedly to the direction of the hospital, among many obstacles which were covering the sidewalks. Avgy was quiet on the way to the hospital. She was spinning around in her head what might be wrong with her father. It was obvious that three years in prison under harsh conditions would not help his poor health. The physical and emotional torture and ill-treatment of the prisoners, eventually take a toll on their bodies. It's true, the body may endure a great deal of abuse and exploitation, but for how long? The soul may support it, and be there for the body and defend it, but the body is made up of bones and skin and flesh, and it cannot bear it forever. The heart may take all the weight and the burden of the body, but it's just a little engine, a small apparatus. It throbs and pounds away in a rhythm. Sometimes it works even harder when the soul is upset and tired, and it's asking her for help; when myriads of devils are chasing it, looking for a reprieve. But the reprieve is not there, the heart gets exhausted and worn out, and it gives up. Then the soul is left alone; it has nowhere to go but to leave the cadaver and start its journey to the unknown. Was that what was happening with Avgy's father? Was his heart getting heavier with all the ill-treatment, and was looking for either to work even harder or give up all together?

We left the hospital heavy-hearted. The doctors said that he had a heart condition, and if he was not released from prison, he would die within three months. He needed special treatment and medication; it was essential that he reduced stress, unruffle and rest. The doctors prepared a letter to send to the ministries of Justice and Health for his immediate release from prison, so that he could be treated, and take care of his ill-health. Meanwhile, he would remain in the hospital for tests and treatment and much-needed rest. Although his potential release from prison was welcomed, his health was deteriorating. Avgy was pondering inside her head how to take care of him. She asked the doctors what she needed to do, to help his recovery; their apartment was comfortable enough, and he would feel very contented and at ease.

"My God," whispered Avgy with fear as we were leaving the hospital, "you're still troubling me, disturbing my heart; until when? Help my mind feel, to make a decision," she said, allegedly, wiping tears from her beautiful face. By all accounts, she was speaking to God.

Was that a moment of weakness? A moment of helplessness, of feebleness? Her father looked very frail and fragile; the bones of his face were protruding, and his eyes were deep inside their sockets, murky and dim with dark rings around them. He had lost a lot of weight. How much he had aged! He faded away; only a few bones, wrapped inside a beleaguered skin; what was left, was enough to give something to the soul to hang on to, so it didn't escape. Those days, that feeble and unfortunate man couldn't sleep; and if around dawn sleep came and took him away, he had a peculiar and inexplicable dream, always the same. Last night he had the same dream; he couldn't take it any longer. He got up; his dream was torturing him. He saw Hades standing at the top of the mountain, with Cerberus at his feet, gesturing at him to follow him down the road to his kingdom. He was a tortured soul.

He struggled and strained himself to form a smile on his face. He spread and stretched out his arm with an effort to take a hold of Avgy's hand and kissed her. Although by nature, he was not a solitary man, yet, he was a man of a few words; his mind worked very fast, and he could be funny at times, as Avgy had indicated about her father. Now lying on his narrow bed, almost forlorn, away from prison, I could almost hear his soul shriveling away. Death was never a long-awaited endeavor, and it was never embraced. The sum of his experiences proved that happiness was rare, elusive, and ephemeral; but to want the impossible? He had a good life, was comfortable, always worked, and enjoyed his family until the death of his wife. But even then, he had to continue for the sake of his daughter; he had to carry on with his life and look after her. Avgy was a young woman when she lost her mother, but he could not and would not be the substitute for her mother. He was her father, and what he had to do was to be there for Avgy, provide for her, without replacing her mother. He had apprehensions and burdens raising a child; he worked hard and many hours, and he tried to spend as much time with Avgy as his time allowed. He inherited the responsibility of taking care of all house chores, entertaining Avgy, and staying faithful to his beliefs. Avgy, on the other hand, as she was growing up, took over more responsibilities. Her father taught her how to cook, and gradually she took over the reins from him, assuming more responsibilities, taking charge of the house and finance. She was now taking care of him.

"Why do you sound so despairing and frantic Avgy? I'm sure with medication and proper care, your father may not completely recover from it, but at least he can control it and live the rest of his life fairly happy and contented."

"He looks so frail and feeble. I don't know if he will make it."

"Of course, he will make it. The human body is very resilient."

"Why are you so optimistic, Daniel? You saw him how he is. He's got heart failure and coronary artery disease."

"I'm optimistic because medicine has gone a long way; there is new medication to control his ailment, heart surgeries have been performed very successfully, and there are more chances now for a heart disease patient to survive and live a meaningful life than ever before."

"I just hope he wouldn't have to have surgery; but medication alone may not be enough."

"As the doctor said, we'll wait until the test result come out, to determine the type of treatment."

"I'll come back tomorrow to see if the test results are out."

We reached Avgy's apartment late afternoon. She opened the door, and piled up on the couch; her face had a fretful and disturbed expression; her eyes were wet, and a few tears were tainting her flushed and tarnished face. I sat across from her, looking at her wretched and desolate face, attempting to make her feel better, in search of the right words.

"Avgy, would you like some tea?"

"I can't believe my father is in such condition; he's the only one I have."

"We had a long day; try to settle down; we'll see tomorrow. Would you like some tea?" I asked her again.

"Yes, thank you."

I got up and went to the kitchen to prepare the tea. I could hear Avgy in the living room sobbing, and my heart was crushed.

"At least look at it from the bright side: he may be released from prison soon and you will have him here," I said from the kitchen, as I was pouring the tea, "then you'll be able to take care of him."

I placed the cups with the tea on the coffee table, and I went and kneeled in front of her; I stroked her hair and kissed her.

"He needs a lot of care, and I don't know if I can give it to him."

"You'll try your best. Also, a nurse will be coming a few times a week to look after him."

"Daniel, I understand all that; but I also know that I will be his twenty-four-hour nurse. Do I have to quit school, and stay home with my dad? Do I have to give up everything I'm doing, and be here with him?"

"I don't think you have to do any of that. He's not paralyzed, and he's not incapacitated. Now at the hospital, he will gain his strength, and he will feel much better. By the time he gets home, he'll be flying. There is no reason to be nervous and panicky, Avgy; at least not yet. According to the doctor, the prognosis is not that bad, and the treatment will be effective," I said and looked at her. She bent her head and kissed me.

"Thank you so much Daniel for trying to make me feel better," she said, contemplating the doomed, as she thought, future. She felt hopeless, and the adverse situation made her contemplate that perhaps she was expecting something different from life; something more palatable and manageable. This awkward and cumbersome situation brought a lot of thoughts into her mind. She was very young when she lost her mother; she still needed her father, and she was not ready to lose him so soon. She remained quiet, gazing into nothingness, while her eyes were strained with an inexplicable expression on her face. She raised her head, looked at me, and she said mercifully, looking for absolution and exoneration.

"My activities at the organization will suffer along with my university work," she said as if indeed that was what was bothering her mind. "Not that my father's condition is not serious," she continued, "but I'm feeling that I ought to bestow and devote myself solely to him. I had surrendered my feelings, my emotions even myself to the *cause*. Now I feel I have to change direction; my studies and the *cause* are not as important anymore," she said as she put her head between the palms of her hands, resting on her legs. "I don't want to lose him, Daniel," she continued, "I will work very hard to help with his recovery," she said, and she got up. She went to the bathroom to splash her face.

Avgy vowed to take care of her father and improve his condition. She would wake him up the same time every morning, and send him to bed at a regular time. He would groan and fuss and swear; she was trying to murder him from the lack of sleep, he would think, but she knew that if he kept a regular schedule, he would have more energy to begin his day. It was simply a matter of patience.

Each day was a little easier; each day he did a little better. It was not wishful thinking, moreover, for she kept a detailed log of every aspect of his convalescence, and in its pages was the evidence of how far he had gone. She tracked down how many hours he slept, when he had difficulty breathing, headaches, heart pain, together with his estimate of the severity on a scale from one to ten. She recorded his complaints regarding dizziness, eyestrain, heart pain, and any other ache that might be related to his heart condition. She made a note of how often and for how long he read, walked, and napped.

In every respect, he was slowly improving. The first couple of months had been terribly difficult, of course, for he was going without caffeine and alcohol, all at once, for the first time since his visit to the hospital, some three months earlier. Had his reliance on coffee been of long-standing, she knew, his recovery would have been far more difficult. As it were, he spent a good deal of the first two weeks nearly drained from nausea, crippling digestive pain, heart pains, and his headaches abruptly worsened. At one point he had all the symptoms of a fever; he was perspiring, he couldn't stop shaking, and he complained alternately of being hot and then cold; but his temperature was perfectly normal when she checked. And then one day, he had felt a little better, and the next day even better. He had gone from strength to strength since then.

"Would you like to go out for dinner?" I shouted from the living room. She walked out of the bathroom wiping her face with a towel.

"Yes, that would be very nice. I would love that."

CHAPTER XXXI

It was indeed an immense protest of prevalent rejection toward the military junta. The Polytechnic uprising began 14 November 1973, although other demonstrations took place before that date, such as the one by the Law students' bloody revolt which took place earlier that year. The November insurrection escalated to an open anti-junta revolt, and the casualties were enormous. That courageous insurgence of the Polytechnic students was supported not only by university students but also by school children, construction workers, and many unions around the country, hoping for the downfall of the regime. The horrendous exile camps of Yiaros and Macronesos had opened again, and many were ostracised, cast out, and ejected into those dreadful islands. Many more suffered arrests and torture which became more frequent as time went by. The vicious and brutal military police, ESA, extorted its fear and terror unambiguously and explicitly on the streets of the city. Fear and silence reigned among the people; *the silence of the graveyard*, as many people characterized the ruthless and atrocious environment that went on for seven years since that fateful *Friday*.

That evening, when I left the meeting, the wind was blowing from the north and it was a cold and raining affair. People were walking by in silence as if the wind was blowing their whispers away. The fear was widespread, and no one dared look at another person in the eyes. Is it the calm before the storm? Could these people, who passed me by on the street, have sensed what the prelude to the storm was? And the storm was coming soon. Maybe not tomorrow, maybe not the day after, and maybe not next month, but it was coming. Did they know what my intends and dispositions were? Or did they just reckon the essence of them?

I should have run or taken shelter from the rain, but the resolutions from our meeting that evening were beginning to sink in. My mind was shaking. I looked up, and the storm, which had fast approached, was dropping a stream of water as if the cataracts of the sky had opened up. The streets had formed small rivers. The sound coming from the rain hitting the sides of the buildings was getting louder. I tried to run but the rain was hitting my face harshly, and it was agonizing and painful. I sought out shelter from the rain under a canopy. A thrust of thunder rumbled close by, and I felt the ground trembled under my feet. The brief light illuminated the dark, and the muted silhouettes of the buildings were momentarily floodlit. The rain started to fall again with greater dominance. The street lights flickered for a second, and they went out. Complete darkness covered the street, which made it a lot more eerie and unnerving. I stayed under the canopy for a good half an hour, until the rain eased up, and relieved the city from the torrent that combatted and surged it for hours.

I left my refuge, and I tried to quicken my pace, walking through puddles of water in the dark. Another blinding lightning, which was pursued by a thrust of thunder, illuminated my way for a few seconds. I was consumed with anxiety. I walked with ponderous legs, chased by my dreads. I tried to collect my thoughts and place them in order, trying to envision what it was going to be like when the pandemonium started. I had a lot to mull over my head, contemplate and plan: design placards, purchase a few obligatory provisions, and visit my parents briefly. Avgy was not at the meeting and consequently, I was compelled to bring her up to date on the resolutions and the preparations. She waited for a long time for this, as were the rest of us.

*

TUESDAY, *13 November 1973.*

It was a quiet evening the time we all gathered in my hotel room. The wind was calm, and the night was warm and tender. It hadn't rained for a few days, and the streets and sidewalks were dry. Earlier in the evening, the storekeepers watered their flowers, which decorated their storefronts, and their aroma infiltrated my room from the open window. It was quiet and serene, as the soft music of a piano concerto, coming from the radio, filled the room with its majestic sound. The events in Thailand last July were going through my mind, thinking of the heroic and brave students who went against the hostile military regime, demonstrating against the atrocities of the junta, seeking their freedom. Now, three months later and the regime's demise and failure came about. The July 1973 uprising would be remembered as one of the darkest periods in Thai political history. It was the *Day of Great Sorrow* when the revolt by the people brought down the military dictator. The student upheavals in France and Thailand brought about freedom and return to democracy, as in the case of Thailand, but not without a detriment to the students. It happened in France, it happened in Thailand, and it's about to happen here now. It had already started earlier that year with the university law students, who stood up against the colonels and the regime; many students were injured, arrested, tortured, and jailed. This city was not immune from those kinds of insurrections. Was it our opportunity now? Were we ready to stand up against the regime for our human and constitutional rights as students and citizens of this country? Truths and moralities had disappeared, vanished, and faded away. Getting hold of our academic and otherwise future was imminent.

*

We all gathered around the table with a pot of coffee and the pastries I had purchased from the shop down the street: Avgy, Ari, Lisa, Mary, Stephan, and Jason. Mary was holding a book, and as she opened it, she looked at the dark and dim faces around the table.

"This will give some life to this gloomy atmosphere in here," Mary said, as she focussed on the book she was holding.

On the secret seashore, she started reading a poem by my favored poet G. Seferis.

> *On the secret seashore*
> *white like a pigeon*
> *we thirsted at noon;*
> *but the water was brackish.*

*On the golden sand
we wrote her name;
but the sea-breeze blew
and the writing vanished.*

*With what spirit, what heart,
what desire and passion
we lived our life: a mistake!
So, we changed our life
Just a little more
And we shall see the almond trees in blossom
The marbles shining in the sun
The sea, the curling waves.
Just a little more
Let us rise just a little higher.*

The words of the poet pierced my heart then and every time I read his poetry. She closed the book, put it back on the table, and looked around at each face again.

"That's where our brothers and sisters are," she said, as she continued perpetually, sustaining our attention and interest. "They are on secret seashores; on desolate islands; in exile. What do they give them to drink when they're thirsty in the heat of high noon? What language do they practice to write their sorrow and grief on the sand so the others are not able to read it? Did the sea-breeze blow and misplaced the writing, or did the guards walk all over it to dishonor and tarnish it? Was the life they lived all their lives a mistake? Were the passion they exhibited, the desire, and the outburst all a mistake? Or did they discover something, which we were unable to see or comprehend and change? We lived our lives for six years under the repression and coercion of the ruthless and callous regime. Was it enough what we endured during the six years of wretchedness and deprivation since that fateful *Friday*, to enable a change? Where is our passion? Where is our desire to change it? Our brothers and sisters are rotting in jails and the islands. Shouldn't they amend that? Shouldn't they forsake and leave behind this kind of life given to them, and embrace and take on another one, unshackled and free? Did they assume the wrong life or were they given a detrimental and objectionable one? But as the poet said, *'just a little more, and the white marbles will shine again, and the almond tree will bloom again; just a little more and we will get higher.'* Freedom is like a sorceress. She steals your soul and you don't even realize it." She took a deep breath, looked around the table, and inserted, "she has stolen *my* soul and heart."

Mary's words were inspiring and heartening, which raised the spirits of us all. A discrete atmosphere was ranging now in the room, as the decision to take immediate action was painted in the faces of all, as euphoria was sweeping the room. There was a general meeting of all the students' unions to take place early the following day at the Polytechnic.

CHAPTER XXXII

*W*EDNESDAY 14, NOVEMBER 1973

In the early hours of *Friday,* April 21, 1967, a group of colonels and military high officials, led by Colonel George Papadopoulos, seized power and established a military dictatorship in a coup d'état, in an attempt to prevent a democratic election, which by anyone's reckoning was going to return to government the Centre Unity Party of ex-Prime Minister G. Papandreou. Consequently, and immediately afterward, the military junta abolished all civil rights, political parties were dissolved, citizens and politicians, especially left-wing sympathizers, were imprisoned and tortured while some fortunate ones fled abroad into self-exile.

By 1973, the regime of Papadopoulos, the junta top dog, was already isolated internationally. To somewhat appease his domestic and international opponents and critics, the junta introduced a *liberalization* process which included the release of some political prisoners – those who did not pose any *danger* to society -- the partial lifting of censorship, and the promise of a new constitution and elections for a return to civilian rule. Many opponents of the dictatorship, including disgruntled and frustrated students, viewed the aphorism of relaxing power as an opportunity to embark on a political action against the regime.

The boldness of its controlling nature, its paranoia, and suspicion, which the military and the regime so successfully had exhibited the past six years, had interfered with students and other organizations. In its efforts to control every aspect of political societal response in the country, the regime banned university student elections, forcibly drafting students into the army, and imposing non-elected student union leaders in the national student's union, EFEE. These impositions and infringements eventually hastened the anti-junta sentiments, already held among students and many others. Until 1974, however, any public display of disapproval of any magnitude toward the military regime were silent ones. In November of 1968, hundreds of thousands of people marched in the funeral of a former Prime Minister, expressing their silent disapproval of the junta; and three years later, in the funeral of the Nobel Prize winner in literature, diplomat and poet G. Seferis, they participated again in another silent march, showing once again their discontentment and displeasure toward the regime.

But it was time for the silent protests to end. The first open public protest against the junta came from the Law students of the University of Athens on February 21, 1973. The students went on strike, barricading themselves inside the buildings of the Law School. The protesters demanded a repeal of the law that imposed the forcible drafting of *subversive youths*, as they were called, a fate many of their peers had endured. The police were ordered to intervene, but many students were subjected to police brutality, as the uprising was stifled and violently suppressed. The event at the Law School was usually considered to be the precursor to the Polytechnic uprising on 14 November 1973.

*

WEDNESDAY, *14 November 1973*
    7:00 A.M.

After spending the entire night sleepless in my bed, the sun shone through the window as it was rising above the eastern horizon. The conversations and deliberations the night before were spinning around my head, which kept me awake all night, delaying the arrival of dawn. Many different scenarios went through my head, as I recalled Mary's words which never left my mind for a second, even though there was a meeting scheduled early morning, which could change the lives of many of us. I hadn't slept a wink.

The morning was cloudless, and a cool breeze was coming through the open window. The long shadows of the buildings were like snakes, slithering across the city streets, as the people were going on about their affairs, unaware of what was coming, considering their intimate matters. The vendors were announcing their merchandise, and the morning traffic was at its peak. I got up from bed, washed my face, and dressed quickly, as I was trailing time. Fresh air hit my face as I stepped outside. Although I was deprived of sleep all night, I was energized by my peculiar thoughts. I walked briskly towards the café where I was meeting Avgy. She was waiting for me at a table with a cup of coffee in front of her.

"Good morning," I said, as I lean over to kiss her.

"Good morning Daniel," she said, returning my kiss. I took my place next to her. I ordered a coffee, and I opened my binder.

"You look beautiful," I said quietly. She looked through me with a stare that was pondering the inevitable.

"I just want this to be over soon," she said with a dejected and desolate look.

"It won't end today, and it won't end next week. It won't be over for some time, you know that. It's only the beginning," I said, and my harsh words restrained her feelings.

"Are you afraid, Daniel?" Her demand was as weak as a whisper. "I am," she said truthfully, and I believed her.

"I'm terrified of failing; I'm terrified of letting this prospect slip away from us; I'm afraid of what may happen, if nothing else in this world ever changes," I said. I turned to face her, as her touch was warm on my hand; I was driven by an inner fear. "That scares me more than dying," I said, completing my thought.

"Demonstrations and uprisings are just a way of getting attention and consideration. Once we attain that, once everyone in this forsaken country is watching, we need something to show them," she said, while her gaze turned to me, calculating, as she measured me up, weighing me against whatever she had in her mind. "I think we'll do quite nicely!"

"Quite nicely?" I dared ask.

"Yes, look at the face of our inspiring revolution," she said proudly, tossing her head back. Her hair trapped the sun, and for a moment she seemed as if she were floating on air. I stayed hovering over the silence, as I wondered my gaze far away, beyond any limits of despair or exultation. I lowered my gaze over my binder.

"I'm not sure what decisions will be taken this morning," I said, as I started going through my binder, "but it will be a decisive one and most likely dangerous for all of us."

"The rumors are that we will go on strike and shut down the school."

"Where will that take us? It was attempted by the law students. Where did it take them?" I said, raising my head to look at her.

"It's a start. We have to voice our displeasure toward the tactics the government is following."

"I understand, but we need to voice other concerns as well."

"Let's see how far we can go. I don't trust the government. We need to be very careful and vigilant."

"So, where do we start?" Avgy asked.

"I think it's time we took a page out of Thailand and the law students' books. France, Thailand, law students. Many were killed, and many were injured. Their deaths were called accidents. We call them, murder. Surely they will be consequences."

My thoughts flashed back to the riots, to the innocent people tortured and killed by a mindless horde of policemen.

"Were those killings our sacrifice?" she snapped, "weren't their deaths worth it to us?" she said, feeling the anger and frustration deep down her heart.

"You sound angry Avgy, but anger gives strength. They knew what they were getting into. We know that as well."

"What about the school children? What happens when the police and the army started shooting at all of us?"

"Think of our history, Avgy; what we have been taught. I believe change is worth the cost."

"I believe our world is on the edge of a blade. Without balance, it will fall. That thought alone gives me a lot of strength."

I had my coffee quickly, and we got up. We hurriedly walked toward the Polytechnic which laid in the center of the city. A lot of students already had gathered inside and outside the campus; there was no police presence yet, but I was sure they were watching us from the surrounding buildings. We met with Jason, Ari, Mary, Lisa, and Stephan.

9:00 A.M.

With all the students' unions present, the general meeting earnestly commenced that morning. It was astonishing to watch all these young people bursting with energy, passion, and thirst for victory, to accomplish something that was in the plans for six years. There were, of course, accords and conformities among the students; but then again, the common goal indeed was to protest against government measures, concerning the planning of student elections and academic freedom, which were pursued for years since that fateful *Friday*. Irrevocably and decisively the decree was to vacate the classrooms and go on strike. Looking back at other more significant revolts against tyranny in our history, we adopted the slogan *Free Besieged* in reference to the poem by D. Solomos who was inspired by the *Ottoman siege of Missolonghi* on 10 April 1826, during the Greek war of independence against the Ottoman Empire.

*

ABSOLUTE unpredictability and randomness, which would, at the same time, be absolutely insignificant and irrelevant, characterized the meeting. Although man's appetites of his nature such as hunger and deprivation are tangible and physical, the spirit's cravings are elusive and abstract. Although the spirit may crave freedom, independence and be free of conditions -- which may be seized and appropriated by outside forces -- the mind is free to think and contemplate. The obscurity of the essence of freedom, which the world has revolved around it and has lost its way by now, puts limitations on one's freedom, thus one yearns to act unreasonably but with a cause. A hungry spirit yearns for freedom which will ultimately derive a sense of *importance*. The conflict, however, between being free from conditions and being *important*, will put further limitations on one's freedom, and consequently one will act pointlessly and superfluously. There must be a cause, a balance, and a foundation for one to seek and obtain freedom and independence. The prisoner may lose his physical freedom, but his spirit, according to external conditions, may or may not be imprisoned. A *free* man may devour his physical freedom but his spirit may be imprisoned. We may be walking the streets free, but our spirit may be imprisoned under the oppression of a government or other outside forces. What is freedom then, if we place it under the assumption that outside forces have imprisoned our spirit? Is that freedom? Is the man, then free, even though physical freedom may be present? No. The absence and deficiency of spiritual freedom inhibit the spirit, the soul, and the mind, presenting obstacles and interferes with the development of the spirit and restraints and obstructs the soul and mind.

*

3:30 P.M.

As the students formed a spontaneous assembly on the grounds of the campus, their determination did not stop them from unexpectedly deciding to occupy the Polytechnic. As the *Coordination Commission of the Occupation* was formed, which had relaxed control over the uprising, more and more students were mobilized and congregated inside and outside the campus. Police had already gathered outside the gates of the campus but did not manage, or at least the time was not appropriate yet, to break into the grounds. This was undeniably the beginning of the turmoil and cataclysm, which started with the occupation of the Polytechnic by the students, and it climaxed to a pan-Athenian mobilization against the regime, as many citizens entered the grounds and joined in to support the students.

Was it warm in that November afternoon, or was I scorching inside and out? The sweat was rolling down my spine and my face, and I was in a state of ecstasy and euphoria. I got the news that the radio station was going to go on the air soon and that Maria and Dimitris, a journalist and author, would be the voices of the Polytechnic. Students were everywhere: on the grounds of the Polytechnic, on the sidewalks, on the gates, on the steps of the main entrance, and inside the hallways. Meetings were going on simultaneously, and committees were formed for decisions ranging from what the students would eat, to the slogans they would shout, to the messages which would be announced on the airwaves. The gates would open and close, and dozens of people at a time would pour in, in support of the students. Some would bring food, others would sing, while others would gather around students to encourage them. I met Stephanie and George, who traveled for three hours to arrive at the school. They expressed their gratitude and gratefulness for what the students were doing. They vowed to stand by and withstand and sustain any brutality and savagery that the police would direct toward them. They believed in our cause and the cause of the enchained and enslaved country; they believed in those who dared lift their heads and stand against the regime, facing guns and tear gas.

There were local and international reporters circulating among the students inside and outside the campus, documenting and videotaping the upheaval, which was unfolding. More and more police were congregating, with their cruisers and their flushing lights and their hands on their holsters. A young man ran across the street yelling something to a police officer, who immediately run after him, snatched him by the neck, and put his face to the ground. Once they put handcuffs on him, they dragged him across the street and locked him up in a cruiser. There was an immediate pandemonium coming from everywhere, as bystanders and students alike witnessed the entire affair. The cruiser then turned and sped away with its sirens blasting, followed by the yelling and shouting coming from the people on the sidewalks and inside the campus. They probably took him away to that *Yellow Building* for interrogation, and presumably for political education. If he were fortunate enough, he might have come out of there with a broken nose, dislocated shoulder, or damaged spline in a week or two. And he was a young man not older than sixteen or seventeen.

I walked up to the lab to probe the preparations of the radio station as Maria was testing the microphones. As she saw me, she nodded and waved at me to come closer.

"We're almost ready. As soon as we get the go-ahead, we'll start. Dimitris will be here soon. He's adding a dynamic and vibrant voice to our struggles," she said, as she was checking the frequencies in which they would broadcast. "How's the situation outside?"

"The police arrested a young man."

"They started already," Maria said, as Dimitris walked into the room.

"Are we ready Maria? Is there anything you would like me to do?" Dimitris said, and he turned to me with a smile.

"I'm Dimitris," he said, extending his hand for a handshake.

"I know of you, and I've heard a lot about you. I'm Daniel," I said, shaking hands exchanging looks of encouragement and reassurance. Maria tested the speakers placed in various locations outside.

"We're ready," she said, raising a victory fist in the air. Her beautiful smile illuminated her face, as her hair fell over her left eye, and a smile painted her face.

6:20 P.M.

By the evening, the slogans and mantras had become political. A well-known Cretan composer, singer, and fighter against the regime joined the students to encourage them and inspire them. Despite the large presence of police and army, more and more Athenians entered the campus to stand by the students.

Although education was the main reason for this revolt, as time went by, the slogans shouted and painted on banners were no longer related to education alone; there were new slogans, broader, which were directed against the regime. Slogans such as: *"Papadopoulos, you fascist, take your washerwoman wife, take Despina and go, the people don't want you,"* were clearly against the architects of the junta and the gallantry and fearlessness of the people were unprecedented. Others were chanting, *"Bread, Education, Freedom,"* *"People break your chains,"* *"U.S.A. out,"* *"Down with the Junta,"* *"Freedom,"* *"Today Fascism dies,"* *"This'll be another Thailand,"* a reference to the student uprising in Thailand in July 1973, which had contributed to the fall of a four-year-old military dictatorship in October of the same year.

The students had won.

8:30 P.M.

The *Occupation Committee,* which was formed that day by the students, had their first meeting at 8:30 that evening. At that time, the gates were shut, and the first manifestos and declarations were broadcasted around the streets, which, by that time, were blocked by crowds of people. The students and all their supporters spent the night barricaded inside the Polytechnic, challenging the authorities, while an enormous gathering of citizens occupied the streets nearby, demonstrating in support of the students. The time had come; and to recall our history, *Freedom or Death* was indeed another slogan chanted by the students, taken from the struggles of the Greek people fighting against the Ottoman Empire in the 1800s.

CHAPTER XXXIII

*T*HURSDAY, 15 NOVEMBER 1973

That November day, the city was obscured by fallen leaves that rippled through the streets and front yards like yellow skins. The sky was clear, and a soft breeze was gusting from the west. It was warm, considering it was the middle of November, and the few clouds, which threatened rain the night before, had dispersed discretely as the sun was mounted in full view. I spent the entire night on the streets or inside the campus, with thousands of people shouting slogans and singing. The police kept their distance, but they were ready for an attack or at least for a confrontation. As the morning succeeded that eventful night, even more people came to join in, to support the students. It was *Celebration Day*, as we called it, for the reason that we celebrated our triumphs of the day before, and what was coming ahead. Triumphs of rebelling and mutinying against the regime, standing up to the threats of the police and the army. There was a great deal to celebrate. The courage and bravery of the students, the defiance toward the authorities, and the gallantry which the students and so many other people had shown. The radio station was raving in full blast on campus and the country's airwaves. The slogan, *Bread-Education-Freedom,* popularized by Maria through the radio waves, gave a new meaning to the struggles not only of the students but of the entire country.

The distant memory of the events of the day before and overnight had granted motivation and enticement to my spirits, or perhaps destiny had decided to offer me a sabbatical from my histrionic afflictions so that I could begin to think again. I was surprised at how few thoughts I had about Avgy or my parents or myself, as if I were encryption, as I was immersing myself into that struggle. By now, I had observed enduring sobriety; a kind of solemnity and thoughtfulness that kept me away from my real feelings toward Avgy, without having to beg a glimpse of her heart or express how I felt. This aptitude was not all mine, I must confess; the events that led to yesterday's incidents, the preparations, and the activities I was involved in for months, had kept me away from spending more time with Avgy. Numerous times she had expressed her feelings to me, and I was at least as much receptive and responsive to that as I could have ever been.

*

My mind grew wings like an eagle or a wild bird as if it were imprisoned inside me; or was it my soul, which was spilling over my body to depart? Did it leave? Was it my soul which was chirping away all day, flying over my head? It wasn't a wild bird neither was an eagle; it was indeed my soul, for I remembered, my body was illuminated, and it was as light as a feather, powerful, like a soul. It soared over the island, the village, the old man's house, and the wharf, where I met Mark. It saw Mark sitting next to me waiting for the ferry, asking me questions which I could not answer. Like a deafening roar, I heard the voice saying: *I will write you, Mark.* It was a lie. I never did. Perhaps he waited for a long time for me to write. I heard his voice: *you didn't write to me, Daniel.* Now that I should remain alone, tell me the truth, don't deceive me; I couldn't continually tolerate hearing voices, coming from every direction; am I a fraud?

My mind, or soul, took the uphill road now and flew like a hawk over the old man's house where his wife, sitting in front of the house, was darning his socks, and the old man, tired from the harsh and crippling work at the fields, was coming back home with his timeworn and lethargic horse, where the table was set for a mid-day feast. Then my mind or soul, climbing up the mountain, saw the shepherd playing his fife, and me, a little boy, sitting on the grass, listening to his majestic sounds. It left that magical and astonishing mountain ridge, and it flew far away, above the clouds, over my dream. It saw me digging, as the lifeless carcass at the bottom of the pit opened its mouth, and screeched again the command. It shouted again the words in the air, which I still carry with me: *"Don't be afraid of your mortality. Climb to your end."* Then, coming back from such a height, my soul, the wild bird, opened his round eyes wider and looked around, gave a shriek, and it stopped at the springs of the village to have a drink of water and diminish the tension and ease my pain…It found my body, which was still under the pine tree, and got in.

My heart melted!

Suddenly and for the first time, my mind emitted a brilliant light with a clear meaning for sure of a dream. Yes, yes, the corpse was right; it told me in my dream: *"don't be afraid of your mortality."* And now and for the first time, I understood the secret meaning of it, and I got goosebumps from contentment. *"Climb to your end,"* he said, and I trembled. What is life without a sense of freedom? How would my soul answer to St. Peter when standing guard in front of the gate he would ask me: *"were you free?" "No,"* I would say with a shaking voice, *"I was afraid." "Afraid of your mortality?"* he would ask, and heaven and hell would agitate, and thunder would be heard in the nethermost edges of Hades. The earth would shake, and the dead would be unearthed, and fire would be unleashed from the underworld… And I sent it back; I sent it back to that *Yellow Building*, to bring me back courage, where there was freedom no more, and policemen and guards, with their double chins and spare pieces of meat hanging from their bellies, sat on their desks, determining the fate of inmates decisively; an inmate who cast a sound and died.

What cobblestone roads should God take, I thought, to come down and brighten and illuminate people's minds? Now his request became a dream, and it came down to my pillow.

I saw myself drifting rootless in a desert, walking on the hot scorching sand, as the sun, following my shadow, was already dangling over my head. My feet were burning in the blistering sand, and I was scanning the ground around, looking to find shade and bargain reprieve from the heat. As I was scavenging around the earth looking for shelter, I heard fluttering over my head: a flock of vultures, were flying over a carcass that was lying peacefully on top of the sand; it was decaying and it smelled horrible.

I covered my nose, and I approached it; the vultures were already on top of the carcass, consuming it. As they saw me approaching, they jumped with annoyance and rage, irritated by my presence; with a mouthful of meat in each one's mouth, they flew away. They circled the air over my head and were screeching at the human being to go away. I bent over, looked at the opened belly of that lifeless creature; the entrails were hanging out and disgust filled my insides. I bent over, and with my bare hands, I dug the sand and covered the carcass. The vultures took after me, wrathful and infuriated; I took away their scrumptious and succulent corpse, and now they were following me hoping I fell, to open my belly and devour me.

The darkness suddenly spilled from the sky and covered the desert. With stretched neck, with my eyelashes closed, I sunk inside me; I heard sounds of water and animals which were sobbing, weeping, and howling in the darkness.

Time became as small as a heartbeat inside me; agonizing like death. I wasn't hungry; I wasn't thirsty; my entire soul gathered inside the sockets of my eyes. I was looking; nothing else; I was looking. Then, at high noon, my eyes became dull and cloudy, the world faded away, and an enormous mouth was opening in front of me; the lower jaw was the sand of the desert, the upper jaw was the sky, and I was walking slowly towards the open mouth, shaking, with my neck stretched. The neck of the world was severed, the voice of the desert was extinguished, and there was no one around to scream for freedom. Slaves? Why then, tell me? Why did God give us head? He gave us head to raise it to the tyrants. The nights and days were passing by like dark lightning and white lightning… and my dream glided away.

*

Dawn was breaking when I returned to where Avgy was resting, after an entire night, keeping ritual with thousands of others inside and outside the campus. The support was coming from third parties, who were allying themselves with the students' protest. First from construction workers, and then from farmers who coincidentally demonstrated the same days as the Polytechnic students. They were expressing their grievances, revealing their discontent toward the regime; they were losing their land to progress. Then the support came from high school students and the populous of the city.

9:30 P.M.

The sit-in drew thousands of Athenians, who flocked the streets and the grounds of the Polytechnic. By 9:30 in the evening, the sit-in was packed, while the rest of the crowds were on the surrounding streets shouting anti-imperialistic, anti-NATO, and anti-junta slogans. The crowds remained all night in support of the students.

PART III

CHAPTER XXXIV

*H*ELSINKI;
February 1998

    While in Laajasalo, east of Helsinki in February of '98 -- for a convention of the International Socialist Youth Organization -- when the air was frosty and bitter cold for jogging, I took extended walks along the river. I liked watching its changing surfaces; in some places, it was wrinkled, or silky, and in other places coarse or turbulent. In clear and fair weather in the summer, it would be sprinkled with the white picks of sailboats sailing to the sea, or in early mornings a parade of the smooth kaleidoscopic and budging of sculls. Other days, the surface turned a shimmering or burnished grey metallic color, something forbidding and unkind about it. At night, the glow and glare of the town lights bounced about on the surface.

    That day, an unkind, frosty windless afternoon, the water was pallid and anemic; an impervious grayish-white that mirrored the snow on the ground. There was only a touch of blue in the white. I walked hurriedly and vigorously, and every so often I brought my hands against my mouth, dosing the tips of my gloves with my warm breath, a puff of white as if that might prevent the fingers from freezing. I liked the coldness of the air on my face; I liked its cold translucence, and its sharp reminder of what life had been, the splendid intensity that was also sometimes painful. As I reached the bridge, I turned away from the water and crossed the bridge that took me to Kultjegranden Street, so that I could make my way along the east side of the park and gardens over to the farthest corner of the library. Daniel came to my mind again and as a phantom, his shadow passed by my eyes as if he were calling me to follow him into the library, as we did many times before at the university. I quickly walked by the library, and it seemed to me that I saw him behind the window with a smile, which neither depicted nor rendered any dejected or distressing sentiments, without indicating any point of view. Of course, it was my irrational and eccentric foolish sentiment that I thought I would see his phantom. My outrageous presumption that the souls of the dead wander around libraries, louring former girlfriends inside, had overtaken my fantasy to higher grounds.

*

THE memories I have of Daniel are adoring and affectionate. Moments that have stayed in my memory untainted and unsullied. Many times, I searched my recollection to find Daniel, to recall his face, his expressions, his smile, and those sparkling bright eyes. His writings have revealed to me his thoughts and agonies from a different perspective. He had always been meticulous with his mind, thorough with his thoughts, pensive, and always brooding deep down inside. Daniel once said that there are coincidences and correlations in life, which are aftereffects and legacies of fate. There are no coincidences, Daniel, there are no legacies of fate; they're only marionettes of our subliminal and intuitive desires. Our subconscious self has stored events and circumstances which pop up from time to time to remind us of who we are. You are the product of your upbringing, carrying with you your brother's memories, his death, and his gentle and compassionate heart. Memories of the sounds of the fife, the old shepherd, the starry sky, and your dreams which chased you your entire life, endeavoring to liberate yourself. Your trips to the countryside, and the people you met and admired and venerated. Your mind has stayed with me as pure and innocent as the blue sky above us. I will remember you sitting in the library with me studying, taking long walks, or reflecting on life and the contraptions which send us every day.

The night that you cried for the people's misfortunes, was the night that I carved my veins and my dreams turned red; that was the night that was in the shape of the sky. The tempest, which came and filled the minds of men, as the moon counted its steps; the time that the sun appeared, escaping from the embrace of the sea. Your voice drifted toward me, and I recognized you and your words, which poured like forceful rivers inside your body. Tomorrow, as the hours would be turning back, I would be waiting for you, there, where the summer left me and you would be coming, like the steps of the sun which were lost in its light. But your face was departing like the light, like water, which would never come back. Your eyes remained dark, and kisses were floating upon them and my protest. The road brought me to the sea again, where, with the sand between your feet, you wrote its name on top of the white walls of the wind, which took them and threw them to the oblivion of the sea. The window opened, and the sea was waiting for you, like an open road in the waters as in the songs, and the morning sun gave brightness to your body. You were naked like an August day in my dreams, but how long would it last? As the sunlight leaned on my roof, deep inside my eyes, red flowers were reflecting from the cracks of the rock, lovely as the sea, though the wind blew them in the direction of death. You talked to me and I dreamed of seas and wind, and I loved you to the endless moon. It was like that when the wind came up and plowed into your waters, as the red flowers in the cracks of the rock were drawn into oblivion. Your large hands held my days, and I followed you to worlds that did not have Sundays. You looked at me, and my palms were filled with your words; and through your thick sea-like hair, my voice traveled. Before you were a word on my chest; now you are a wound of sorrow. An apparition in the world of grief and melancholy. A spirit like a marble statue, with a smile which is frozen.

"*Exiled poet, tell me, what do you see in your century?*"

*

HE often adopted the tone of a dry, puzzling, slight inexplicable face in his communication with other students or members of the organization, although they all liked the expressionless delivery of his words. He indeed liked the other students; at least he did not dislike them, trying not to show dismay at their sometimes-shocking lack of knowledge, or curiosity, as they stood there, taking in what Daniel had to say to them, and there was no response or reply. But should he have expected otherwise? It had what he had been purposely avoiding, really. For a long time, the idea had gnawed at him. But grief and disappointment had paralyzed him; and only as they lifted, did he find out he could imagine, trying again to speak to fellow students about their struggles.

*

It was a rainy day, which seemed to explicitly define all the beauty and sadness of being merely human. Such was the day when Daniel came in all drenched, soaking wet to the bone, and somewhat agitated and distressed. His wet hair was sticking to his forehead, and with a book under his armpit, he looked like an absent-minded poet. He was at a meeting, which seemed something might have happened to upset him so fundamentally. He took off his jacket and sat down looking at me with a distracted look.

"I had to take my leave," he said, "I can't explain it, only that I felt I had to detach myself or I would have become less authentic, less genuine. So, I took my leave early and perhaps rudely, but with that priceless feeling of sudden, exquisite freedom," he said, wiping his forehead with the back of his hand.

"It was as I was leaving," he continued, "that I saw Kostas walking toward me. There was a sadness that was covering his face, and he greeted me with a soft, indulgent manner. He asked me if I wanted to sit down and talk for a while."

"There was a day one time," Kostas started, "when I showed frustration at the current situation in our country. My father did not share my anger and rage, and I yelled and argued with him. 'How can you put up with it? How can you tolerate it and act as if nothing is wrong?' He walked away wordlessly because of course, it was dangerous to do what I was doing. Later that day he came back, and sat down next to me and said to me very quietly, he said, 'Don't you see, Kostas, I have to believe in them' he meant the colonels. He said, 'I have to believe in them, otherwise, how can I get up out of bed in the morning and face the world as it is?'"

"What is that supposed to mean?" Kostas queried his father.

"This world, where people that we love are taken away in the middle of the night never to be seen again. Where they are hounded nonstop, and they cannot read or listen to music as they wish, and have their very reputation and professions stolen from them," his father said with conviction and condemnation.

Michael came to Daniel's mind, as he was listening to Kostas.

"But I'm sure it's only for now. Temporary until things change. A necessary wrinkle. You cannot make a stew without killing a rabbit. Things will change when everything is sorted out," his father said persistently.

"How can you even say that? Is Michael just a rabbit? Stephan?" Kostas probed his father.

"Certainly not."

"Oh, quit it. I don't understand how you can keep up with this," Kostas said to his father, and his face barely moved as he said that; but his intonation changed so that Daniel wondered if, as he said it, he was hearing his father's voice.

"Although we are enduring all this," Daniel said, "justice will prevail. We abide by directives and imperatives but our attitudes have not changed from the standpoint of searching and fighting for our freedom. But I would rather get up out of bed in the morning with a firm and undeniable plan to obliterate and annihilate the junta, and tear down the kingdom of oppression, rather than put up with the current situation, just for the shake of my insanity," Daniel said, as Kostas beheld Daniel's gaze for a few seconds and shook his head.

"He understands, my father," Kostas said, "but he's scared, because of our family's background. My uncle did time on the island, and we have been stigmatized." He stood and he seemingly looked unburdened, but he was not, really. He wished Daniel a good day and walked into the meeting.

Kostas' revelations to Daniel were striking. Was it fear which guided that man, Kostas' father, to say what he said and believe it? Was it a sense of uncertainty that he had to believe in the colonels, to get up out of bed in the morning? Although it sounded absurd, it was human nature to be fearful of powerful people. Especially if those powerful people were the government. Daniel, having reached the end of his conversation with Kostas, which ended rather abruptly sad, and which created a sense of guilt within him, walked out into the rainstorm.

*

As he took a puff of his cigarette, now in the confines of his room, he unfolded the newspaper (always hiding its name from habit, the same way he listened to his music in secret, alone, or with me or the books he was reading) and started reading the depressing articles first. But the cocoon of his room was no comfort to him. Realizing that he was pacing, he forced himself to stop. In front of his eyes the city was raised, turbulent, dipped in blood, at the summit of despair, from where hope began. But the city had vanished suddenly, the people sank inside its entrails. The room had become narrower, the four walls touched him; he was flabbergasted; he threw the newspaper on his desk, grabbed his coat and gloves, and without saying anything, he ducked out the door to make his way down the narrow staircase and out of the hotel. Something came over him, a longing for the misty air.

*

WHEN it came out, Daniel, that you were a poet, I waited for you to mention it to me; but you didn't. When I asked you if you read poetry, you said that you had found a taste for it. That's how you said it: *you had found the taste for it*. I asked you how that can be, to regain your taste for poetry, and you said that you disagreed with Aristotle's notion that poetry is a medium of imitation that seeks to represent or duplicate life through character, emotion, or action. But you also said, which I have engraved deep inside my brain, that there was something dishonest about it. I was of course horrified about your categorization, and I pressed for an explanation. You said that you disagreed with the word *imitation,* because you believed poetry comes from inside the heart and soul of the poet and that, although the poet creates a duplicate life, it's real, and the emotions and characters outlined in a poem are offspring of the poet's mind. The reality you wanted to believe was right there, it existed, it endured, and so you had to restore it on the page.

It was original.

There were moments that the questions, which had once seemed to me so dominant and pivotal, became less urgent and imperative now. My short life with Daniel (almost four years until his murder) overtook those other mysteries and ambiguities, grew larger than the past, created a new bygone and new times of yore. With him, who I knew as no one else had, life was tranquil and effortless. Oh, Daniel! The years with you had been that much tender and kinder, for the way that your heart had opened up and was getting exposed it seemed, more and more every day; the wanting and the needing were not there as you were trying to find your way back, somehow. Your ideals, your struggles had taken over you, as you rummaged around trying to find the non-existent, surviving only in your thoughts.

As years went by, I wanted to believe that Daniel was the man I had fallen in love with. I had wanted to believe that we would manage to keep on going on in the aftermath of the Polytechnic uprising, with intermittent spurts of deprivation and hope, which were human virtues and behaviors. I wanted to believe that Daniel had died and had returned in another form or shape, as a character in the pages of a book. In the pages of his writings, which I was still exploring. But he had stayed in my tender memory as the man who was kind, loving, and dedicated to his cause, to the extent that he gave his life for it. As humans, we are subconsciously willing to believe anything rather than the veracity and authenticity of life. That's how I came to discover you, Daniel. You were the antithesis to all this. I realized early enough your potential and your pursuit of shadows accelerated your life and led you to your ultimate and eventual mortality. Shadows that chased you all your life. The beasts and demons inside you which never seized to hunt you down and contest with you. Your arena was the world, the ladder, which I'm sure you inevitably climbed, to reach the imminent predicament and liberate yourself from **the turbulence of your soul**. The commands, which you received from deep down inside you, asking you for the unbearable and the incredible. Asking you to liberate yourself, to climb high up and become another eagle, gazing from the heights of society the unjust and discriminatory behaviors and fix it. As you once wrote:

My first anxieties.
We're nothing but clowns in the circus of life.
They're nothing but forms,
Which, we shoulder and take on,
Their shapes.
They're our lost dreams
Where someday,
The stars,
Will fall
And be crashed in the dark chaos
And melt in the burning heat of darkness.
And then, with them,
Nestling in our hearts,
Will be drowned in the turbulence of our soul.

The turbulence of our soul. That was your battlefield, Daniel. You fought your demons and you won. You fought your anxieties and you liberated your soul. You fought for your freedom, for your soul's liberty, for your mind's autonomy and you died for it. Now you are free. Now you have the permission to rest.

*

NINETEEN ninety-eight: the year of reflection. Twenty-four years have elapsed since the fall of the junta, and although the bruises could be felt every day, each one spoke about it openly now. Now people talked also openly about the other struggles in other faraway places. They talked about other students who gave their lives to liberty and emancipation, who fought against the forces of fascism which had polluted the entire world with a stench of suppression and containment and which would never go away. The struggles against tyranny and dominance. The halfway between repulsion and disgust. That was where our society was headed. That was why we had to stop its descent into oblivion and obscurity. Many lives were lost, but none in vain and with a great deal of hope. The reminisces and recollections of those days stayed vividly in my memory. The heroic broadcasting of Mary and Dimitri's, the bravery of the students and the people on the streets, had engraved my heart and soul, and it warmed up my spirits, as I recalled the events of those three days.

*

I often remembered conversations I had with Daniel, which always took an existential angle and which was incredibly difficult to preserve an autonomous endurance. He was exceedingly idealistic, uncompromising, and unwavering with his beliefs, which made it very difficult for me to argue his urgings. As romantic and passionate as one can be, Daniel always had the right argument which one could carry on an entire long conversation based on his logic and lucidness. Our conversations lasted well into the early hours, and always started with an unpretentious question or a meek statement.

"Avgy," Daniel would start each conversation by decreeing my name first before he made his statement or ask his question.

"Avgy, when the colonels say *control, authority, might* they mean *force, potency, muscle*. *Skill* and *adeptness*, however, refer to the mere and ordinary things they do daily, such as torture a subversive, push one off a train, or shoot one on the head."

"That may be true, Daniel," I said buoyantly, "but we neglect to realize how much power we have now and how much we can control. Our organization as well as the other ones are too radical and far-reaching for some. But we can control the change and how we go about it. That will convince people. We are on the slow burner which at some point, it will quench an uprising."

"Oppressing and trapping us in an endless cycle of poverty, death, and injustice, any student anywhere will tell you that coercion and subjugation do not last for too long. At some point, it will end well and successfully, but many lives will be lost."

"Changing the world has costs, Daniel. Yes. Many will die, mostly students, but it must be done if we want to preserve our dignity and freedom."

"Our minds have ripened Avgy, and now our heads don't bow to any masters or chiefs. Life for the chiefs and masters has no value, without people in it to dominate and control; but life is a spark, which illuminates just for a moment between two infinite abysses. The endless fight is demanded always, to compel the heart and soul to act and exploit; with it, come sounds and actions, so we don't hear the secret voice which cries inside our heart, quietly like the monotonous slow rain. Everything is frivolous, and the only action, like wine, will deceive us and uplift our spirit for a while."

I reflected on what Daniel had said to me, as my mind wandered off into another world. The students at Penn State University, the students in France, The Law students here in our city and so many others who dared raised their heads above the filth and ordure of an oppressive and totalitarian regime. The soul worked, the heart guided and the spirit opened the way. Our ephemeral stay on this earth required and demanded sacrifices; many had to be sacrificed to achieve what we were fighting for.

My mind flickered back to other attacks by other organizations without any civilian casualties. Those attacks debilitated and destabilized the regime for a while. But weren't there consequences? Of course, there were. They rounded up many suspected citizens who were imprisoned and tortured. During the riots, innocent people were tortured and killed, as my thoughts flashed back to those years. Were those people their sacrifices? Were their deaths worth it to them? I suppose they were both, for them and us but, for different reasons. We gained poise and conviction, they gained vengeance and retribution. Uprisings needed a spark, but even sparks burn out eventually. Our catalyst was still alive nonetheless, and it would inspire many.

*

I don't take well to being dejected and woeful. My memories of Daniel were sometimes ecstatic and generous, while other times were miserable and dismal. Time and again I recalled his generosity with words, his face the way it would light up when he saw me, the time we were caught up in a thunderstorm, or the time Michael was sent to exile. His emotions, his mental and emotional state would change, and he would be quiet, stricken by grief or he would be cheerful and jovial in other instances and in good spirits.

It was astonishing, really, to hear his voice through his writings so many years later. I opened his manuscripts again and I imagined, that between its covers there was Daniel's entire life. I looked at the old dry ink, thinking that perhaps Daniel was relating; bonding with me through these pages. I realized my eyes were teary, and I wiped them with the back of my hand. I started reading his scripts again, amazed how just a few pages revealed so much about Daniel. His outlook, his good nature, and despite his lack of training as a writer, his intellect and sense for language were attuned and in harmony with the plight of the people and his own. Those empty pages at the end of the manuscript were not simply blank, but unpretentiously painful in their blankness. He didn't have a chance to fill them. Only he knew which letters of the alphabet he would choose to express his sentiments, emotions, and viewpoint, accommodating his dispositions and frame of mind, revealing the essence of his being. The inquisitiveness and marvel I felt reading his poetry and prose, were as compelling and formidable, as when I read them years ago for the first time. His words were concerned not with art but simply with the truth, which in its way revealed the beauty of art. Daniel was a man who took the time to transcribe his inspirations and reflections of his life. How many other men like Daniel, unknown, had left such documents behind? How many manuscripts, diaries, letters had been confiscated from those people by the police, and now they're sitting in the police department's archives? How many of these scripts are sitting there waiting for someone to read them? Someone to take a look and let the world know of those unknown creators!

I learned a lot about him from his work and inscriptions. He would dispense himself into the pages of his book, cascading his ideas through his words, painting his mind and soul with the pen, and every letter of the alphabet, every word, was a testimonial of his intellect and convictions. The writing he did at that island he went one summer; at Delphi and Sounion; at his village, he loved so enormously. Wherever he went, each time he found himself emerged so deeply into his thoughts, and all his anxieties came out onto the surface to torture him, attempting to fight his demons. And he did right to the end. But his ultimate goal was to defeat the regime.

He fought his entire student years for the liberation of the mind, the spirit, and deliverance from tyranny, persecution, and repression. I remember his bright dark eyes illuminating every time he talked about his goals, his aspirations, objectives, and his ultimate intentions. Daniel was a poet, a fighter, a rebel, a warrior. He had a very deep understanding of the emotions that people went through, their sentiments, and passions. He understood very deeply the plight of people, their agonies, their anguishes, and their woes. Daniel was a protagonist of liberty, of autonomy, and self-determination.

*

Friday 16 November 1973

It's dawning. Ashes of the events, deadly shapes, processed the fibers of the day; and then, it was blue and yellow and green, as in a dream. Their hearts were longer than the trees, as the sun was born over and over again, among the legs and the bosom of the nymphs. Let me be free again, among haughty cypresses and pine trees, so I can race my wishes through the white temples, and nothing I would care more, than the sky and the earth which would allow me to run with my naked feet, among the waves and the friendly winds of my thoughts. Such was the day when the troops arrived. Death was already spreading like a disease on the city streets, but the people had many hopes, bursting with anticipation and eagerness for the events which would fill the new day. The demonstrations continued throughout the night and into the early morning. The sun was awakened and was coming to life, emerging from behind the eastern mountains, as more people were gathering outside the Polytechnic and on the streets. It was chilly that early morning, but soon it would warm up if not from the sun, at least from the people themselves, who felt the fire burning inside them. They had conquered their fears and their trepidation, without any apprehension of any consequence. Daily nightmares were gone; they were absent that morning. Anxiety was a former feeling which had been replaced by reassurance and encouragement. Torture, islands, *Yellow Building*, and death did not exist for them at that moment. They were not startled and were not alarmed by the tanks, the soldiers, and their weapons. They had persisted and endured the fight now for three days, and they were not about to give up. The mental insurrection was elevated in their hearts, and their cerebral sub-consciousness was guiding them ahead.

9:00 A.M.

By 9:00 o'clock in the morning, the pandemonium was launched and instituted. Two massive demonstrations were roaming the downtown streets. Thousands of heroic and fearless people shoulder to shoulder were walking the streets chanting and singing. The main downtown streets were buzzing, and the police, yearning to get into a confrontation, eager and fretful at the same time, were getting ready. How can one stop such a crowd? How can one stop the furious downpour of a rainstorm? Because that's what it was: a furious downpour. Their weapons and tanks cannot stop them. Suddenly and as the massive crowd was marching towards the Polytechnic, a banned revolutionary song was on the lips and hearts of the protestors.

10:30 A.M.

The gallantry and fearlessness of the students had reached the pinnacle of courage and bravery that morning. Coming out of the Polytechnic, an announcement was made by The *Coordination Commission of the Occupation,* proclaiming that the students and the people of Athens were aiming and intending to bring down the regime. Such was the valor of the students at that time. They could not and did not conceal their anger and resentment towards the government. For six years their quiet calm melted into a barely concealed rage, which now erupted and spilled all over the streets of the city. No need to hide it any longer. The proclamation was made, the people of the city and the students were ready to follow through, as their intentions were made clear: six years under extreme oppression were enough. The boots of the colonels were dripping with blood; the prisons and islands had no more room left. The besieged and beleaguered students blockaded inside the university campus were ready for the showdown. The announcements and encouragement coming from the radio station, reaching hundreds of thousands of people, were a success factor to this affair. The massive demonstrations were sweeping the streets of the capital, as they were progressing toward the Polytechnic.

2:45 P.M.

The demonstrations on the streets of the city by the students and the Athenians were intensified, as their rage was spilling out against government buildings and the police. Some attacks targeted neighboring ministries; those ministries which had caused so much grief and anguish to the students and the entire population at large for so long. From banning books, films, and music, to the suspension of certain articles of the constitution, to arrests and holding people in prison with no grounds or charges. Fires were set in the middle of the streets while Molotov cocktails were thrown at government buildings and the police.

That was the first time that a considerable amount of fury and indignation was shown by the people of that oppressed and beleaguered nation, even though the police were present, ready with tear gas or worse. That was the first time that Molotov cocktails were thrown, and the junta was deranged, maddened, and disordered. At that point the government decided to repress and contain the riots, stifling the population. The repression, however, was lethal and fatal with extreme and irreconcilable consequences. Snipers were placed at buildings around the Polytechnic. As a result, hundreds were assassinated, others were severely injured, while a number of the demonstrators were arrested. The students had no choice but to barricade themselves inside the Polytechnic and behind the iron gates which protected the perimeter of the university campus. They believed that perhaps they were safe on campus behind the locked iron gates, with the deceptive notion that the police were not allowed to enter the grounds of the university.

The provisional radio station of the Polytechnic was blasting its broadcast in loudspeakers on campus and around the city.

"Attention. Attention. In operation the radio station of the Polytechnic. It broadcasts at 1150 kHz next to the 'Enoplon' station. Listen to it."

That radio station reached many people, who eventually poured into the streets in support of the students. Thousands of construction workers, farmers, high school students, and people of all walks of life came to voice their fury, rage, and their resentment toward the government inside and outside the campus. The farmers' committee from Megara, protesting the expropriation of their land, visited the *Coordination Commission of the Occupation*, while the radio station was broadcasting:

"The people of Megara promise to stand and fight at the side of the students and workers... This is a common struggle... It is not just for the town of Megara or the Polytechnic, but for Greece. For the people of Greece who want to determine their own lives. To walk on the path to progress. The basic requirement is the overthrow of the dictatorship and the restoration of democracy."

7:00 P.M.

The clashes between the demonstrators and the police began in earnest with grave and sober consequences. There were many injuries and deaths among the students and the demonstrators. At 7:00 P.M. another massive march headed towards the Polytechnic, as the police chose to strike again. Police in armor cars came closer and shots were fired. There were deadly clashes in many downtown streets.

The students along with school children had to shelter from snipers' bullets in Hotel Acropol, across from the Polytechnic, where the manager went around with sandwiches saying to the students, *"it's not good to fight for the freedom of our country on an empty stomach."* Those images were broadcasted on television screens around the world. A young school student-run from the hotel toward the Polytechnic, when a sniper bullet found his young body and fell. Two schoolgirls run outside, as if they were in a battlefield, to retrieve the fatally injured schoolboy, only to be yanked out of their hands by a policeman. He was left to die in the middle of the street. A Norwegian girl, an unsuspecting tourist, was hit in the neck by another sniper bullet as she ran to a telephone booth to make a phone call to her parents in Norway. And when the students were calling desperately, using their loudspeakers, for medical help and ambulances, the ambulances arrived indeed with their incessantly screaming sirens, but there were no doctors or nurses in them. There were blood-thirsty policemen, camouflaged as doctors, wielding their batons and pistols.

9:30 p.m.

At 9:30 at night, the police declared curfew in the center of the city until further notice. But despite that, the streets remained occupied by the people, still singing and uttering slogans. The radio station meanwhile was broadcasting antidotes to tear gas, as the police were using that weapon to disperse the crowd.

"Attention. Ways to fight tear gas: cover your nose and mouth with a wet cloth, and wash your eyes with a sufficient amount of water. Courage brothers and sisters. They will fall."

11:00 P.M.

The radio station and loudspeakers asked people not to abandon their efforts, despite the retaliatory threats by the police, because of the curfew order that was declared. The area around the Polytechnic was blanketed with choking teargas.

The radio continued its broadcast, encouraging people.

"Polytechnic here! People of Greece, the Polytechnic is the flag bearer of our struggle and your struggle, our common struggle against the dictatorship and for democracy."

In a nervous and excited state, anticipating what would happen next, the entire city, the country, and indeed the world watched the events, as they were unfolding minute by minute, with bated breath. The message of struggle aired by Maria and Dimitri was broadcasted to the entire city, as people were gathering by the thousands downtown.

"Polytechnic here! Polytechnic here! This is the radio station of the free-fighting students, the free-fighting Greeks. Down with the junta, down with Papadopoulos, Americans out, down with fascism, the junta will fall to the people. People of Greece, come out on the streets, come and stand by us, to see freedom. The struggle is a universal anti-dictatorial, anti-junta struggle! Only you can fight in this struggle. Greece is governed by foreign interests! The dictator is trying to hide behind a mask of democracy with the fake government of Markezinis and the fake elections it is proclaiming."

CHAPTER XXXV

THE BRIGHTNESS OF THE moon was shedding light on the darkest corners of my soul, as it was traversing the sky, hiding behind the clouds, and then again reappearing in the vastness of the universe. The stillness of the night was overwhelming, engulfing me, devastating my senses, annihilating the peace I had felt some time ago, expecting something to happen. I was wonderfully fearful of the fate of most of us on campus, as the minutes were going by, and the silence was overthrowing the peacefulness around.

The brightness of the moon, which shed light on this internal darkness, rained upon me the strength I needed to carry on. It was a night in November, warm, tender, and it was the stillness of the night which was heard in the endless silence, and it was time for reflection. Muteness blanketed the city. It was almost midnight when I heard the thunder of gunfire fill the tranquillity of the night. And then again silence. Only the sirens of police cars were heard now and then, racing down the streets in the blackness, among buildings and empty littered sidewalks. As the silence was stifling the senses and anticipation was high of what would happen next, a distant humming was heard which was like a rumor, a whisper of the night. The buzzing was intensifying, becoming more and more concentrated, mounting the anticipation and eagerness of the students barricaded inside the campus of the Polytechnic. It was midnight or shortly after when the first tanks appeared with their headlamps on. The government had ordered a blackout of the city. The regime had sent the army in the dark, in the middle of the night. The tanks circled the campus, and eventually settled all in a row, surrounding the buildings of the Polytechnic. The showdown was apparent. The students, clinging to the gates, were singing the national anthem.

Daniel was pacing back and forth, along the iron railing which confined the campus. He would stop in front of the iron gates, glance at the tanks surrounding them, and he would walk away again. He wanted to repel the feeling he felt, enfolded and fenced like a wounded animal in a cage, he sensed the need to run and yell and ask for his freedom. He needed to keep his feelings and emotions at bay and drive back his frustration which was escalating by the minute. His revulsion toward the regime, the colonels and the police were crushing his sentiments for collectiveness and social order. No words, declarations, whispers, or promises would ever unruffle to pacify his heart.

Suddenly, and as I was looking at Daniel, walking around like a wounded animal, gazing at the tanks and the soldiers, gales of winds lifted, trembling the earth; he came out of the dust, dressed in a long white robe, standing there, in front of the iron gates. That wasn't Daniel, I thought; that was a creator, a constructor. His vision like a menace, holding a sword, whirling it around in the wind like the sword of Democles he looked like a warrior going to battle, to eradicate the enemy and build his new world; the new world without perimeters and obstacles; without religion and oppressive politicians; without peril and thorn in the flesh. And there, with a sword in hand, he was building towns and cities and countries in the air with the swing of the sword. He would run hither and thither, building white columns, raising temples, and houses, creating new towns with people in them, free of oppression and dismay. He built crosses where he hung his executioners, the executioners of freedom and decency; he unfettered the world from tyranny. His towns and cities and countries did not know of oppression or autocracy; they didn't recognize the cursed and anathematized souls, which were prevailing and administrating the feeble, who had turned the beautiful islands into tormented and beleaguered jails for the righteousness souls to disintegrate and die.

The vision, as quickly as it came, disappeared in the dust of the wind. The storms relinquished, and the dust settled down. I could now see Daniel, still like a wounded animal, walking up and down, along the iron fence, looking at the tanks and the soldiers outside. I was sitting at the steps of the Averoff building watching him and the rest of the students, talking with each other or planning something unattainable and inaccessible. Were we losing the battle? Had we misplaced our priorities or simply lost the game? Was that a defeat we were all sensing or was it the feebleness of the strength we felt three days ago or even yesterday? I got up and approached Daniel.

"Daniel, there is nothing we can do now. We are surrounded like caged animals. We lost the battle."

"No, Avgy, we haven't. There must be something we can do. They are our brothers. We surely can bring them over to our side. They can sense justice. Liberty is not a subjective notion, a concept which changes with circumstances."

"We're not dealing with the soldiers in the tanks Daniel; we're not dealing with the snipers on the rooftops; we're dealing with the regime which has shown over the years how atrocious and fierce they can be." Daniel turned and looked at the tanks through the iron gates. The silence was insistent and unrelenting.

Beyond the lights of the campus, which were powered by the university's generators, there was darkness. The campus felt like an oasis in the middle of a dark desert. Amid this calmness and serenity, the radio station resumed its broadcast. The loudspeakers were blasting again, sending messages to the people on the streets and the soldiers in and outside their tanks. It was calling on the soldiers to put their arms down and join them. They were brothers and sisters, and brothers and sisters do not murder each other.

Saturday 17 November, 1 A.M.

By now, the Polytechnic had been surrounded by tanks. The radio station was broadcasting messages, and the loudspeakers were carrying those messages as far away as the middle of downtown.

Don't be afraid of the tanks.

Down with fascism.
Soldiers, we are brothers. Don't become murderers.
Saturday 17 November, 1:30 A.M.

But the silence did not mean defeat. The students once again broke the stillness of the night and began once again shouting slogans and messages to the soldiers, as the tanks were surrounding them. They were calling them *Brothers*. They were asking them to join them and "*together in the fight to defeat fascism.*" Then the unthinkable happened. An enormous AMX30 grey monster tank (still kept in a small armored unit museum in a military camp in Avlonas, not open to the public) took position outside the main iron gates of the campus as if they were battling to annihilate a well-fortified fortress and not a university campus full of unarmed children calling for freedom. As the students were begging the soldiers not to use force and not to harm them, an army officer appeared with a gun in his hand shouting at the students that they would not negotiate with anarchists. Meanwhile, the students at the Acropol Hotel were crying, praying to God to stop the madness. The military gave the people inside the Polytechnic 20 minutes' notice to get out, as the *Coordination Committee* was trying to negotiate the students' safe exit.

Saturday 17 November, 2 A.M.

Tanks are ordered to crush the student rebellion at the Polytechnic.

Saturday 17 November, 2:15 A.M.

A group of students from the *Coordination Committee* ventures out of campus to negotiate a surrender and safe passage for the students, asking for half an hour to evacuate the campus. The officer in charge said, "*we will only give you fifteen minutes, but don't even wait for ten.*"

Saturday 17 November, 2:50 A.M.

I remember that early morning so vividly, as the harsh images engraved my recollections so deeply which will never leave the depths of my memory. It was a cool early morning. The stars were bright, as the rest of the city had descended into darkness. As the tanks (approximately thirty of them) were positioned surrounding the campus and as the monstrous AMX30 tank was facing the main campus gate and the huge cannon was pointing in our direction, their headlights on and soldiers surrounding the tanks, I felt that our time had come. The time of reconciliation and resolution was far gone. Divergence and discord were almost eminent, as the tension within and outside the campus was escalating. As the students were gathered in small groups discussing options, a thought crossed my mind that perhaps we failed. Perhaps we misjudged the degree of brutality and the viciousness of the Junta, their intentions, and heartless actions, which were so evident during the past six years. Overestimating our potency and intensity, we ignored our vulnerability and how defenseless we were. Many images rushed through my mind; the good times I had with Daniel; our meetings at cafés and restaurants, where we talked about so many things, pleasant and unpleasant; our visits to the island of the exiles and my father at the hospital; the preparations we went through for this particular moment. Did we fail? Did we miscalculate the outcome? The preparations for this rebellion were in the works for many months, but what were we expecting to achieve? Changes, as they happened in France? The overthrow of the regime as it happened in Thailand? The eagerness and passion to regain our liberty? But how? We were besieged within our confinements. We were physically blockaded, but our spirit was not; not our hearts and soul; we were merely *Free Besieged*.

Many students had climbed the main gate, yelling and shouting at the soldiers not to kill them. They called them *brothers* and asked them to join them in the fight against injustice and for their freedom. Daniel was among them. I ran to plead with him, and persuade him to come down from the gate. My senses were alerting me that something dreadful would happen. I yelled at him, I yelled his name and screamed over the sound of the engines of the tanks and the pandemonium which was unfolding. He didn't hear me. At that moment the commanding officer, with a pistol in his hand, waved the AMX30 tank forward. The engine of that monstrous tank roared with such a deafening sound and resonance that the ground shook, concealing my screams and those of the students. The gates were falling. As in slow motion, I watched Daniel tumbling down from the gate, facing the sky with his arms wide open. At that moment, everything seemed to me to come to a standstill; everything was frozen in its place. There were no sounds, no yelling or screaming; I could not hear the roaring sounds of the AMX30 any longer; but only Daniel, who was falling, and it seemed he was falling forever. It seemed as if there were a spotlight on him, shining on every flex of his muscles, every nerve, every artery of his arms, trying to get away from the approaching tank.

The sky was dark and closed; neither fire nor staircases were coming down for him to climb; not even a small sign that perhaps Daniel might be hoarded and taken away; he was vanishing, accepting his fate. Daniel was dead.

He didn't retain anything and regarded nothing for later. He vanished and departed from this earthly life, or he perhaps stepped into the boundaries of salvation and redemption. Don't solicit answers. Every moment, he placed in the hands of danger the entire world. But he was not the only one; he was part of an army. One moment under the sun, and his face was illuminated; all of a sudden, his face was extinguished, and another face illuminated behind it, and another, and another. His forefathers were the greater body: the previous, the present, and the future. He was an expression, a manifestation of his mind; that was the face, extraction of the body. He was the shadow; the forefathers were the body. He was not free; Myriad invisible hands were holding him down and they shuffled him. When he was angry, a past forefather foamed in his mouth; when he loved, a past forefather embraced the woman and loved her; and when he slept, the tombstones opened up inside his mind and his head was filled with predators and parasites.

*

THE students scattered around, jumping from the gate to get out of the way, as the AMX30 was approaching. Daniel did not have time. He fell back and the gate came down and crushed over him, as the tank roared over it. It was all as in a dream. As if it were not happening; as if it were not happening to Daniel. He was a fallen soldier. He was not wearing a white robe; he didn't have a sword in his hand, but he went to battle, naked, with only his soul and the brilliance surrounding his body. His fierce look, a defiant stare tacked in the sky, as if he were looking at the towns and cities and countries he created. I screamed and started running to get away from the tank. I was crying, washing my soul with my tears. I was struggling to extinguish from my memory that horrific vision: the gate falling on top of Daniel crashing him. Forgetting everything, the good and bad times with Daniel, permitting our souls to be reborn, virgins and start all over again.

The tank continued up to the front steps of the main Averoff building, as the voices of the radio station carried on to an emotional outbreak, reciting the lyrics of the national anthem.

I recognize you,
By the fearsome sharpness
Of your sword;
I recognize you,
By your face,
Which hastefully defines the land.
From the sacred bones,
Of the Hellenes arisen,
And valiant again as you once were,
Hail, oh hail, liberty

The AMX30, which roared toward the main Averoff entrance of the school, was followed by men of the security forces and the LOK Special Forces.

In unclear footage, clandestinely filmed by a Dutch journalist, the tank was shown bringing down the main iron gates to the campus, to which students were clinging. Other documentary evidence also survived as well as recordings of the *Athens Polytechnic* radio transmissions from the occupied premises.

Soldiers and police jointly stormed the campus relentlessly, spreading death and destruction, at which time the Polytechnic radio transmission ceased. Shots were fired; many students fell; some dead, some badly wounded. Several soldiers helped students escape, but plain-clothes policemen were waiting at the exits. As the gates crashed to the ground, with students clinging to it, other students rushed out through the open gate to escape. Some were beaten with clubs, and others were arrested. Many students and demonstrators were killed. The number of dead that circulated in the media early in the event was 34 but many reports claim that the number was significantly higher. Perhaps hundreds.

Twelve hundred dead?

Soon after the events at the Polytechnic, the government was asked by senior officials to re-impose martial law.

*

Saturday 17 November, 3:20 A.M.

By 3:20, early morning, there was no one left on the grounds of the Polytechnic. At least not a living soul; only corpses. The city was still hidden behind the veil of darkness, as was the campus of the Polytechnic with corpses scattered around, littering the yard. Many wounded were helped by paramedics, doctors, and nurses. Some of the tanks left, leaving behind devastation and death. They were followed by the sound of their engines, which was contracted and faded, as they drove away. The student rebellion was crushed, and this time with devastating and demoralizing results.

Daniel's body was recovered the following day.

*

The 17 of November 1973 confrontation was the turning point of the events, following that ill-fated *Friday* of April 1967, which brought dictatorship to the country. Although the students did not bring about the overthrow of the regime immediately, their intense and persistent actions, however, the new voice which was heard from the Polytechnic and the Law Students' sit-in earlier that year, shook the Junta to its rotten core. It would be less than a year later which the decaying and disintegrating regime finally rotted away and fell.

CHAPTER XXXVI

*Y*EARS *L*ATER

When I contemplate, after so many years, what stood as the ultimate and supreme moments in my life, I think of the moments when my life had changed fundamentally from its roots, and memories were left unattended in my heart, there were two: the day the regime fell and Daniel's death and my eyes still get teary and they trickle. What was, then, the crust that covered the earth, archaic, irresolute, and uncertain as the people, muddy and bloody slithered on it, looking for freedom? Sadness covered my soul, when I saw them climbing the endless uphill, opening the path sometimes with their bare hands, and sometimes with their swords to find it. They stared at the open meadow, anticipating and envisioning her coming: did she show up, she didn't show up, now she should show up. Sometimes a tree or an animal fooled them, and other times, in the depths of the night, a dream. But the animal ran away, and the dream was extinguished like the flame of a candle; and then, they stared all over again at the horizon, over the meadow to get a glimpse of her.

Was she coming?

Such was the anticipation of her arrival, hoping the regime would fall soon, and she would appear in her white gown again, with a wreath on her hair, holding an olive branch.

But now, look, the ground shifted and shuffled; the old tombstones opened up, and a voice was heard from the depths of the earth: *"look, she's coming, she's coming!*" and the old warriors and rebels ran down from the mountains with their heads wrapped up and bloody, with their limbs missing, with one eye, were coming with their swords, some limping, some running to salute and greet her, shouting, *"she's here, she's here!"* In the taverns people were drinking, they were dancing; the squares and the streets were ornamented and garnished with flowers and greenery, and *Freedom* was standing there, in the middle of all this, and the sky was brilliant above her.

I never felt it so deeply as when I thought of our dead; our dead had not died; and in those crucial and critical moments, they jumped out of the soil, they took possession of our hearts, our eyes, and minds, and conquered our beings. All the young men and women who died in the hands of the police and the army, all the unfortunate prisoners and exiles who vanished, they were all shouting and screaming and dancing from happiness, when the road was empty, and nobody was there to hear and see them. When I contemplated that day, I was grateful I was around to witness it. And then, when all was over, and happiness was sent to rest, and the rains came and cleaned up the streets from the blood and the dirt, life came back to normal, sober, within its borders. The streets were radiant and luminous, the people, washed and shaved, were gathered at the square; sometimes one would hear an exhausted and worn-out voice singing in a tavern. Then, I would go out, and I would dance and scream from the top of my lungs to soothe and subside myself when the road was empty, and nobody was around to see me and hear me. And with me, all our dead were dancing and screaming to soothe and pacify themselves.

*

ONE morning, as the sun was sweltering and scorching the soil and the stones, I set out to visit Daniel's grave. It was a quiet morning, hot, as the shrewd long arms of the sun were piercing and stabbing my skin. My thoughts were muddled in my head, as my mind was occupied by mystifying and enigmatic notions and brainwaves, that he was up there somewhere, ready to welcome her. He would be around to witness her arrival in spirit. Freedom and death had liberated him. He could now see the square and the streets decorated for her. But I was sure he screamed and yelled and dance on the street with her. He was resting, gratified, and convinced now, that the battle he gave was over, and his struggles and efforts did not go to waste. He was assured that she had arrived triumphantly and jubilantly. Her white veil was blowing in the wind and her hair, propelled by the wind, was flattering within the rays of the sun. He was free.

Nothing I cared more
Than the night of my death,
When everything will be green and white,
And the sea will be singing my hymn,
Under the sun,
Which will be born that very moment;
I will celebrate the event of my existence
    Only once,
Running down the hill, July or April,
Where the sun will grow round, once again,
And time will allow me wishes,
Raised through the fields of green,
Before it takes them away,
Under the shadow of my hand,
In the moonlight,
As I ride, forever, to sleep.

It was one of Daniel's final poems; he predicted his death, enveloped and draped under *the moonlight* as it was written by destiny, wishing that *"… time will allow* [him] *wishes…"* So much melancholy; so much dejection, but so much optimism. Rebellious – as time allowed him -- even describing his death as such; but there were no regrets, as the sky and the earth were not dark and gloomy, but full of color and life. The earth was covered with the colors of his existence, and *"everything* [was] *green and white"* as the sea sang and chanted his hymn, under the sun. It had passed the censors of his heart, and the spirit had conceded. He died under the moonlight, and time did indeed grant him his wish, as scandalous and appalling as his death were.

Man's soul is just a flame; a blazing bird, which jumps from branch to branch, from a hilltop to a hilltop shouting: *"I can't stand still; I'm burning; no one can extinguish me."* Where are we coming from? Where are we going? What is our purpose in life? The heart shouts, the brain asks, thrashing and pounding on chaos. A flame inside Daniel suddenly moved to give him an answer: *"the day will come when that flame will scrub and cleanse the earth and the soul will become a hot tongue which will leak the world, aiming to extricate and detach the dark structures from it."* But there was another flame: the flame of the unknown and inexplicable beyond; we danced and cried between those two flames: life and death. Our manifestations and bodies remained brilliant and radiant. Peaceful and composed, he stood between these two flames; his mind and intellect remained motionless in vertigo we call life, and he said: *"time is very short and the space between the two flames is elongated."* Very sluggish and laborious was the rhythm of life; he had no time; he had no place to dance; he was in a hurry. But all of a sudden and abruptly and as the rhythm of the earth became vertigo, the dance disappeared; the moment became a tornado, it became eternity, and the prison was there no longer; the moment melted and evaporated from the heat of the flames, and the powers inside him were freed. Eternal these two battlefields were: light and darkness; life and beyond: the battlefields of life and death. Endless these two divergent and hostile powers were; they fought, they clashed with each other, they declared victory, they were defeated, they capitulated and submitted, and they started all over again. The spirit scrutinized and dissected the marvels and wonders of life, and established and set up rules and laws; then new roads opened to bridge the chaos, to help the soul and spirit march. Such was Daniel's struggle; he was an edgy and apprehensive soul. Many questions were troubling and harassing him. Flames engulfed his soul and spirit, as the doubtful and cynical questions consumed them both: what is life? What is death? What is our purpose? He turned towards the sky to explore life; he turned towards the stars to understand and justify his existence. His heart was agonizing and distressing, pounding at the abyss, as his flame wiped clean and polished his world, exposing and confessing his apprehensions and fears; his soul, like a blazing tongue, leaked the world, to extinguish its composition and arrangement. His spirit flew up to astonishing and incredible heights. He looked for his ladder to climb and liberate his soul. He scuffled and wrestled between those two flames: life and beyond, as his equanimity and carcass remained brilliant and radiant, he stood peacefully and composed between them. He felt life's vertigo engulfing him, as his mind and intellect remained in place; but time was short for him and the space between the flames was narrow and restricted; and so, the rhythm of life became arduous and laborious. The soul felt distressed and tormented and had no time and no place to dance: he was in a hurry. Then the rhythm of the earth became vertigo; he tumbled and plunged into it. The dance ended and disappeared; the moment became a tornado, and it was eternal and infinite; but mercifully, the moment melted and evaporated from the heat of the flames, and the powers inside him were unleashed and were freed. Then the battle begun in the soul's arena: life and death; light and darkness; existence and nothingness; that was the battle of life and death. That was his battle: at his village, the islands, the city streets, and the iron gates. Did he lose the fight? Was he holding on to the trees, the animals, the humans, stepping on solid ground, shouting? He climbed the endless dark precipice of death and he trembled. His soul and spirit fought with each other; they won, they lost, they compromised and they fought again; they marveled at the wonders of life, as the chaos was bridged, for the soul and spirit to march. He bridged the chaos with life. Daniel was able to climb his ladder, from life, across the abyss to eternity. He was free.

*

ON days, when he felt loose-tongued, Daniel would reminisce about his childhood, growing up with his brother in the green fields surrounding his village. He described it in such detail, the house that he lived, the mountains, the hills, and the dry river bed with the pebbles and rocks and sand. Sometimes I would picture it so vividly in my mind, that it seemed to me as if I had lived there with them. But he was gone, leaving behind many memories and recollections with his writings, as his heart and spirit had always stayed with me. We had made plans for the future, even during those turbulent times, but destiny was making plans as well. He was taken away very young, but he accomplished what he wanted to accomplish. He was immersed in his fight and struggle with his entire being. He couldn't sleep at night. He would get up in the middle of a deep sleep, put aside his dreams, send them away, and he would sit on his bed reflecting on a different life. A life free of doubts, fears, and apprehensions; a life without poverty, deficiencies, and destitution; clean, white-washed sidewalks, without the stains of misery, blood, and death. His unshackled soul flew away, to reach and climb his staircase, to fight the vertigo of eternity and perpetuity and liberate himself. His heart spoke to him and he followed; he received a command, he accepted it, and executed it. He got hold of his soul and guided it, following his footsteps; time allowed him wishes, as it seemed, and the wishes became commands and commands became his path. Oh, Daniel, how free you must be!

*

NEITHER when it was over nor a long time afterward, did I regret having been involved with the organization and the uprising which shook the core of the regime and caused it to fall less than a year later. Looking at it from the perspective of several years, the fact that Daniel's death endured in my heart for many years afterward (and I'm sure for many more years to come) seemed of great importance. His death did not become emaciated and waste away. It did not go uncultivated, nor did it lessen the importance and significance of his death and the deaths of thousands of others, which had a bearing in the aftermath and the results of our uprising, months later since we started. The fact that many young men and women lost their lives for their beliefs and ideals, was of great importance and significance for the human race. There was a great deal of sufficiency, of symbolism and vivid images about their deaths and the grief that followed, to stamp itself in my mind.

That bloody November dawn, the aftermath of three days of fighting, had gone like a wildfire in dry grass. The rumor, the story, whatever it was, something about the language which the colonels and the high officers used to describe the demonstrators, did not stain the cause; it did not detain and confine the students from carrying on their activities, whether they were called anarchists, *Reds*, nihilists or radicals. These characterizations went far beyond any human comprehension and intellect; far beyond the root and the origin of the frustration and the level of tolerance of the people, and particularly of the students who brought about change, seemingly, and triggered off the downfall of the junta. The general perception, however, rooted deeply into the fearful and terrifying tactics of the junta, was that, it was inconceivable that a handful of students can bring about change. But they instigated it, inaugurating their spirit, inducting their souls into the long lineup of national heroes. The grounds and the perimeter of the Polytechnic and the streets and sidewalks of the capital were painted red from the blood of the students and so many others. But, was justice done? The legitimacy of their fight and their struggle, which was allowed to the students, also allowed them integrity and validity, contesting the colonels with such determination and fortitude.

Yes, justice was done.

*

I got hold of my life after so many years, since those fateful days of November of '73. The events had carved a deep wound into my soul and heart, which took extraordinary measures to heal and stop the bleeding. It mutilated and lacerated my spirit, witnessing the destruction of human essence, as the students and the Athenians were falling from the bullets of their army; those same people who were supposed to protect them. That ill-fated *Friday* of April 1967 that all began, was wiped out; it took many years to restore and heal the countless wounded souls and mend the damage and repair the wounds, which were inflicted on numerous people around the country. The aftermath though was not an ideal situation, although the colonels had left, I would say on vacation to some resort --because that's what their prison's cells looked like -- their imprisonment was a mockery and travesty to the dead. A parody that many people could see even through a smoked piece of glass. There were trials indeed, misrepresenting the number of dead during the three-four days of that November at the Polytechnic; misrepresenting their intentions, their actions, and prosecutions, which the people suffered during the seven harsh years of dictatorship. People knew who they lost and how they lost their loved ones; there was no need for the junta to advise and enlighten them, whether or not their son or daughter was dead, murdered at the Polytechnic. The morgues, the hospitals, and clinics were overwhelmed with the number of dead. But one thing was certain and conclusive: there was no doubt, freedom from the colonels was attained. It was not only the fascination of a few of the *anarchists* or the *Reds* as they were called; it was the fascination of an entire nation. Was it complete freedom? Was it that justice was done punishing the perpetrators of that fateful *Friday*? The perceived notion was that it was not. They deserved worse than what the courts had allowed them: restricting somewhat their freedom and that was the extent of their punishment.

CHAPTER XXXVII

I SAT BY THE POND. The sun was spiraling down behind the western mountains, as the clouds were revealing their colors: orange and purple and red, I had a thought. As the ducks were peacefully floating around the pond, and the birds were diving in the cool waters, I had a thought. "I feel peaceful," I thought, "I feel serene and the weight of the world is off my shoulders, as a liberated Atlas would have said. I like this place," I thought, "the people, the things I've accomplished, my creations. My inspiration and innovation were put into work, and I fashioned little people in a box who run around orderly, picking up things, politely, restricting things, and suggesting others. It's a little box which, looking at it objectively and empirically, it's a metropolis, a microcosmos, a town, or a nation in which things happen. The microcosmos of an orderly place, with no revulsion or aversion, one cannot find it insufferable and be repulsed by. A place where things and order are respected; a place where there is no hate, misunderstanding, or jealousy."

The sun was down by now, and the colors of the clouds were more intense and penetrating, as the sun withdrew its fiery hand, and the earth became colder and darker. "It's peaceful and quiet here," I thought. Only the sounds of the leaves of the poplars could be heard dancing in the wind and a distant animal looking for its mate. "I'm serene," I thought, "my soul is serene." My spirit had settled, and I got hold of my life. I got hold of my life among the trees, the sky above me, and the sounds of purity and innocence. My mind was wandering in distant lands. I could hear the waves crashing on the rocks of my secret island and the seagulls above my head, as the hot sun was piercing my skull and my skin became dry and red. I was left alone, at the mercy of my thoughts. I had no chains, no masters—and it was getting dark. I heard something in the woods. A blue heron flew above my head heading toward the lake, disappearing behind the tall birch trees.

I moved my body toward the water, which was getting dark that very moment. The water was cold, and a toad jumped just ahead of me. I felt good and accomplished. There was no competition in nature; everything was well placed.

I turned toward the house. A familiar face smiled at me from behind the window. Daniel, my son, was sitting on the veranda, playing. He always reminded me of him; the Daniel I never had a chance to enjoy; the Daniel who stayed in my memory as a long-gone forgotten dream; the Daniel who dedicated his mind, soul, spirit, and body to his cause. But he loved me. He loved me with all his heart and in his way, and he was only twenty-three. I wiped my cheeks, and I smiled back. The dinner table was set with a candle in the middle of it. It was the same one, which I carried down the aisle the day I confirmed my devotion to him. I sat down. I filled the glasses with the nectar of Dionysus, I placed my finger on my lips requesting silence, and I raised my glass. He smiled. There were no words spoken, as I stared into his eyes. The clock tolled nine times as the night was settling in. I was free.

About the Author

Peter Routis received his degree in English Literature from Wilfred Laurier University, Waterloo, Canada and his degree in Computer Science from Humber College, Toronto, Canada. His career as a Systems Analyst lasted until his early retirement in 2016. Since then, he has devoted his full-time to writing. His first play, "The Rats" was staged at the University of Waterloo in 1974. He has published three plays: The Rats, The Tragedy of Job and The Tragedy of Eli. Mr. Routis has been writing since his teenage years and off and on during his time as an I.T. professional. Born in Athens, Greece, Mr. Routis is married with two children, two grandchildren and three step daughters and lives with his wife Joy in Toronto, Canada.

www.ingramcontent.com/pod-product-compliance
Lightning Source LLC
Chambersburg PA
CBHW071654090426
42738CB00009B/1521